SMALL HOURS

THE LONG NIGHT OF **JOHN MARTYN**

SMALL HOURS

THE LONG NIGHT OF **JOHN MARTYN**

Graeme Thomson

OMNIBUS PRESS

London / New York / Paris / Sydney / Copenhagen / Berlin / Madrid / Tokyo

Contents

Prologue
The Road to Ruin

In the opening scene of the movie that will never be made of John Martyn's life, the camera pans slowly across Island Records' Basing Street studio. A band recently signed to the label is playing an informal showcase. Fellow artists have come to watch, listen, drink, gossip and offer encouragement.

Through the smoke and sound, a Gorgon crown of golden curls bobs up, then down, then up again. Beneath it is John Martyn. He snakes between the throng, bopping lightly to the music, tossing out jokes, trying on voices, cultivating connections, curling an arm around familiar shoulders. The music never stops and neither does he.

Island in the early Seventies was something like an extended family. Musicians gathered at its offices at 22 St Peter's Square in Hammersmith, at the Cross Keys pub across the road, or in the studio at 8–10 Basing Street in Notting Hill. By habit and through choice, they played on each other's records, toured together, often lived together.

If Chris Blackwell was Island's unflappable paterfamilias, then John Martyn was the favoured wayward child. Full of wit and bounce and bite, he pushed his luck into corners and charmed, or slugged, his way out almost every time.

There is something hugely attractive about a young musician in bloom, on top of their game and acutely aware of the fact, confident bordering on arrogant, flying not just with their talent, but the *idea* of their talent, the possibilities stretched out before them like the outline of a new country. It doesn't last – it cannot and should not last – but for a long moment it seems to be that everything they do possesses an intuitive, essential rightness. Their spell charms almost everyone it touches, even if it touches only relatively few. It is the kind of meaningful contact that travels deep rather than wide.

Martyn in the first half of the Seventies was that artist. He and his music walked hand in hand in a kind of golden glow. The best vocalists sing like they speak; Martyn sang like he *looked*, in hazy, honey-coloured tones, barbed and fuzzy around the edges. He was stoned, certainly, but wired-stoned. Head spinning, feet twitching, fingers flashing; always in motion. Softness and abrasion. Irresistible, seductive, unsafe. He was so good he didn't trouble himself with the plain art of precision. He made it up anew each time. Martyn was the kind of artist you travelled towards with your heart in your throat, as you travel towards unrequited love or a fire in the woods.

He wrote, sang and performed simple songs with dazzling dexterity and an intensity that bordered on outright aggression. Rocking back and forth, slamming the strings with his index finger and thumb – his great friend and foil Danny Thompson called him 'Badfinger' – his energy on stage was volcanic and confrontational: are you with me or against me?

Martyn's best songs travel down, or up, or around and around, but rarely in a straight line. Melodies blossom then wilt. Time signatures stretch and snap. Rhythms steam, bubble and deliquesce. He loved water and used it again and again as a lyrical and musical motif. It is the element which best fits the sounds he created: ripples, waves, currents, eddies; rocks plunging, stones skimming, whirlpools boiling. He drew fat circles in wet sand, surrendered his anchor to tidal drift, echoed the irregular patter of snow-melt.

Having grabbed a foothold in the rather earnest Sixties folk scenes in Glasgow and London, he soon outgrew what he regarded as their limitations. Folk rock, when it soon came, was firmly 4/4. Martyn kept his own time. He immersed himself instead in spiritual jazz, skeletal blues, reverberating dub, pushing his guitar playing and his voice, stretching his capabilities. It did not carve a route to fame or fortune. He never had a hit single; a sole album scraped into the Top 20. It was just as well. Martyn sold as many records as his life could stand.

The art was magical and unerringly beautiful, fearsomely personal, feather-light and somehow pure. It was also capable of being coarse, aggressive, wayward and indulgent, not to mention repetitive and downright dull on occasion. Its great recurring theme is love, which, given the way Martyn lived his life, is not so much a contradiction as evidence that a sincere belief in the power of love is not the same thing at all as having the desire or the ability to practise that creed. It was certainly not enough to sustain him peacefully through the world, or to protect the world from him. The heart that was always present in his music was a divided one, the beauty mirrored by what Ralph McTell calls 'an awe-inspiring darkness'. It didn't always require words. A divine, whirling rage is powerfully evident in 'Outside In', just as one can discern a profound commitment to some higher healing force flowing through 'Small Hours'.

It must have been exhausting being the John Martyn that John Martyn presented to the world. So much so, one suspects that playing music was the only time he was able to get out of the way of himself, to allow himself a break, a breather. 'The great thing about music,' he once said, 'is for those sections of my life that I'm playing, I don't actually exist and I'm quite convinced that, while other people are growing old during that time, I'm not.'[1]

Even during the pauses on stage between songs he was 'on', jiving and joking, jousting with the audience, his band, himself. To watch him perform was to witness an unsettling dance between deep revelation and blunt, sometimes brutish, concealment. The music said too much, and he spent the rest of the time – his life – living it down. Some curse: to be so hopelessly in thrall to beauty as to fear it and seek constantly to undermine it. The innate prettiness Martyn possessed – in his face, his voice, his music, his words – was a gift he at first exploited and then actively mistrusted. In the end he simply destroyed it.

Lost inside the music, however, he dropped all fronts, and some purer form of his true self emerged – a romantic, vulnerable soul, minded to love, curving towards peace, no stranger to tears. Did any musician in the Seventies fly so free as Martyn did on *Bless The Weather*, *Solid Air*, *Inside Out*, *Live At Leeds* and *One World*? Did any fall quite so far?

So much for the movie.

We were in the beer garden, John Martyn and me, and I could think of no useful means by which to measure the distance his life had travelled from his music. It was the autumn of 2005. Martyn had a little over three years left to live, and the hard fact of his mortality was cruelly apparent and yet somehow seemed absurd.

At this stage in the proceedings, fifty-seven years deep and scored with the irrefutable evidence of a long spell of hard weather, Martyn was a man who tested the limits of the powers of description. He tipped the scales at twenty-something stone, his huge face scarred, his fingers grey and pale and thick as butchers' sausages. A plump pink abscess poked out from under his shirt. When he stood and leaned on his walking staff, he resembled a fallen Shakespearean king, a titan damned to a dotage of impotent rage. By now, he spent much of his time in a wheelchair.

He had lost his right leg below the knee in 2003 when an infected cyst burst and septicaemia flooded his bloodstream. He had, in effect, poisoned himself to the point of amputation. He now wore a prosthetic where it used to be, which had not been a success. He was on his ninth 'false leg' and had put on six and a half stone in the past eighteen months because there was no exercise to be had. He was constantly at war with his absent limb. He explained that now, when he tried to swim, he went around and around in circles. 'No rudder.' It seemed a fitting phrase.

There was not the faintest trace of self-pity. Though demonstrably wounded, he still gave off an aura of dangerous power. The trouble was all in the eyes. Even when Martyn was young and terribly beautiful, you noticed it: the potential for lights to switch from green to red at great speed. I had known other men like this. I'd met them in pubs in Glasgow, Bristol, Dublin and London, big men vibrating dangerously on little bar stools, hunched over their medicine, filled with a febrile bonhomie. Big men raised too quickly on stickle-brick foundations, governed by mercurial mood swings that were impossible to read until they had swung right at you.

When I met Martyn, those fires had dampened down, though the embers were still smoking. His predicament seemed karmic, suggesting that the bountiful gifts of his youth had been granted as the down payment on a debt which was now being ruthlessly called in. If anybody else had inflicted the damage on the beautiful young man Martyn had once been, if some third-party aggressor had taken pains to so brutally dismantle and erase all trace of the fellow Danny Thompson calls, over and over, as though summoning him back, a 'wonderful curly-haired boy', then it would have been a police matter. As it was, Martyn was both perpetrator and victim of this crime. He looked in the mirror and had all the evidence he needed. No charges would be pressed.

Earlier, Martyn and his partner Teresa Walsh had met me off the Dublin train. I had clambered into the back of their car. Teresa was driving because Martyn was no longer able. I'm not sure he ever had been, though it hadn't always stopped him.

We tore through Thomastown, an unremarkable county town in Kilkenny, and as we did so I totted up the misfortunes suffered during the last few years alone by the man squashed into the passenger seat. Broken bones, whiplash and abrasions sustained when a heifer smashed through his car windscreen – 'this black cow jumped into my lap'; a fractured toe caused by stumbling drunk on stage; a split head suffered during an altercation with a rock during an underwater swim. Before that, a punctured lung, a serious stabbing, pancreatitis, prostate trouble, punishment beatings. Then the leg. This was before even contemplating the daily toll taken by the drink, the drugs, the terrible carelessness. With the kind of grimly humorous flourish Martyn fully appreciated, a bankruptcy notice had been served on his fifty-third birthday: September 11, 2001.

We headed to Carroll's bar in the centre of Thomastown. The sky was a stale grey, the pub sunflower yellow – a popular combination in Ireland. Martyn was clearly well known here, not so much a regular as a one-man income stream. We ordered drinks. Fizzy water for me; cider and quadruple vodkas for Martyn, which he mixed by taking a gulp of the cider and then tossing the spirit into his pint glass. Shake and serve. I'd never seen anyone chance this particular combination before, nor have I since. Another favourite tipple at the time was dark rum and orange.

We passed through the main bar and into the beer garden. A toasted cheese and onion sandwich arrived and was swiftly demolished. Writing this now, I'm reminded of what a musician told me about touring with Martyn in the Seventies. 'He was like a hyperactive kid. He had to either damage something or at least play with it.' A toddler kicking a football nearby was bewitched. You could see why. Martyn had charm to burn and presence by the barrowload.

Martyn lived in Thomastown for the last years of his life. What brought a man here? Hard weather, for sure. Money trouble. A fresh start. A good woman. Bed and board. It seemed an odd place to pitch up, until you remembered that Martyn had been pitching up in odd places all his life. There had been formative spells in Glasgow and outer London, but more characteristic had been a desire to lay low in the broom, like some fugitive robber baron making his home in the margins, close enough to strike for the towns when a job called. Places with good fishing nearby and a decent view from the kitchen window to gaze at while cooking. Places where, when you ran out of supplies at midnight, you could call the minicab firm in the nearest town and they would deliver the required dose. Forgiving places.

We talked for a couple of hours, a conversation which will be called back at points during what follows, alongside the recollections of scores of people who knew him, played with him, laughed with him, lived with him. People who loved him and feared him – often at the same time.

As though confirming the well-versed suspicion that there was a range of personalities lurking within that vast broken frame, his accent shifted between matey Cockney-lite and rather mellifluous Glaswegian, sometimes travelling over borders in the space of a sentence. Two men, I thought – and the rest.

In terms of his social status, he aspired downwards. Slummed it. Though his Scottish roots were respectably middle-class, he often adopted the persona of the erudite Glaswegian hard nut. His mother was a light opera singer from Surrey by way of Belgium, but in England he preferred the guise of East End roustabout, all apples and pears and bish-bash-bosh. There are schoolboys who want nothing more than to grow up to be villains. One suspects that Martyn never quite grew out of that ambition.

He expressed his love of Nick Drake, Buddhism, Davy Graham, Teresa and *The X Factor* alongside his desire to send the royal family to Elba and most of the record industry somewhere worse. At turns he was sweet, tough, slightly terrifying and very funny, exhibiting roughly equal measures of scholarly eloquence, quicksilver intelligence and macho roguery, with flashes of tenderness. If there was guilt – and there must have been – it was not offered up. He seemed cheerfully unrepentant about the many bad choices he had made.

There was an unexpected courtliness, an old-school refinement and a pleasing precision and dryness in his choice of language which reminded me of the great Scots comic Chic Murray, one of his favourites. In some other life and time Martyn might have been a tweedy rural doctor, serially seducing his patients' wives. Like many brawlers, he was an incurable romantic and terribly sentimental, as given to tears as violence, often in close proximity. The hug and the head-butt were not strangers.

When I left, I did so with some sadness, and I confess a degree of pity. Hard to fear a one-legged man. He must have hated that. As we parted, he appeared concerned that I would miss my train to Dublin. Teresa drove me to the station with minutes to spare. A few days later, when I had flown back home to Edinburgh, my phone rang. It was Martyn, niggled by some relatively innocuous misgiving he had aired regarding a cover version of his much-loved – though not by him – folk anthem, 'May You Never', which had been released by an obscure Seventies band many years ago and long forgotten by most sentient beings. The gist was, he recalled, that he had told me he thought their rendition was shit. Please would I not print what he'd said? It was a long time ago, and he didn't want to offend anyone. I assured him that I wouldn't, and I didn't. As I did so, I thought, Why would you worry?

'He was a one-take man,' Chris Blackwell told me on the day, three and a bit years later, that John Martyn died. 'A true one-take man.'

Martyn lived his life the same way he made his music, improvising as he went, with no safety net, admirable in one sense and impossibly irresponsible in another. He tore through it, scattering brilliance and destruction in his wake. He blackened the eyes and broke the spirit of women he professed to love, abandoned at least one of his children and neglected others. He wore his volatility and rage as armour, perhaps, but it was volatility and rage just the same.

xiii

Despite the murk of his life, the good heart of the music shines through. Whether it shines sufficiently brightly to penetrate the surrounding darkness is perhaps the wrong question: one would not exist without the other. His first wife calls Martyn a 'Luciferian' and his stepson sums him up as 'a disaster; this guy was demolition man'. His daughter Vari describes her relationship with Martyn as 'one of the best of my life'. To Danny Thompson, he was 'totally beautiful'. He has been called a waster and a genius. Softness and abrasion. You either take your pick or wonder whether it may yet be possible for one person to be all these things, and more.

PART ONE

The Winding Boy

1

We are in the beer garden, John Martyn and I, talking about and around Philip Larkin's most famous line of poetry. They fucked him up, he says, his mum and dad.

'I don't care what anyone says, a good gran beats a good mother anytime. They have all the experience, so they're not learning on you. That said, I'm quite sure that any flaw in my character has to do with the divorce of my parents. I'm very sure of that.'

There's much here to untangle: a tight hard knot of abandonment issues, armchair psychology, insecurity, projection, love and hurt. Before all that, the cavalier reference to 'any flaw'. That there were indeed character flaws – armed to the teeth and hunting in packs – is hardly open to question. The flaws, in a sense, are why we are here. In the pub in Thomastown, lines from Martyn's wonderful song 'Head And Heart' seem to float in cartoon speech bubbles from the super-charged cider. This is the man who desired to be loved '*like a child*'.

The divorce of his parents occurred at an age when Martyn was still soft fruit, ripe for bruising. It was not simply the painful matter of the end of their relationship, but the fact that, in his reading, he was not claimed by his mother in the spoils of war. Instead, he was raised by his father and grandmother, visiting his mother during summer holidays. In the early Fifties, for a young child to live apart from his mother was unusual to the point of social transgression. For a two-year-old, it was simply incomprehensible. The confusion spread through his life, spilled ink on a blank white page. At least, that was the way Martyn felt about it.

His parents were Thomas Paterson McGeachy and Beatrice Ethel Jewitt. At the time of his birth both were professional singers. 'They weren't *real* singers, they were light opera singers,' Martyn told me. 'It was all ever so upmarket and highbrow, or so they thought. Not really my caper. In fact, they rather detested my voice. They said I was a trickster, because I didn't do' – and here he made an awful shrill noise – 'the opera thing.'

Beatrice was born on December 10, 1924 to Maud and Harold Jewitt, into a Jewish family that had moved, after her arrival, from Belgium to England.* Her father was a broker for a shipping company, her mother a housewife. They lived at 34 Compton Avenue, in the new and affluent garden suburb of Gidea Park in Romford, Essex. Beatrice had an older brother, Harold Jr, and a sister, Ivy, six years her senior, to whom she remained close.

Martyn's paternal family was big and boisterous by comparison. His father was the second oldest of seven children born to William and Janet McGeachy, who married in 1916. Tommy was born in 1919 in Greenock, a port on the Firth of Clyde, where his father worked for Scotts, the shipbuilders. During the First World War, as a marine engineer, William had sailed to Calcutta and Rangoon. Later, the family moved to Edinburgh, where William bought a major shareholding in Lothian Motors on Gorgie Road, and where Tommy's three younger sisters were born. They later settled at 10 Tantallon Road in Shawlands on the Southside of Glasgow.

The Second World War broke out when Tommy was twenty. He served in Italy as a volunteer temporary sub-lieutenant in the Royal Naval Reserve and sang opera for the troops on the radio. Everyone who knew him, at all ages, remembers his gift. 'I could be coming down Tantallon Road and you could hear this incredibly beautiful

---

* Much later, when he fought – which was often – with his first wife, Beverley, née Kutner, who was herself Jewish, Martyn would shout, 'I'm Jewish!' Beverley would say, 'Oh, shut up!'

voice ringing over the streets,' says Linda Dunning, Martyn's girlfriend and latterly fiancée between the ages of sixteen and twenty.

It was a talent Tommy shared with his wife-to-be. In her late teens, Beatrice began singing under the stage name Betty Benson. A soprano, she was a regular on the General Forces Programme and the Home Service from 1943 onwards, often performing with the Harry Fryer Orchestra. As one of the titular attractions in *The Three of Us*, which aired on Sunday afternoons, she sang alongside Sally Douglas and Lorna Martin. 'Three newcomers,' announced the *Radio Times*, 'three girls still in their teens.' In 1947 she appeared in *Music in the Home* on the Light Programme. According to family lore, one of her friends was a young Julie Andrews.

Mostly her career involved performing in variety shows, revues and pantomimes. She was singled out in the *Burnley Express* as 'the sweet of the party' and performed often with Chalmers Wood and His Scottish Dance Orchestra. Heavily trailed in the *Daily Record*, she sang as a featured vocalist at the Kelvin Hall in Glasgow on December 23, 1945 – which is where she may have first met Tommy McGeachy.

By the following year, the pair were performing together, often in Scotland, billed as Betty Benson and Russell Paterson: Paterson was Tommy's middle name and the maiden name of his mother. They garnered brief but admiring notices in the local press. The uncredited reviewer for the *Dundee Evening Telegraph*, watching *Hello Summer* at the Perth Theatre on June 21, 1947, observed that 'the soloists are in good trim. Russell Paterson and Betty Benson are sweetly sentimental.' Later in the season, a writer for the same paper noted 'the fine tenor and soprano voices of Russell Paterson and Betty Benson... [They] carry the audience with them in their song numbers.'

In September, shortly after the end of the summer run in Perth, they married in New Malden, a town in Surrey on the suburban fringes of London. They were staying at 58 Beechcroft Avenue, a handsome, semi-detached Thirties villa, with a front and back garden, on a horseshoe-shaped road.

Almost exactly a year later, on September 11, 1948, Ian David McGeachy was born in New Malden.* Tommy returned to treading the boards, in short order appearing in *Giggles & Girls* at Dundee's Palace Theatre the following month and in *Goldilocks and the Three Bears*, a pantomime at the Glasgow Pavilion, in December. Betty was back home holding the baby. She wouldn't do so for long. The marriage was a short season. It did not run and run.

Martyn claimed he once saw his parents perform together before they separated. 'About fifth on the bill would be Mummy and Daddy, Betty Benson and Russell Paterson – "Scotland's Troubadour". They sang stuff like Gilbert & Sullivan. I remember them singing [Émile Waldteufel's] "The Skaters' Waltz" in the Gaiety Theatre, Ayr, with my mum in a dazzling Victorian outfit.'[1]

If this is true, he possessed excellent recall of his earliest experiences. Within three years of his birth, his parents had not only divorced but Betty had already married again, in October 1951, to Peter Donaldson. In the fallout, it was agreed that their child would be raised in Glasgow by his father and grandmother, and that he would visit his mother during the school holidays. Within the family, it was believed that Betty had wanted to continue her career and felt she could not do so while looking after her son.

Martyn once told me he was bequeathed a sense of decency from his father and a wandering morality from his mother. She was, by several accounts, a fascinating woman. Independent, clever, direct, funny, free. She married three times, became a mother twice more in her forties, and lived with a certain resistance to convention. In his teens, his mother's lifestyle opened Martyn's eyes to the attractions of the bohemian life, but, as both a child and a man, he also resented the implications and consequences of some of her decisions. Those who witnessed them together are in no doubt that she loved him, and he her, but it was a complicated relationship. 'His mother gets a bad rap as the person who abandoned her child, and it just wasn't as

---

* His given name is often incorrectly written as Iain, but on his birth certificate it is spelled 'Ian'; it is written this way in his school yearbooks and also on the birth certificates of his children.

straightforward as that,' says Linda Dunning, who knew Betty well in the mid-Sixties. 'This certainly wasn't a child whose mother didn't care about him – that was far from the truth.'

Nevertheless, it proved difficult to foster a traditional mother-and-son dynamic with a woman he saw for only six weeks each summer. Periods of sustained closeness in his late teens and early twenties were followed by longer periods of minimal or zero contact. Martyn's own children met their paternal grandmother only once or twice, and never formed a relationship with her.

Both parents continued to sing professionally once the marriage had ended. For Betty there were theatre runs in Bolton and Eastbourne, and in the summer of 1952 a season not far from Glasgow, at Troon Concert Hall, which may have provided an opportunity for Martyn to see her perform and spend time with her. Otherwise, her visits to Scotland were, at best, infrequent. For all the McGeachys remember, his mother never came to see him at home, and the divorce and its aftermath were not discussed, even as Martyn travelled through childhood into adolescence and adulthood. 'Nobody really talked about it; they would shut things out,' says Martyn's cousin, Alison McGeachy. 'Betty lived down south with her new husband. I don't ever remember her being mentioned, actually.'

Tommy subsequently appeared in several Harold Dayne productions: light comedies with musical interludes, variety shows and pantomimes called things like *Cinderella Sally*, *Autumn Leaves* and *For the Love of Pete*, often forming tenor and soprano acts with Grace Calvert or Greta Hagan. In October 1951, the month his ex-wife remarried, the *Arbroath Herald and Advertiser* announced a forthcoming attraction, *The Fighting Flanagans*, at the Dundee Palace Theatre, featuring Russell Paterson among the cast. The *Winter Show* of 1952 found him performing at the Empire in Inverness.

While his father was away, Martyn was looked after by his grandmother in the family home. He had grown into a happy, garrulous child. His father later recalled that, on one of the first occasions he had brought his toddler son to Glasgow on the train to visit his family, the boy talked non-stop for the whole journey, charming everyone in the carriage. One school friend recalls that his mother called Martyn 'Mr Speak-A-Minute', because when he came around to play he never stopped chattering. As he sang many years later, silence never was his thing.

In later life, Martyn often turned up the temperature of his raising on the mean streets of Glasgow. To hear him tell it, adolescence was a blizzard of razor fights, gang wars and back-alley rumbles. Yet he was not a rough boy and he was not raised in roughhouse ways. His grounding in Glasgow was firmly middle-class. The Gorbals would have swallowed him whole. 'He couldn't fight his way out of a paper bag,' says Brian Stanage, who first met Martyn when they were both four years old and who remained a close friend throughout their school days. 'He was the most passive guy. It was like wrestling with a blancmange.'

Situated near the end of a leafy street of fine sandstone tenements, 10 Tantallon Road was a beautiful old flat occupying the top floor and attic space, overlooking the entrance to Queen's Park, one of Glasgow's finest public parks. There was a playroom with a snooker table, a scullery, more bedrooms than could be counted on one hand, and a sitting room with fine bay windows looking onto the street, with furnishings which included a piano, comfortable couches and vases filled with fresh flowers. Martyn's close friend at secondary school, Davie MacFarlane, remembers Tantallon Road as the first time he had been served spaghetti that hadn't been decanted from a tin, and where he first tasted home-made lemonade.

Most of the bustle took place in the kitchen, with its large wooden table and Rayburn stove. At the end of the long downstairs hall, a staircase led up to the top floor, where Tommy kept both budgies and lodgers, who occupied many of the upper bedrooms. Number 10 Tantallon Road was a comfortable, substantial and somewhat eccentric family seat.

'It was such an interesting house,' says Brian Stanage. 'A strange house. There was a samurai sword which held a fatal fascination for us, which belonged to his father. He had these collections of knives and he would bring them out and show them to us. Sleepovers were a bit spooky. We used to sleep in the attic with the door locked.'

For many years during Martyn's childhood, the extended McGeachy clan spent much of their summer holidays, Easter breaks and the period between Boxing Day and New Year together in the house in Shawlands. On his father's side, Martyn had six aunties and uncles – Eddie, William, Robert, Janet, Agnes and Catherine (known as Kitty) – and twelve cousins spanning a considerable age range.

His uncle Eddie was a PE teacher at Waid Academy in Anstruther, Fife. Another uncle, Robert, worked as a forester at Carradale, on the remote Kintyre peninsula in southwest Argyll. Martyn's aunt Agnes lived at Tantallon Road during his early childhood. He would engage her as a surrogate parent, asking her to walk him to school or to accompany him to sports day, saying, "Can we just pretend that you're my real mother?"[2] When Agnes later married, Martyn would look after her daughter, Janet, eight years his junior, taking her for ice cream at the Bluebell Café and teaching her how to guddle for trout in the River Cart or at Patterton dam.

Martyn's father taught him 'the manly pursuits. I was very lucky. No better thing can happen to a young boy.'[3] Fishing and shooting became lifelong passions, ones he sought to pass on to his own children. 'John had a terrific eye for beauty, and a terrific love and respect for nature,' says his daughter, Vari McGeachy. 'He was very happy when he was in it, whether it was fishing or foraging for mushrooms or out shooting rabbits.'

His cousins idolised him. He grew particularly close to Eddie's eldest son Kirk, who was eighteen months his junior and shared his love of music.[*] Many of his younger cousins entertained schoolgirl crushes. Alison McGeachy remembers carefully rehearsing what she would

---

[*] Kirk McGeachy emigrated to Montreal in 1972, where, alongside an accomplished academic career, he established himself as a highly regarded amateur folk musician in a number of Celtic-orientated bands, including Orealis. He was also a prolific songwriter and performed widely as a solo artist. He died in 2006.

say to Martyn before she saw him, so painfully bashful was she in his presence.

Tommy McGeachy is remembered by his nieces, nephews and Martyn's childhood friends with great fondness. He was loquacious, good-humoured, pleasingly idiosyncratic, a fine singer, hospitable host and committed bon viveur. His portly frame and curly moustache lent him a physical resemblance to Frans Hals' classic self-portrait. Tommy had learned to cook spaghetti bolognese in Italy during the war, and at Tantallon Road he turned the meal into a piece of living theatre. He tended the sauce for hours on the Rayburn, teaching the children how to twirl the spaghetti and to carefully spoon out the correct measures, insisting the dish must be eaten by all, regardless of age, with a sip of red wine. 'It was a religion to him,' says Linda Dunning.

At the centre of it all was Martyn's grandmother Janet. Her husband William had died two years after Martyn was born, having suffered from severe arthritis for many years. At the end, Janet was unable to look after William. The McGeachy family had their roots in Kintyre, and William was shuttled back and forth to his family in Dalintober, near Campbeltown, until his death in 1950. Ever since, Janet had been the head of the household. She was a stern matriarch and a firm disciplinarian. 'Victorian, and very strict and old-fashioned,' Martyn recalled. 'But lovely.'[4]

'My granny was very good to Ian,' says his cousin, Fiona McGeachy. 'She was his surrogate mother. She was very loving, she made a big fuss of us all, but she was a bit no-nonsense, too.' It was an unfashionable kind of love, tough but true. The kind that cast an unsparing eye over her grandson's potential girlfriends and caused acute unease among some of his other friends. Brian Stanage recalls a 'babushka of a grandmother who was absolutely terrifying. On sleepovers I couldn't sleep; I thought she was going to get me.'

She instilled a little fear, but also a deep love of music, in her children and grandchildren. As late as the Seventies, not long before Janet died, Beverley Martyn remembers her as 'a great old woman who could still thrash out a mean ragtime on the piano'.[5] Tantallon Road was filled with music. Everybody sang. Tommy's sisters played piano.

His brother Eddie not only played guitar but was instrumental in setting up the school folk club at Waid Academy; Eddie's wife Ella played, too.

In what was still largely a pre-televisual era, a typical family gathering started with food and drink and ended with everybody in the sitting room, the fire lit, with Martyn's granny or one of his aunts playing piano. Everybody performed their party piece, a slightly more refined example of the Glasgow tradition of one singer, one song. Martyn claimed to have been an 'innocent bystander'[6] in these proceedings, listening and watching. The range of songs and styles was wide.

Music was one inheritance. There were others. There was a slightly wild outer edge to life with the McGeachys – a trace reading of hysteria. Kirk McGeachy's widow, Pat, recalls a 'hammy' side to their collective nature, a characteristic passed down to Martyn, who in his adult life was highly gesticulatory, flamboyant in speech and gesture, even at times ever so slightly camp. Another family member mentions a streak of anxiety in the genes, a tendency towards high-strung nervousness. 'I don't know if Ian had that or not. I wonder.'

Martyn believed that after his wartime experiences his father was never quite the same. 'When he came back, he could only think of having a good time,' said Martyn. 'Didn't want to work. And as far as I can see he lost faith in the whole of society. He was a very sweet man but the war just destroyed his brain, took his illusions and his innocence away.'[7] One thinks of the ragged character in Tom Waits' 'Swordfishtrombone' who returned from the war with a party in his head.

After his singing career ended, Tommy was involved in the wholesale grocery business for a time. He also worked for a local newspaper, the *Glasgow Citizen*, but he was better known around Shawlands as a nightly fixture at the Corunna Bar on the corner of Langside and Pollokshaws Road. 'I think John and he had quite a tricky relationship,' says Vari McGeachy. 'From what I heard, there was quite a lot of John hanging about outside of boozers waiting for his dad.' When Billy Connolly first became acquainted with Martyn on the Glasgow folk scene in the Sixties, he recalls that 'John was scared he'd become alcoholic, because his father was alcoholic'.

'It runs in the family, from my grandmother on down,' Martyn told me. While Fiona McGeachy says she never saw Janet drinking 'except when we had our little soirees', Martyn remembered her imbibing secretly in the scullery, using egg cups instead of glasses to avoid detection. In contrast, Tommy's illness was acute and widely known. Martyn later told Paul Wheeler, a singer-songwriter and one of his closest London friends, that he would accompany his father to Alcoholics Anonymous meetings. 'He wrote a song called something like "How Could You Let Life Do That To Your Love" about his father,' says Wheeler. 'I don't think he ever recorded it, but I remember him singing it to me.' Tommy grew steadily more reliant on alcohol. When he died, aged eighty-four, 'he was still drinking, big time,' said Martyn.

It was not perfect, but which family is? Martyn enjoyed a loving home life. He was an only child, but it hardly felt that way much of the time. He was short of neither attention nor affection, which would not change. Indeed, he was destined to be forever indulged. 'He had a wonderful family in Glasgow,' says Fiona McGeachy. 'There was no misery. He just accepted it and got on with it. People say he got a deep dark hurt from his mother. I don't buy that. I didn't get that sense at all.'

On the surface, he skated through. Deeper down, those closest to him believe the absence of Betty as a constant in his life had the impact of a branding. 'I felt John was obviously looking for love, from an early age when I knew him,' says Davie MacFarlane. 'It wasn't from lack of love from his gran and his father; there was just this big hole where his mum should have been.'

'He never forgot the fact that he wasn't brought up by his mother, that his grandmother and father brought him up in Scotland,' says Beverley Martyn. 'There was this intrinsic sadness that went right back to him being a small child and not seeing his mother; writing to her and never getting any reply. Many letters were found that his mother had kept: "Dear mummy, why don't you write back to me? I love you so much, I miss you so much, when can I see you?" It was heartbreaking. There was a lot of lies and covering up, and he mistrusted women, which turned him into a misogynist.'

Childhood summers tend to lodge in adult memory as a series of unfocused Polaroids, each one a smudged sunburst of yellows, greens and blues; all the dull greys edited out. For Martyn, these idealised memories felt truer than most. His visits to his mother occurred mostly during the long school summer holidays in July and August and assumed a significance which bordered on the mystical.

Martyn's wavering accent bounced between Scottish and English his entire life, sometimes to comically exaggerated extremes. The initial impulse was likely rooted in a desire as a child to bridge the divide between life at home and life with his mother, a wholly understandable attempt to fit into his surroundings and smooth the process of transition.

Betty hadn't travelled far. The homes she made in the Fifties and early Sixties were within a mile or two of New Malden: Lakehurst Road in Epsom, Ferry Road in Thames Ditton, the kinds of streets typically favoured by television sitcom writers as visual shorthand for the humdrum stupor of middle-class English suburbia. Yet the reality was rather different. 'My stepfather was a terrible beatnik,' said Martyn, who recalled spending time with his mother and Peter Donaldson on houseboats in Surrey. 'Very sophisticated compared to Glasgow: there were Chinese restaurants! We smoked dope, and all my stepfather's friends played the bongos and guitar very badly.'[8] Later, towards the end of the marriage, the Donaldsons ran pubs in the West Country towns of Devizes and Bradford-on-Avon.

According to Martyn, Peter Donaldson was an alcoholic who didn't care for children in general and his stepson in particular. 'I only got to see my mother for two months of the year, and I never got to stay with her because my stepfather didn't like me, so I stayed with her sister and her husband,' he said in 1974.[9] His aunt Ivy was married to

Ray Gloyns, and the couple lived close to Betty in Hampton Court Way, in Surrey. It was here that Martyn stayed when he was visiting. Here too, he later claimed, that Ray first got him drunk at the age of nine: two cans of cider and a proud vomiting.

Being banished to a relative's house during summer visits to see his mother may have added fresh layers to his sense of rejection, yet the mixture of mild intoxication and the enchantment of the Surrey suburbs cast a spell over Martyn that drew out his softness like sap from a tree. He fell hard for Green England: the green parks, the green waterlilies, even the green trains which rolled out to Surbiton on the Southern Line. This was an idealised country of riverbanks and willow trees, sleepy, sun-dappled and serene, a bucolic pastoral which spoke to something deep in his nature. It was an emotional as well as physical space in which he maintained a connection to his mother, and within it he recognised the potential for a new way of being.

During a series of Edenic Surrey summers some fatal romantic spirit entered his soul. Glasgow was cold, hard and real, whereas 'London was like a dream to me'.[10] The feeling travelled deep into his music. The proximity to the river, the parks and the sunshine at first made an unsophisticated literal impact, in early songs such as 'Knuckledy Crunch And Slippledee-Slee Song', where he lived '*on a houseboat*', fed the swans, and even his uncle Harold, Betty's brother, makes an appearance.★ 'Dusty' was inspired by the vivid spectacle of the Hampton Court Fair, the colours swirling through the '*chestnut tree night*'.

Later, the mixture of profound beauty and deep melancholy in much of Martyn's music would radiate more meaningfully from these childhood summers, where he felt both a peaceful sense of belonging and raging isolation and rejection. It runs through his work like a thick verdant vein, though it is strongest in the first decade. By the time of

---

★ The lifestyle made a lasting impression. According to Ralph McTell, he 'bought a bloody canal boat on a whim one day. I always had this vision of the peaceful canals of England, driving along in a narrowboat with only the back end in the water and the front sticking straight up in the air with John at the helm.' In the Nineties, Martyn lived for a time on a boat in Chester.

Grace And Danger, the memory seemed to have faded and lost its potency, and the compelling oppositions in Martyn's work no longer sparked much creative friction. The taste stayed with him, however. Almost half a century later, he rhapsodised that *The Wind in the Willows* was his favourite book.

At the time, he brought it all back home and tried it on for size. 'I had always seen myself as a bohemian, since the age of about thirteen,' he said. 'I liked walking the streets of Glasgow in my bare feet; that seemed a fine piece of rebellion to me... it was the desire to be something different.'[11] It offered a crucial point of departure from the prevailing orthodoxy. In a city which did not generally encourage deviations from the norm, here was a way to stand out.

The uniform at Shawlands Academy in the Sixties comprised a white shirt, navy-blue jersey, grey flannel trousers, blazer and school tie. It was not strictly enforced and became a minority fashion choice, but even so, the newly liberated Master McGeachy pushed the school's tolerance to the limits. 'He was always a one-off,' says his schoolmate Tommy Crocket. 'He would come in with a string vest on top of his T-shirt, a pair of jeans and a pair of white sand shoes without socks. He was a character.'

Martyn was educated first at Langside Primary School, a few hundred yards along Tantallon Road. In these early years, his sartorial choices were equally striking. 'He had a three-piece suit with short trousers and a bow tie,' says Brian Stanage. 'That was his gran's influence. He was different, because it was ascertained very quickly that he was English, and that was a bit of a stigma.' At primary school, there were typical instances of teasing and name-calling. 'He didn't get involved in any altercations as far as I can remember; he just walked away.'

Aged eleven, in 1960 he moved up to Shawlands Academy, five minutes' walk to the other side of Shawlands Cross. It was a big school, and a good one. Pupils were expected to work hard and to aspire to higher education. Discipline was firm. The headteacher,

Archibald Bell, was nicknamed Ding Dong by the pupils, though only when well out of earshot. There was little in the way of bullying or fights. When indiscretions did occur, the belt was used to punish those who overstepped the mark.

By the time Martyn was going through the school, the social sands were shifting. There was a developing schism between the pupils who lived locally, in relative comfort, and those who arrived on the bus from the new council schemes of Nitshill, Pollok, Carnwadric and Arden. 'Shawlands Academy was quite a grim conformist place in the mid-Sixties,' says former pupil Norrie MacQueen, who attended at the same time as Martyn. 'Inordinately pleased with its "Senior Secondary" status and infused with petty snobberies: Shawlands and Newlands owner-occupiers versus we "schemies" from the corporation estates further out.' Another pupil in Martyn's year, Ruthie Zorgenlos, recalls how shocking it was to encounter the influx of pupils from the outlying estates. On one occasion she was taunted in the playground for belonging to a family that owned their own house.

According to MacQueen, Shawlands witnessed the formation of a 'sort of dissident circle' of working-class students who challenged the norms. This faction would not have been accessible to someone of Martyn's status. To his undoubted chagrin, as a natural disrupter and 'lifelong socialist', he found himself stationed on the more conservative side of the barricades. He would have to cook up his own rebellion.

The class divide was not something to which many of his friends paid heed. Folk singer Linda Thompson was at this time still Linda Peters, a year older than Martyn and living on a housing estate in the Southside. Martyn had found part-time work delivering milk and newspapers in the area. He first became her paper boy, then her friend. 'We hung out at a café in Calder Street, smoking and playing the jukebox,' she says. 'He was very handsome, but there was never anything romantic – he was like a brother. I was in a council scheme in Merrylee, and John cultivated a bit of a hard-man image. I would have thought of him as working-class like me but, no. I think his family owned their flat.'

In one of the most fervent football-supporting cities on earth, his disinterest in the national obsession made him 'stick out like a sore thumb,' says Brian Stanage. 'It isolated him from most of us, who were football mad. He had no natural ability at all; it was incredible. We used to take the piss out of him – he kicked a ball like a girl, we used to say. Just no natural rhythm at all.'

His preferred sports were rugby and cricket, pursuits which, in Scotland, came with clear middle-class connotations. He was also partial to snooker and darts, more earthy diversions in the city's clubs and bars, as well as the decidedly un-rock 'n' roll pastime of lawn bowls. In the Seventies, Camphill Bowling Club, just across the road from Tantallon Road, would occasionally enjoy the dubious honour of a visit from Martyn and Danny Thompson.

He remained a fan of rugby in particular throughout his life. When the author and poet Andrew Greig bumped into Martyn in London in March 1969 outside Les Cousins club in Soho, the talk was mainly of Scotland's First XV beating France 3–6 in the recent international in Paris. Only after re-enacting the highlights did he offer Greig's folk duo an opening spot before his headlining show the following night. In later life he claimed to have played fly half for the South of Scotland team and to have once scored a winning try. One schoolmate, Eric English, recalls playing rugby with Martyn at school, but the yearbooks for Shawlands Academy during his tenure feature photographs of the football First XI and rugby First XV and he is not pictured in any of them. Nor is he mentioned as participating in any of the school's musical productions.

His academic prowess, however, is noted. He did well at school. Upon moving up from Langside Primary, he entered 1LF and was streamed into the top set in all subjects. 'We did every class together for the first two years except PE,' says Sandra MacEwan. 'He was very smart, very bright and very confident. I wouldn't say he toed the line. He wasn't a rebel, but he could make waves when necessary.' In a school with a clear hierarchy, and where the staff demanded respect, 'he was always quite happy to question what was being said,' says MacEwan. When it came to teachers most susceptible to being riled, the Latin master, 'Chunky' Cowan, was top of the list. At times, Cowan would lose patience. He once flung a heavy wooden board duster at Martyn's head – 'Boy, turn around!' – while he was talking to another pupil.

Martyn was an amiable live wire. Trouble with a lower-case 't'. Ruthie Zorgenlos recalls Martyn as 'the life and soul of mischief in the class and a really affable guy. He was always the one in the middle of any bother – but not nasty bother, just hijinks. Bravado. Devil may care.'

In third year, pupils made specific course choices. Martyn leaned towards classics and the arts. Entering class 3B1, in 1963, he was in the boys' first stream, swimming near the front. That year, he was chosen to represent his entire year group in Scottish Television's inter-schools quiz programme, *Round Up*. His two fellow team members were a girl from fourth year and the girls' school captain. They lost by three points and 'John stole the show,' says Davie MacFarlane. He was commended in the school yearbook for being the top student in his year in English and was selected for a pilot project where the brightest students studied Latin and French at the same time. A gift for language stayed with him. On his first date with Beverley Martyn, he impressed her by ordering in French. He also had a little Italian.

He formed close bonds with a small circle of friends rather than running in a pack. 'He would gang up with you for one night, then you wouldn't see him for weeks,' says Brian Stanage, who, alongside Davie MacFarlane, became Martyn's closest friend. They called him McGeachy, never Ian. MacFarlane came from a staunchly socialist family in Strathbungo and worked on the milk round alongside Tommy Crocket. Despite their contrasting academic levels – 'I was in one of the dunces' classes' – he and Martyn hit it off. 'You could see they were on the same wavelength,' says Crocket.

MacFarlane had longish hair and wore ex-army combat jackets provocatively accessorised with a school cap. He and Martyn spent weekends record shopping in town and listening to music at each other's houses. They embarked on silly pranks. MacFarlane had found a Labrador wandering in Queen's Park and was looking after it until it was claimed by its owner. Martyn would walk the dog around the neighbourhood with his father's antique stick and a pair of sunglasses, keeping a tally of the number of good Samaritans who helped him across the road. They both loved to fish, in the local rivers and dams. In time, they explored a shared enthusiasm for alcohol.

There was already a tendency to present himself differently depending on the context. While Ruthie Zorgenlos recalls a 'character, a comic, a big personality', MacQueen remembers a boy with 'a rather distant demeanour. Ian was not standoffish exactly – he was friendly enough – but a little shut off.' The memory of another pupil, Gordon MacIver, is that 'he sat behind us in French wearing a parka and a scowl. Never said a word. He seemed to have zero pals and less social skills. I remember him as a sourpuss who appeared aloof and a bit arrogant.'

Some pupils resented his intelligence. 'They called him "Kichie McGeachy"* at one stage,' says Davie MacFarlane. 'I wouldn't say he was a teacher's pet, but he was so bright that he got a lot of encouragement from teachers.' One English master, Mr Cochrane, 'raved about him and encouraged his storytelling abilities,' says Stanage. 'He almost promoted him to prodigy level.'

He sat his SCE exams in 1964, at the end of fourth year, and stayed on to study Highers, the Scottish equivalent of A levels. University was the obvious next step for a pupil of Martyn's ability – he later said he considered medicine – but other distractions took precedence.

At sixteen, Martyn starting going out with Linda Dunning, his first serious girlfriend. She lived in the well-heeled suburb of Newton Mearns and attended the city's top independent school, Hutchesons' Grammar, less than a mile from Shawlands Academy. The relationship was meaningful for them both and would last until the end of 1968, when Martyn met his first wife.

He and Dunning – nicknamed Dizzy – clicked at a dance at Whitecraigs tennis club, a regular Saturday-night fixture. No matter that, immediately prior to that first encounter, Dunning had been

---

* 'Kichie', pronounced 'keechie' to rhyme with 'McGeachy', is Scots slang for 'shitty' or 'filthy'.

stepping out with Davie MacFarlane. 'We were really pissed off and angry with him,' says Stanage. 'She was Davie's first girlfriend, and she was suddenly snatched from him.' Here, perhaps, was an early glimpse of the 'wandering morality' Martyn later spoke of, the single-minded ability to set aside his finer feelings which proved characteristic throughout his life. There were other examples. A little later, Stanage bought a hand-tailored three-piece Harris tweed suit, which was instantly coveted by Martyn. Having ended up in hospital after overindulging at a weekend dance, Stanage woke up the following morning to find that the suit had disappeared. 'Your mate took it,' the nurse told him. 'He wasn't for giving it back,' says Stanage. 'He claimed they had had to cut it off me and that it was ruined. I eventually had to go around to the house and force him to give me it. That's the kind of guy he was. He was a bit of a chancer.'

From the moment they got together, Martyn and Dunning were joined at the hip. 'He was a beautiful young man,' she says. 'Tall, long legs, curly hair, this character that walked around in long fur coats or army greatcoats with no socks. My mother despised him.'

Martyn was never allowed across the threshold of Dunning's smart semi in Newton Mearns. Undeterred, whenever he came to collect his girlfriend or drop her back home, he did star jumps on the street outside the house, shouting hello to her mother at the top of his voice.

They became a rather glamorous sight around the city's Southside. She with her long hair, short skirts and hippie threads, which included a flowing black cape with a silk purple lining. He with his bare ankles and blond curls. Fiona McGeachy recalls her older cousin in his teenage pomp. 'He was very good-looking. He had a lovely sheepskin coat with a curly fur collar and stripy jeans. All the mod fashion.'

At the local tennis club dances, the girls drank Babycham and Martyn would have a few cans of beer. He liked getting drunk but chose his moments. Despite his later tendency to talk up trouble, he largely avoided the gang violence and indiscriminate aggression that could often mar nights out in Glasgow. 'There was a lot going down around us, but John certainly wasn't part of it,' says MacFarlane. 'Later on in life he had to fight because he upset people – but not back then.'

20

Together, Martyn and Dunning enacted the standard teenage rites of passage: after-school rendezvous, late-night bus rides, long walks home, deeply professed declarations. 'It was first love, and a great time. He was a very charming person, and he mixed easily with people. He was carefree.'

They hung out at the local Wimpy bar and the Embassy café and went to the beautiful art deco Embassy Cinema, which was demolished in 1965 to make way for an ugly shopping arcade. After school, they often met at Shawlands Cross and walked to Queen's Park. 'He always had his guitar, and he would sit down strumming and picking, teaching himself,' says Dunning. 'I had no idea that it would evolve into what it became. I wouldn't say there was a burning ambition, but, as he became more proficient, it was what he wanted to do.'

The guitar was a new passion. In a home filled with song, it's little wonder Martyn eventually took the bait. He sang in church – in a city where religion mattered, the family was Protestant – and at a young age had been encouraged to learn the fiddle, which he struggled with and soon gave up. The first instrument he played 'with any joy' was the harmonica, keeping the beat as he walked the long miles home late at night – perhaps why, in his prime, he careered through the world with the accentuated swing and bounce of a 'Gatemouth' Brown harp riff.[12]

Shawlands was not an especially musical school, although one of the French teachers was Morris Blythman, who performed as Thurso Berwick, a left-wing activist and prolific contributor to the oeuvre of Scottish political songs. A peer of singers such as Hamish Imlach and Josh MacRae, Blythman 'was big in the folk revival movement and he used to mentor some would-be folkies,' recalls Norrie MacQueen.

Perhaps Martyn was one of them. If so, it's not something he ever mentioned. He had found his way slowly to folk music. Having enjoyed an eclectic musical upbringing, hearing everything from Debussy, Saint-Saëns and Segovia on his mother's side to traditional

Scottish music, Tin Pan Alley and *The Pirates of Penzance* on his father's, in his early teens he started shaping his own tastes. 'I was desperately trying to become a bohemian by playing guitar, wearing shades and attempting to grow a beard to be cool, *man*. A beatnik thing, I suppose.'[13]

He wrote poetry and read the Beats, Ken Kesey and Hermann Hesse's *Siddhartha*, set texts for many switched-on teenagers at the time. He enjoyed Lenny Bruce. There was a long flirtation with the Mod movement, which involved 'two Vespas... ska and soul, The Temptations and Four Tops, Prince Buster.'[14] When the high tide of this passion receded, it left in its wake a lifelong love of soul.

By 1965 his interests had turned to folk and blues. One catalyst was seeing Joan Baez perform 'Silver Dagger' on television. It was the song rather than the singer which fascinated him, and in particular Baez's fast, finger-picked guitar playing. Another revelation was hearing a Davy Graham record at the home of Davie MacFarlane, a household which was more progressive than most. MacFarlane's older sister was a student at Glasgow School of Art, and his father had been a conscientious objector during the war. They were politicised, inclusive and culturally aware. 'I had [Graham's 1964 album] *Folk, Blues And Beyond* before a lot of other people in the area,' says MacFarlane. 'John and I loved Lead Belly and the blues guys; that's where we first hit it off. Then it was Bob Dylan and Davy Graham.'

Born in Leicester to a Scottish father and a Guyanese mother, Graham's complex tunings and intricate fingerstyle playing galvanised the folk scene and lifted the veil on a world of new possibilities. His classic solo guitar piece, 'Anji' (also sometimes known as 'Angi' or 'Angie'), a descending corkscrew of a composition, was first released in 1962 on the *3/4 AD* EP, although by then it had already been taped informally by Len Partridge and passed around the folk community like the commandments of a new religion.

'It was a real eye-opener in terms of guitar technique,' says Archie Fisher, one of the leading figures of Scotland's folk revival. 'Davy was more jazz guitarist than folk guitarist. He adapted his tuning to play Indian and African music, and adopted the DADGAD tuning, which is now the gospel tuning for all folkies. His influence was that the guitar didn't have to stop at the three-chord trick and a bit of picking. People started to make arrangements inspired by that possibility.'

Folk, Blues And Beyond and *Folk Roots, New Routes*, the latter recorded with Shirley Collins in 1965, sealed Graham's status as the godfather of a new breed of British acoustic players which included Bert Jansch, Martin Carthy, Wizz Jones and John Renbourn.

Graham and Jansch became lodestars for Martyn: their desire to pull away from folk into more exotic territories proved inspirational to his developing tastes. A sheen of film-star romance clung to Graham in particular. He was mercurial, mysterious, a little dangerous and troubled. Heavily narcoticised, politically radical and utterly unclubbable, he lived to his own code. He had ventured to India and Morocco, bringing back knowledge and enlightenment from ancient cultures. He tuned into obscure bluesmen and found inspiration in modern jazz artists like Thelonious Monk, Charlie Parker and Mingus.

As soon as Martyn heard him, he became fascinated by the possibilities of the solo acoustic guitar, a style he had previously associated solely with classical players like Julian Bream and Segovia. He borrowed a guitar from a friend in Glasgow, then bought his own, a Rolif acoustic. 'I actually begged my father for a guitar,' he said. 'I was in love with the thing; I used to run home from school to practise.'[15] He would lock himself in the scullery at Tantallon Road to practise in peace.

Although this distracting infatuation initially caused 'many an argument between him and his father', according to his cousin Janet, Tommy McGeachy was the kind of man who was inclined to help.[16] He was a Mason, and one of his friends in the local lodge, a guitar maker called Billy Synott, pointed Martyn towards Hamish Imlach, who ran guitar classes at the Glasgow Folk Centre.

Eight years older than Martyn, Imlach was a broad oak in Scotland's traditional music landscape. A popular folk singer-songwriter, he was a consummate blues guitarist and charismatic entertainer, as adept at penning anti-nuclear protest songs as he was at writing wry social comment or winking comic doggerel. He honed a highly successful career in Scotland and further afield with his mixture of traditional material, American blues, risqué parodies and shaggy-dog stories. He recorded for Transatlantic Records, sang in pubs and at peace demos, and for a short while was resident MC at Clive's Incredible Folk Club in Glasgow. His heart was huge and his mind wide open. He became a critical link between old and new folk currents.

In Imlach's biography, which he co-wrote, the musician and author Ewan McVicar summed up the range of his gifts succinctly as 'a raconteur who taught Billy Connolly, a singer who taught Christy Moore, a blues guitarist who taught John Martyn'.[17] He was a large man, and larger than life. Says McVicar, 'I only met one person who had a bad word to say about Hamish, and that was a girl whose flute he'd sat on and bent.'

Imlach gladly welcomed all manner of waifs and strays into his home. He lived on the top floor of a three-storey council block at 152 Muirhouse Road in Motherwell with his wife Wilma and their four children, who were turfed out of their beds whenever a visitor needed it, which was often. Christy Moore remembers first meeting Martyn at Muirhouse Road. 'It was open house,' says Phil Shackleton, a good friend of both Imlach and Martyn from the mid-Seventies until their deaths. 'The door was always open, the neighbours were in and out using the phone. You were always guaranteed some kind of entertainment.'

Martyn joined Imlach's ragged coterie, and in time became part of the family. Wilma Imlach – who died in 2019 – would always talk about his 'wee angelic face' when he had first appeared seeking guitar lessons. Mothering was a recurring theme in Martyn's life. He became a favourite surrogate son of Beryl Moyes, wife of Drew Moyes, who ran the Glasgow Folk Centre. All his life, he tweaked the maternal instincts of kindly women, though they did not always get their due in return.

Imlach became Martyn's new school, where he learned the rudiments of a bluesy acoustic guitar style. The education went deep. Imlach loaned Martyn many key records – Robert Johnson, Reverend Gary Davis, Brownie McGhee, Blind Lemon Jefferson, Bukka White,

24

the Folkways *Anthology Of American Folk Music* – which he blended with his own interests. He had heard Bob Dylan, Pete Seeger and Phil Ochs at the home of Davie MacFarlane and liked the rousing feel of protest music, which chimed with his own worldview. 'I've been a socialist all my life,' he told me. 'Natural-born socialist, but the folk clubs really brought it out of me.'

As an aspiring guitar player, he graduated from Duane Eddy and The Shadows to pieces by Lead Belly and Blind Boy Fuller; 'Don't Think Twice, It's All Right' by Dylan; the ubiquitous 'Cocaine Blues'. 'Anji' was regarded as the Matterhorn of achievement. 'That was the test piece,' he said. 'If you could play "Anji" you were taken kind of seriously, you had the basics.'[18]

It was an obsession, and he got good very quickly. 'The development of his guitar playing was phenomenal,' says Tommy Crocket. 'Nobody could believe it. His talent was unbelievable.' At school, Martyn began to get noticed. 'There were a few of us in my own year aspiring to be blues guitarists,' says Norrie MacQueen. 'This was the high tide of Davy Graham, Jansch and Renbourn. The shared target was getting "Anji" right – and [John] was already way, way beyond that. So we were a bit in awe of him. I do remember the occasional ad hoc performance, or demonstration, for us in the playground.'

It was immediately apparent that he possessed a natural gift, but from the very beginning he displayed unusual levels of application when it came to music. His work ethic was fearsome. Returning from a session with Imlach, he would practise for hours in his big, sparsely furnished bedroom in Tantallon Road, or locked away behind the scullery door, losing himself in the music. 'When he first started out, his fingers were nearly bleeding,' says MacFarlane. 'He put in an incredible amount of work. He would turn up at my door at 11.30 at night: "I've just worked out this chord. I've got this new song – do you want to listen?" Wouldn't leave until about one o'clock.'

Throughout his life, or at least for a good part of it, Martyn possessed a trance-like ability to tune out distractions and home in on his craft. 'I had never seen anyone so wrapped up in his playing, so concentrated as John,' Beverley Martyn said.[19]

The 'how' of making music was already becoming clear to him. The 'why' was always a little less obvious. He was rarely inclined to look too closely. 'I was a little isolated, I think,' he recalled two decades later. 'I played to alleviate or release some feeling. I wouldn't say it was a conscious move to minimise an unhappy feeling; it was just an urge to sing... It was just something romantic to do.'[20]

2

Martyn's first live performance was a home fixture. Langside Halls is barely one hundred paces from the McGeachy end of Tantallon Road: two verses and a chorus, around the corner and gently up the slope. It's still there, a grand Victorian public building with multiple function rooms dominating the corner of Queen's Park where Langside Avenue meets Pollokshaws Road.

Sometime in the second half of 1965, Martyn made his public debut at Langside. Like so much that would happen subsequently in his life and career, he framed ambition as happenstance. The Scottish singer Josh MacRae 'got drunk in the pub and couldn't appear,' he recalled. 'So I was given the gig, because I was the only one in the audience who could play the guitar and sing.'[1]

He was one of several people that night to get up to do a turn – folk concerts generally not being short of audience members who can sing and play guitar. What is notable is the confidence. He had been playing guitar less than a year. His recollection was that he sang 'Candyman', 'Cocaine' and his own composition, 'Run Honey Run', all betraying an obvious debt to the folk-blues repertoire of Jansch and Graham. But still – 'they shoved me up there and everybody liked it'.[2]

Significantly, the set also included his most noteworthy early original song, 'Fairy Tale Lullaby'. Martyn gained a head start on his peers by beginning to write before he had fully mastered his instrument. He wasn't much interested in a dutiful apprenticeship working his way through the folk canon. He was gifted linguistically, an astute listener and an excellent mimic, all crucial attributes for an aspiring writer. 'He started writing at a fairly early age,' says Linda Thompson. 'We both came up in an age where songwriters wrote and singers sang, [but] writing was fostered in us by listening to Dylan and Phil Ochs and The Beatles.'

Some weeks after his first appearance, he played again, at the Black Bull pub in Dollar, a well-heeled country town near Stirling. He claims he was paid £11 for his troubles, the equivalent of almost £200 in 2020, which seems unlikely for an unknown teenager starting out.

On both occasions, Martyn was presented with the opportunity through his connection to Hamish Imlach, who was performing as the headline act. 'His patron at the time was Hamish, who used to take John around,' recalls Archie Fisher. 'I can remember Hamish complaining about John leaving too many sweetie papers in his car. He was just a nice, innocent, curly-haired young boy, who would do a spot in a folk club before Hamish.' He was company for Imlach, rather than competition, although his attendance could cause some frustrations. Phil Shackleton recalls, decades later, Imlach still complaining about the fact that Martyn would sit in the front row and jump in with the punchlines to his jokes just before he said them. 'Hamish threatened to kill him one night!'

It was Martyn's fine fortune as an embryonic artist that he found a mentor and a platform at a time when Scotland's folk music scene was loosening its collar. Where previously it had been rather regimented, with all the formal rules and fussy subclauses of a closed society, it was now tuning into the rather more ragged tenor of the times.

Edinburgh set the pace. In the post-war era the city was outwardly staid, but below the austere façade lay a wild and woolly cultural underground, shaped by hard-left politics and the annual Festival and its Fringe, which 'brought all sorts of people through,' says Robin Williamson, the Edinburgh-born singer and songwriter who founded The Incredible String Band. 'Notably some wonderful Indian and African musicians, like Ali Akbar Khan.' At the 1963 festival, one memorable after-hours jam session involved Carolyn Hester, Larry Adler and Ravi Shankar.

During the festival, poets, actors and musicians rented out derelict shops and performed. An unlicensed venue housed in an old toffee factory, Edinburgh Late combined a gallery, cabaret and café. Organised by the Young Communist League in conjunction with Glasgow Art School, it mixed the earthy and the glamorous. Albert Finney dropped in. Eventually it was closed down by the police.

The Paperback Bookshop in the university quarter was a countercultural nexus run by Jim Haynes, an American émigré who co-founded the Traverse Theatre, and later co-launched the progressive anti-Establishment publications *I.T.* and *Suck* and the Drury Lane Arts Lab in London. After hours, people would congregate for wine and smokes, talking art and politics, playing music. The CND movement was in its embryonic stages. Communism and nationalism were popular causes. 'It was very cosmopolitan,' says Williamson. 'There was a left-wing, slightly radical element. A lot of the early gigs I did were for the Communist Party. Edinburgh was very receptive. A lot of students and beatniks.'

Folk music was tightly stitched into this landscape. Old Town pubs like Sandy Bell's and the Waverley Bar held regular music spots. At the centre of it all, by the early Sixties, was the Howff, a former hillwalkers' club located at 369 High Street, opposite St Giles' Cathedral on the Royal Mile. Founded by the English impresario Roy Guest and his wife Jill Doyle, it was here that Bert Jansch, a sixteen-year-old guitar prodigy, first began to play publicly.

Born in Glasgow but raised in Edinburgh, Jansch had recently left school to work as a market gardener. He blew in one day in 1960, attracted by the club's guitar classes, and impressed everyone instantly. Jansch became a rather introverted fixture in the Howff where he frequently drove patrons to distraction, sitting on the floor, picking at his guitar incessantly.

Rarely more than the length of a bothy ballad from financial catastrophe, in early 1962 the Howff finally folded. The vacuum was filled by the Crown, a pub in nearby Bristo Street where Archie Fisher and Jill Doyle started a folk night, held in the back room every Thursday. 'It was very stark: sawdust on the floor, no stage or PA, a few benches and stools,' recalls Joe Boyd, the American producer, manager, publisher and talent spotter who first visited Edinburgh in 1965. Performers were paid 50 per cent of the door takings, with a couple of drinks thrown in. The male dress code was tweed, flannel shirts, kipper ties and cords. The counterculture had not quite swept into the world of folk music, but it was knocking at the door.

Before long, Williamson started his own folk night at the Crown. One of his most memorable bookings was Davy Graham, hired for the princely sum of £100. Graham was Jill Doyle's half-brother, and a regular visitor to Edinburgh. 'He was worth every penny,' says Williamson. 'At his best, he was a unique and stellar figure. We were all a bit scruffy, and he arrived wearing a white suit, white shirt, white tie, white socks and white shoes. He was absolutely immaculate and played so beautifully. He influenced everybody.'

The Crown was where The Incredible String Band formed and took wing, initially as a union between Williamson and Clive Palmer, a fully fledged beatnik from London who enthralled his friends with authentic troubadour tales of busking around Europe. Palmer landed in Edinburgh in 1962, living in a cavernous communal room in the Society Buildings, a dilapidated Quaker meeting hall on Chambers Street. It was a vast space, big enough to accommodate a game of football, with a basin at one end and a toilet cubicle at the other. In the middle they constructed a Bedouin tent as living quarters, to avoid having to heat the whole room.

Palmer and Williamson played together throughout 1963 and 1964. The music was changing with the culture. Hashish began appearing on the scene, challenging alcohol as the stimulant of choice. 'People say that hash didn't really become available in Edinburgh until 1962, which was about the time that Clive arrived,' laughs Mike Heron, another Edinburgh musician, who joined The Incredible String Band in 1965. Acid crept in, too. At the same time, the influence of American, Indian and African music, alongside the medicine cabinet, began twisting the music into interesting shapes. When Joe Boyd passed through Edinburgh in the spring of 1965, he saw Williamson and Palmer perform in the Crown. 'It was great,' he says. 'It was Scottish tunes, taking them to Appalachia and back via the Balkans and North Africa. I thought, This is really wonderful.'

By 1966 Palmer and Williamson had added Heron to the ranks, and the original three-piece incarnation of The Incredible String Band was born. Boyd signed the band to Elektra and took them to Sound Techniques in Chelsea to produce their debut album. Alongside Bert Jansch's version of 'Anji', the String Band's 'October Song' is the quintessential sound of mid-Sixties Scottish folk. Though built around a traditional finger-picked riff, it has a hazily exotic edge, dense with metaphysical musings about *a door behind my mind*. Heron began writing, too, and would soon compose 'A Very Cellular Song', a 13-minute opus which 'was meant to be a description of a trip, how you go through all these different levels and come out at the end'.

This was the febrile culture John Martyn stepped into as a young musician. He was booked at the Crown at least once, recalled by Williamson as 'a wonderful player. He had a handsome fresh face, which he later managed to destroy completely.' Shortly afterwards, he appeared at Clive's Incredible Folk Club in Glasgow, a memorable if short-lived venture set up by Clive Palmer for ten weekends in the spring and early summer of 1966, housed in the fourth floor of a disused office block at 134 Sauchiehall Street.

The whole room, including the windows, was painted matte black. Access was via an ancient cage-like lift 'or way up a rickety set of stairs,' recalls Rab Noakes, one of the legions of local musicians who made the pilgrimage. It ran from 10 p.m. on Saturday until 5 a.m. on Sunday and everyone came and played, including the String Band, Davy Graham, Bert Jansch, Billy Connolly, Wizz Jones and Les Brown, whom Martyn claims gave him his first taste of hashish around this time. The more traditional end of the scene was served by Matt McGinn, Alex Campbell and Hamish Imlach, who was the resident master of ceremonies.

Martyn would come to watch and also to perform, arriving after midnight, often after taking Linda Dunning home to Newton Mearns.

'We booked everyone we could,' says Mike Heron. '[John was] one of the young guys that we thought was outstanding, so we got him to do a set. He was really just into the music back then. He wasn't really [wild].' When the club emptied in the early hours of Sunday morning, many of the throng travelled fifteen miles out of town to Temple Cottage, the home of Mary Stewart, an American veterinary doctor with five children whose farmstead became a freak-folk HQ.

In Glasgow, folk music had until now largely been the preserve of societies like the Iona Community, the Jordanhill Folk Club and the Glasgow Folk Song and Ballad Club, held in the Grand Hotel at Charing Cross. Founded in 1960 by Ewan McVicar and Drew Moyes, the Glasgow Folk Song Club changed the tone. A Sunday-night gathering in a lunch club called the Corner House, situated opposite the Tron Theatre on the Gallowgate, it was a spartan affair. 'We used to have to stop singing when the tram came by, as it was too loud,' McVicar recalls. In time the club was blessed with a rudimentary PA, slung on the top of a pole.

After a couple of years, Moyes opened the Glasgow Folk Centre in a disused industrial space on Montrose Street, behind the City Chambers. Like many similar venues which were beginning to appear, the Folk Centre moulded itself into being from the most unpromising raw material. It had previously housed sewing machines and consisted of a large open room with a smaller room at the rear, and a stage with a battered piano on it. It became a hub for all manner of emerging local artists, alongside well-known national and international acts. A music programme ran every night of the week. During the day, there were workshops and instrumental lessons, even a record-lending club.

'It was brilliant,' says David Philip, a frequent visitor, who later worked in Bruce's Records in Sauchiehall Street and befriended Martyn. 'The guys who ran it were cable-knit-jumper types, but they knew which way the wind was blowing, and they were getting all the new acts in. The String Band would play a lot of Sunday afternoons, which was fantastic. Ron Geesin took a piano apart on stage. There were a lot of really good guitarists, semi-blues singers, coming off the back of Bert Jansch. It was so small, you'd be sitting on top of people, and you'd get a bacon sandwich at one o'clock in the morning.'

The high turnover of artists ensured the Folk Centre thrived on the kind of variety which began to attract younger, fresher faces. Martyn was one of them. He performed floor spots in exchange for free entry. Some nights he brought Davie MacFarlane along as a plant. When Martyn asked the audience for requests, his friend would immediately call for 'Anji'. Martyn would ponder the request, nod, then reel off a note-perfect and apparently spontaneous rendition.

Finances were a recurring issue for Moyes, who gained a reputation for fiscal unreliability. When Irish balladeers the McPeake Family came to play, there wasn't enough cash on the door to pay them – a situation which caused considerable consternation. Many years after performing there, American bluegrass guitarist Doc Watson could be heard bemoaning the fact that 'that bastard Moyes still owes me £45'. But then Moyes owed practically everybody money. He would later go bankrupt, to no one's great surprise.

Martyn left school in the early summer of 1966, aged seventeen. He was more than capable of going to university, but 'Ian being Ian, he just did his own thing,' says Fiona McGeachy. 'Tommy was always asking my dad [Eddie] for advice, about how to set him straight and get him on the right track academically. He was worried that Ian was drifting off into the music.' Following a period during which they were at loggerheads over his compulsive guitar playing, Martyn always maintained that Tommy was relatively lenient. He didn't lecture his son about his behaviour, was permissive on matters of drink, sex and soft drugs, and, once it was clear that further education was not going to be an option, supported his ambitions and let him run more or less free.

'I never heard him talking about university, even though he was extremely bright,' says Linda Dunning, who started a teacher training course at Jordanhill College after leaving school at the same time as her boyfriend. Instead, Martyn found a job as an office boy for Petrofina, a global oil firm with premises in central Glasgow. He would often meet up with friends at lunchtime and vent. 'He went out in a suit every single day and he didn't like it one bit,' says Dunning. 'I think it triggered the realisation he needed to be somewhere else.'

'I don't think he lasted very long, because the late nights that he kept ate into his ability to turn up early in the morning,' says Brian Miller, a fellow folk musician whose father was Martyn's boss at Petrofina. 'I know he kept late nights, because I saw him perform in the small hours in the Glasgow Folk Centre!'

He worked for a spell for a company which manufactured lanolin and supplemented his income any way he could, including occasionally skimming the takings from collection boxes intended for the RAF Wings Appeal. When Donnie Barclay first met Martyn, at the Kind Man pub on Pollokshaws Road, he was playing darts for money in a pair with Davie MacFarlane. Barclay already knew Martyn by sight from the Folk Centre, where he cut a rather aloof figure. 'He kept himself to himself,' says Barclay. 'Everyone wanted to speak to him because he was so good on the guitar. He would be polite, but he never seemed to form any close friendships.'

Appearing regularly at the Folk Centre, Martyn began to register on the radar among his peers. 'He was a good-looking young man, confident, with a really good voice,' says Rab Noakes, who made his debut during the same period. 'He had a wee bit of a swagger about him that was rare in one so young. It wasn't anything obnoxious; he was just quite cool and aware of his own capabilities.' The influence of American blues was strong in the clubs at the time. This suited Martyn, whose guitar style, shaped by Imlach, betrayed his love of artists like Mississippi John Hurt. 'It was mostly a bluesy repertoire,' says Noakes. 'He had a really interesting finger style. If there was any Hamish Imlach influence, it would be in his guitar playing, and the subtle art of stagecraft. From an early age he knew how to hold people's attention.'

Even then, Martyn was the kind of presence who tended to fill a room. Not all rooms desire to be filled; some prefer a little elbow room. His boisterous self-belief could occasionally grate. 'We'd go to folk clubs together and have fun,' says Linda Thompson. 'He always said, "I'm going to be terribly famous, because I'm fabulous!" He was physically gorgeous and preternaturally confident. I never met anyone so sure of himself till Rufus Wainwright decades later.'

He rapidly progressed beyond Davy Graham's 'Anji', the scene's ubiquitous instrumental, to performing his own material. 'Every time I saw him, he had written a new song,' says Barclay. 'It seemed to pour out of him.'

Billy Connolly was a member of folk trio The Humblebums, with Gerry Rafferty and Tam Harvey. A regular presence at the Glasgow Folk Centre, he recalls first hearing 'Golden Girl' there, a song which later appeared on Martyn's first album. 'I remember him singing [about] the green stream that meanders round [his] mind,' says Connolly. 'He was a good guy, a good laugh. He did an instrumental on the guitar using the capo; he'd slide it up and down, going up a half tone each time.' This was 'Seven Black Roses', which became Martyn's undergraduate party piece in the clubs of Glasgow and London, a flashy flourish of cheerfully contrived theatre which always went down well in the room.

Already, the rigidity of sections of the traditional crowd rankled. Many Scottish folk musicians were conspicuously reverent to the purity of the source material, a notion that didn't much interest Martyn. He saw himself as liquid to their stone. 'A lot of people didn't like him, because he queered the pitch,' says Linda Thompson. 'There was that thing of folkie people thinking, "Oh, he could be really good if he was more traditional." John was very versatile, but because there was an American feel to him a lot of people disregarded him. I think he fell a little bit between pillar and post.'

As an artist who, more than half a century later, is still most often categorised for convenience as a folk musician, Martyn presents awkwardly. He loved the more elemental forms of Celtic traditional music, drank down its mystery and magic, but, while socially and superficially he clearly transected the folk movement, to squeeze Martyn into the straitjacket of such terms is to mislabel him. He modelled himself as a bluesman, and when he turned to the traditional repertoire, it was to the house of the blues he most frequently called; by the end of his life the affiliation was glaringly obvious.

When he sought an outlet for the explorative side of his creativity, it was jazz which offered a guiding principle. He loved reggae, soul and dub, and borrowed liberally from them. He was not averse to a jaunt down Tin Pan Alley. Folk in the most traditional sense, however, with a few notable exceptions, was not his calling. Crucially, he was temperamentally at odds with the communal impulse so fundamental to that world. 'He wasn't the kind of guy who would sit in on a session with other folkies and sing with them, like the Fishers would,' says Brian Miller. 'He was a singer-songwriter.'

As a practising bohemian, he forged his own path. The most serious and successful collaborations he sought during his life did not belong to the informally inclusive world of folk, where everyone met as equals. Martyn's alliances instead relied on the versatility of other artists, their willingness to stay with him no matter where he led, and their ability to push him even further out into the wilds. He may have been hard to follow, but follow him you must; he did not readily or regularly bend to the requirements of others. And, unlike so many young musicians starting out on a musical adventure, 'a band never appealed… Very selfish. I've always had a vision of a lonely bluesman going down lonesome tracks into the setting sun. Mississippi blues is my kind of thing; I like that solitary approach.'[3]

He was a little too angelic at this stage to make a convincing Blind Boy Martyn. 'He had a very pretty voice, which irked him a bit,' says Linda Thompson. 'He wanted to sound rougher.' Life, craft and experience would grant him his wish. For now, he was a lone wolf who more closely resembled a spring lamb.

When he played outside Glasgow, Martyn would often rendezvous with Imlach in the Montrose Bar or the Marlin before setting off in Imlach's Mini to clubs, bars and hotels around Scotland and northern England. It was a generous apprenticeship, a chance to hone his skills playing a 15-minute set as the opening act to an established name.

Often, he impressed the organisers and they would book him again, billed as the main attraction next time. Before long, he was taking the bus or hitchhiking to gigs all over the country.

As he and Imlach saw more of each other, their bond deepened. Martyn became a surrogate son, visiting Muirhouse Road for Sunday lunch, post-gig sessions, parties, family gatherings. 'They kind of adopted me, really,' he said. 'Hamish was an incredibly generous man, wild in spirit but just totally socialist with a wonderful sense of humour.'[4]

His flat was not merely a music hub. It was an informal seat of learning, where wit, erudition and staying power were traded as precious metals, and which provided endless social stimulation. 'Hamish was a movable party,' says his son, Jim Imlach. By showing rather than telling, Imlach taught Martyn how to live large. 'If you bought one of something,' says Phil Shackleton, 'Hamish would buy two. John got a lot of that from him.'

At Muirhouse Road there was good food, and plenty of it: curries, spaghetti bolognese, soups and stews simmering on the stove at all hours. It was open house, with beer, wine, spirits, music and dope on tap. Come all ye and stay awhile. Last man standing wins. 'In the Sixties my capacity for spirits was phenomenal,' Imlach wrote in his memoir, *Cod Liver Oil and the Orange Juice*, recalling how he would challenge all comers to drinking competitions. Martyn was not yet up to anything like full speed, but he observed with admiration.

When it came to the guitar, however, student quickly outstripped teacher. 'The difference [between] John and my dad was that John had the application to practise for ten hours a day,' says Jim Imlach. The public dazzle of Martyn's playing was polished hard in private. Each performance was an event, with elements of intuitive spontaneity, but he always gave himself the best chance by laying down the groundwork. 'He was confident, because he was good at what he did and knew what he was doing,' says Linda Dunning. 'He wasn't going to mess up.' Even during the madness of the Seventies, there was 'a lot of energy, and an incredible work ethic,' says his stepson, Wesley

Kutner. 'I remember him keeping me up all night long, tuning and practising all night.'

He took his gifts seriously. He wanted to be better than everybody else. Clive Palmer, who had left The Incredible String Band and headed for India with almost indecent haste after the release of their debut album in June 1966, later returned to Scotland and spent time on the road with Martyn. 'He was always a very determined player, he used to practise a hell of a lot,' said Palmer, who died in 2014. 'He never put the guitar down when I knew him... he was going in a straight line towards being successful on his own terms.'[5]

He thought deeply about ways in which he could stand out from all the other earnest young men playing acoustic guitars. Brian Miller recalls Martyn removing the metal pin from an old elastic capo and sellotaping it over the sound hole of his acoustic guitar. 'When he played, this thing rattled up and down and gave a very odd sound indeed. Even at that stage he was experimenting, trying to manipulate the sound. He was obviously influenced by Davy Graham and Bert Jansch, following in the wake of people who had paved the way for him, but he developed his own style.'

He was already testing out different tunings, some of which he was shown by the String Band, according to Davie MacFarlane. While certain songs were written and played in standard tuning, he largely forswore the popular DADGAD tuning in favour of DADDAD, in which the third and fourth strings chimed in unison. Other songs were written in drop D, where the bottom E string was lowered a tone, and in open C. Ewan McVicar recalls that early on at the Folk Centre Martyn played his songs in the same order each time, because he 'didn't know how he had got from one tuning to the other, in terms of the theory of it'. Instead, he simply memorised the entire routine.

In time, as is the way of these things, Martyn forgot that he had ever been a student at all. He had a lifelong aversion to any whiff of structured tuition, and would tell people, mock-indignantly, 'Nobody taught me how to play guitar!' – which was not entirely true, but one could see his point. He simply took what he needed and built on it. Jim Imlach studied his technique and came away baffled. 'I watched my dad for years – he was great – but watching John up close, I couldn't recognise one thing he was playing. There were no chords. The left arm was playing stuff that was unbelievable, and the right arm was going along with it. John's thumb could come right over the top of the guitar and reach the second string. How do you even do that? I thought I knew how people played guitar, but he was truly unbelievable.'

Martyn may have transcended Imlach in musical terms, but much of what he learned about the texture of life as a touring musician stayed with him. Imlach typified the old-school showbiz values of the Scottish west coast folk scene. 'Edinburgh was a bit more academic; people *studied* folk there,' says Mike Heron. 'In Glasgow, they didn't give a toss, they just wanted to have a good time. It was more boisterous.' The city's folk stars tended to be garrulous and versatile entertainers like Imlach, Matt McGinn, Alex Campbell and Billy Connolly. Cheek and chutzpah were highly valued. When that arch-traditionalist Ewan MacColl visited, he cocked an ear to the locals and their irreverent mix of sardonic humour, blues, skiffle, trad ballads and originals, and dismissed the whole bunch of them as tartan cowboys. Martyn, however, was practically allergic to reverence and felt at home on the range. He never forgot the value of putting on a show.

From Imlach he also learned by heart the troubadour's code. 'They had the exact same outlook,' says Jim Imlach. 'If you look back in history to any bluesman, you take bits from other people's work, you pass things on to the next generation, and you drink the whole time, take drugs and have fun. That was his outlook, and that was Hamish's outlook. John was tied up with all of that. It didn't come separately [from the music]. It was the old blues tradition: you travelled, you played, you drank, you met women. I absolutely know they both felt like that. They laughed at someone like Bert Jansch, because he took the whole thing too seriously. They were a couple of wasters and they loved it.'

Throughout his life, Martyn returned regularly to Imlach's flat in Motherwell. When he moved back to Scotland in the early Eighties, he stayed within striking distance of the family. It was his North Star, a kind of refuge, immune to airs and graces, where he was accepted entirely as he was. The door was always open, as was a bottle. Phil Shackleton, another of Imlach's musical surrogates, remembers a conversation he had with Martyn many years later, in the small hours, as the snow was falling outside his cottage in Roberton. 'He said to me, "It was always great to stop at Hamish's. You'd get up in the middle of the night and peep in the bedroom, and Wilma was laid in bed there with all the kids cuddled up around her. It was beautiful." That was Ian McGeachy talking. He was soft as hell, really.' One of Imlach's three daughters was called Vhari. Martyn named his first child after her.

'There was a bond there that I never really got to explore,' says Jim Imlach. 'They were very, very tight. As John got older, he even started to look like Hamish. Even my mother commented on it. A lot of it was about mutual respect. They never had a falling-out. It was just about the music and having a good time.' They did once engage in a heated argument about rhubarb. Martyn told Imlach that rhubarb was poisonous. Imlach told him he was talking rot. He had eaten rhubarb many times and was still here to tell the tale. 'This was before the internet,' says Imlach. 'They put a fiver bet on and John was right. That was typical.'

Falstaffian, Rabelaisian, selfish, wildly immoderate and endlessly generous, Imlach died, hugely overweight and somewhat diminished, on the first day of 1996, at the age of fifty-six. The parallels with Martyn are striking. Perhaps the pupil learned too well.

3

The manner of Martyn's departure from Glasgow balanced brazen ambition with a certain cinematic flair. It happened in the spring of 1967, when he was eighteen. While Linda Dunning waited at Shawlands Cross for her boyfriend of two years to turn up for their arranged date that evening, he was already on the train south. Tunnel vision.

'He didn't tell me that he was going,' she says. 'I waited and waited and waited, and finally I went around to the house, and his dad was very upset. He said, "I'm sorry, my dear, but he's gone. He left on the train to London." I was heartbroken.'

It was no whim. His friends knew he was going. Martyn had realised that he was not where he needed to be. He went to London in a concerted effort to make money, live out his imaginings of a bohemian lifestyle, and avoid clocking into a regular job – ambitions which he fulfilled, on variable terms, for the rest of his life. As he would sing four years later, on the shrugged mea-not-quite-culpa which opens *Bless The Weather*, nobody glancing at Martyn would ever mistake him for a man devoted to a life of labour.

Yet he *was* working, on his guitar skills, his songwriting, his contacts. 'John's rise on the folk scene was meteoric,' remembers Christy Moore, the Irish folk singer making his own way at the same time. 'He seemed to go from support slots in Scotland to headlining in Les Cousins in a short period of time.'

41

Opinion divides around the force and nature of Martyn's ambition. 'He was certainly not interested in being famous,' says Brian Blevins, who worked with Martyn as head of press at Island Records for much of the time he was signed to the label. 'The last thing he wanted to be would be a pop star. I think he had more of a jazz musician's approach and mentality to things, which meant that the size of your audience is going to be fairly small but fairly intense.' For Paul Wheeler, Martyn was 'terribly career-conscious, for all his apparent rejection of that. In all the time I knew him, he always knew the right person to chat up in terms of his next career move. He was very calculating like that. I saw that right from when he was in his teens.'

Perhaps the two positions are not so contradictory as they first seem. Perhaps Martyn was an artist who displayed little compunction about being ruthlessly single-minded when it came to achieving his aims, but whose goal in doing so was not a conventional notion of fame and fortune, but something more idiosyncratic. In other words, he chased down success, but success defined on his own terms. Money was certainly never much of a spur. It is also worth noting that ambition is not a fixed appetite. It waxes and wanes.

He was without doubt driven as a young man. By the end of 1967, he had fulfilled his first great ambition, which was to become a regular in Les Cousins, the heart of the capital's singer-songwriter scene, a cellarful of tatterdemalion folk royalty and a circling court of acolytes and pretenders. He could be spotted at all hours bounding through Soho with a copy of his debut album cradled in his arms, a gesture which goes a long way to capturing the slightly infuriating charm of Martyn during this time: bullish, vulnerable, cocky, excitable; everything pushed up front for the world to see, fingers, head and feet bopping in time to some complex, irrepressible internal rhythm.

He had performed in London before April 1967. Folk singer Alec Milne told the writer John Neil Munro he saw Martyn at Bunjies Coffee House & Folk Cellar, a folk hub at 27 Litchfield Street, on the fringes of Soho and Leicester Square, in the autumn of 1966, performing much of the material that would end up on his first album. There were other shows during darting expeditions which garnered experience but no real foothold. On one occasion, he returned north with at least two tangible accomplishments: he had seen Davy Graham play at Les Cousins and been mesmerised; and he had adopted a stage name.

He became John Martyn on the advice of Sandy Glennon, the owner of the Excelsior Club and a contact of Hamish Imlach. Glennon was an old-fashioned Soho impresario and 'well-intentioned hustler'[1] who acted as a booking agent for many emerging folk artists, including Sandy Denny, Diz Disley, Johnny Silvo and Alex Campbell. He would in time handle Martyn's bookings, but for now he simply suggested that this ambitious young man might want to consider a more easily pronounceable professional handle.

'John went down to London and said he had to change his name,' says Ewan McVicar. 'He said that he would go in and ask for a gig, they would ask for his name, and he would say, "Ian McGeachy." "What?" He'd repeat it. "*What?*" It was just pragmatic common sense.' 'Changing my name did me no harm,' Martyn told me. 'The legend is that Martyn came from Martin guitars, but I didn't play a Martin in those days. I had a Yamaha. John Yamaha hasn't got quite the same ring, has it?'*

His breakthrough in the capital during the spring and early summer of 1967 came courtesy of the Folk Barge in Kingston-upon-Thames, run by Theo Johnson. A stocky rugby fanatic, Johnson was a chancer with limited musical skills, a ton of front and a backstory more suited to a secondary character from a cheap potboiler. On the heels of Hamish Imlach, here was another rotund, larger-than-life surrogate to help Martyn on his way, even if his motives were not entirely pure. 'I didn't like Theo,' says Donnie Barclay. 'It was just dollar signs in his eyes. He knew John was good and he thought he could make some money off of him.'

Born the eldest of six children in Flood Street, Chelsea, in 1930, Johnson grew up in Whitley Bay in the North East of England, where

---

* He didn't start playing a Martin D-28 until the early Seventies. Before the Yamaha, in the very early days he had a Harmony Sovereign. John Sovereign does have a certain ring to it.

the family moved during the war to avoid bombing. After the Johnsons were abandoned by their father, Theo went to sea at fifteen and served on a factory whaling ship in the Antarctic. Still in his teens, he was jailed for six months for stealing a gas meter from a bombed-out house. While in prison, one of the guards noticed his aptitude for drawing. He ended up taking classes and becoming a successful engineer.

According to his younger brother Van, Johnson helped design the heating and ventilating system for the Queen's Building at Heathrow Airport, which opened in 1955. He was chief design engineer on the Russian-Siberian gas pipeline which pumped gas to the Mediterranean, and one of four engineers who designed the first concrete platforms for the North Sea. Also according to his brother, 'he was both highly intelligent and a complete idiot all at the same time. He had no concept of money and was generous to a fault. Any money he had he spent on friends.' It perhaps comes as no surprise that he married four times.

Johnson had a strong voice, a taste for innuendo and a rousing manner. By the late Fifties, he was singing with Dave Waite and Roger Evans in Bunjies. When they went off to form the successful trio The Countrymen, Johnson became more heavily involved in the mechanics of the London folk scene. For a time in the Sixties, he ran Bunjies and was a key figure in several other clubs, including the Crypt in St Martin's-in-the-Fields and the Cabbage Patch and the Crown in Twickenham. He booked many notable performers. When Paul Simon pitched up from New York in 1964, broke and unknown, Johnson arranged a gig at the Labour Rooms in Richmond. Only eight souls turned up. Simon also stayed with him for a time, in common with several other American folk artists, including Tom Paxton and Jackson C. Frank, some of whom had come to Britain to avoid the anti-Communist purges sweeping America.

Johnson lived in a first-floor corner flat at 400 Richmond Road, a red-brick apartment above Vogue Interiors on the Twickenham side of Richmond Bridge. It was an elegant flophouse, with mattresses scattered throughout several rooms. The sparse living room had two essentials: a couch and a stereo. Open to all comers, Richmond Road became a rent-free mecca not only for folkies but jazz and blues players, local and global. 'He would tell people, "Take the tube to Richmond, then walk over the bridge and ring the bell at the house with the blue front door on the left side of the street,"' recalls Bridget St John, one of numerous musicians who gravitated there. Twelve-string guitarist Dave Shelley occupied the converted attic flat above.

'We had several other musicians living across the courtyard at the back and we used to sit with the windows open and sing and play to each other,' says Van Johnson. 'Almost every folkie around came or stayed at some time or other. Diz Disley and Stéphane Grappelli used to practise in the lounge. Noel Murphy was always around. Jackson C. Frank stayed with Theo and tried to commit suicide twice. He wanted to dedicate his first record to Theo, but Paul Simon talked him out of it, saying no one would know Theo in America; he was ever a self-centred little shit.'

By the time Martyn landed in London, Johnson was in his late thirties and had established the Folk Barge, a club which convened three nights a week in an old Dutch sailing barge moored just below Kingston Bridge, a couple of miles downstream from Richmond. It had blacked-out windows, fusty damp walls and a condemned air. A dipsomaniac couple called Geoff and Helen owned the place. The cover price was two shillings and six pence but you would get in for free if you played a floor spot, a trick Martyn had already turned to his gain in Glasgow. The main room was big enough to hold around 120 people and was full most nights.

The regular crowd was known as the Whalers or the Barge Crew, and included Theo Johnson and his wife Kate, Dave Waite on banjo, Van Johnson and Dave Shelley on guitar. Others who sat in included Disley, Jonny Silvo and John Renbourn, who was studying nearby at Kingston College of Art. The young Sandy Denny was taking a foundation course at the same college and made her first public appearance on the barge in 1965.

Martyn jumped aboard in April 1967, soon becoming a regular. 'John turned up at the Barge one night and Theo immediately

45

recognised a great voice and told him so,' says Van Johnson. 'Theo told him he was too good for the folk world and said he could make him a star. John said in his own imitable style, "Fucking go on, then!" Theo gave him his phone number and the next day took him to the studios and began recording his first record.'

That, at least, is the version a screenwriter might use in the film that will never be made of Martyn's life. In reality, it took slightly longer for Johnson to manoeuvre Martyn into the studio. First, he settled in at the Folk Barge, playing there several times throughout April, May and June. During that time he played elsewhere in London, notably at Bunjies.

Between stints staying with his mother in Surbiton and accepting the hospitality of other friends, Martyn joined the parade of musicians who crashed at Johnson's Richmond flat, among them Robin Frederick, a singer-songwriter originally from Florida who had recently returned from studying in Aix-en-Provence, where she had met a young, beautiful, meandering and tantalisingly unattainable young Englishman called Nick Drake, who was spending time there before beginning a degree in English Literature at Cambridge University in October. Frederick came to Britain and 'spent the summer of 1967 in London with John Martyn, listening to *Sgt. Pepper* and The Incredible String Band, watching John learn to play sitar in about ten minutes, living on toast and tea'.[2]

Produced by Joe Boyd, The Incredible String Band's expansive explorations of folk, blues, jug band and world music, heard on their eponymous debut and its follow-up, *The 5000 Spirits Or The Layers Of The Onion*, released in July 1967, afforded Martyn glimpses of how far he might take his own music. The fact that he knew the members from the Scottish scene only heightened the possibilities. 'We listened to [the first album] over and over for hours, sitting on the bare wooden floor in the living room,' Frederick told the writer Rob Young. 'You can hear the same naive, childlike quality in The Incredible String Band that you hear in John's songs.'[3]

She was one of several young female musicians with whom Martyn at this time enjoyed a close relationship. Frederick's friend Bridget St

John had also studied in Aix-en-Provence and was now in her final year at Sheffield University. She became tight with Martyn after visiting Richmond Road.

'He was young and confident and very approachable, very likeable. I would say you could see his soft edges quite easily. Or I could. I don't know if innocence is quite the right word, but [he was] really quite open and super helpful to me, a really, really good friend and brother.' Martyn took St John shopping for a steel-string guitar on Richmond Hill, showed her the ropes at Bunjies, and introduced her to new music. 'He was always broadening my whole experience of what being a musician could be like, because I had no experience of it.'

On occasion, Martyn gently abused Johnson's hospitality. One day, 'skint and bored', he and a visiting Hamish Imlach drank a bottle of his Haig whisky and replaced the contents with cold tea.[4] Van Johnson recalls that the scene involved 'a bit of drinking, not much in the way of drugs, which would only have been dope'. Martyn was often stoned, and already experimenting with the pills and hallucinogens doing the rounds among the Thames Delta set. 'It was a very strong part of my life, a real stretcher for me because I'd led a very closed sort of existence up until then,' he said.[5]

In this orbit, he made several small-time but meaningful industry connections, among them André Ceelen, who also lived at Johnson's flat for a time. A Dutch folk enthusiast who worked for Saga Records, Ceelen played an instrumental part in Martyn becoming a recording artist.

It was an era when many tiny independent and budget record labels were taking a chance on folk music. Among those who worked as opportunistic interlocutors between artists and the industry were Theo Johnson and Sandy Glennon. The releases they oversaw were shoestring affairs, taped live in a single homespun session with little paperwork involved, following a template pioneered by Bill Leader at Transatlantic. As Dave Waite recalled, 'just to be recording was a feather in your cap. It was a step up the ladder and you might get a session fee of £5 per song, or a nominal flat fee of fifty quid. If it was a traditional song, the producer would claim the arrangement credit.'[6]

One such label was Saga, a budget imprint run from a suburban house in Finchley, where the MD, Marcel Rodd, was wont to interview prospective employees while propped up in bed wearing black silk pyjamas. The primitive studio was located in the basement. The label specialised in cheap – and often excellent – classical and jazz recordings, but was branching into folk, seeing the chance for a quick, easy profit.

Johnson had already paid for and produced Sandy Denny's earliest recordings – first, *Alex Campbell And His Friends* and then *Sandy And Johnny*, on which she and Johnny Silvo performed alternate tracks. Both albums were recorded in the spring of 1967 and released on Saga. Johnson also discovered Maddy Prior and organised the recording of her debut album, *Folk Songs Of Old England, Vol. 1*, made with Tim Hart and licensed to Teepee Records. It was produced by Tony Pyke in circumstances almost identical to those in which Martyn made *London Conversation*.

André Ceelen recalls that there was never any talk of Martyn signing for Saga, which is perhaps surprising, given Johnson's existing association with the label and the fact that Ceelen worked for the company. Instead, Johnson pitched Martyn to Chris Blackwell at Island Records.

Blackwell is one of the industry's great music men. Born in London in 1937, his father was a scion of the Crosse & Blackwell brand, his mother a Costa-Rica-born heiress. He grew up in Jamaica, albeit with long periods in Britain, where he was educated at Harrow. In 1959 Blackwell started Island with a $10,000 investment from his parents, recording local pop acts with rudimentary equipment and selling their singles at local markets. In the early days, he was supported with a £2,000 annual allowance from his family. His Jamaica was very different from the one experienced by his future signings Bob Marley and Lee 'Scratch' Perry, but somehow their worlds came together.

Blackwell and Island relocated to London in 1962, where he sold ska records from the back of his car. His breakthrough came in 1964, when he produced a cover of 'My Boy Lollipop' by teenage Jamaican singer Millie Small. He leased the recording to Fontana, and it sold six million copies worldwide, giving Blackwell a crucial entrée into the mainstream recording industry, and putting Island on a firm and self-sufficient financial footing. Shortly afterwards, he signed The Spencer Davis Group, forming a long and successful partnership with Steve Winwood.

Handsome, urbane, loyal, charming, laid-back but fiercely committed to fine music and good people, Blackwell had excellent taste and the kind of principles which did not often survive prolonged exposure to the world of music-selling. He betted on the long game rather than short-term options and won more often than he had any right to.

With a direct line to many of London's independent labels, by 1967 Theo Johnson had already come into contact with Blackwell. The following year, billed as Big Theo, he released *Bawdy British Ballads* on the Island subsidiary, Surprise Records. 'Ah, Theo Johnson,' says Blackwell today. 'A big guy on a small moped. I remember him very well. I liked him.'

'John Martyn, Theo and I went to Chris Blackwell's office just to get acquainted and get some understanding,' says André Ceelen, 'but nothing was signed then.' At the meeting, Johnson played Blackwell a primitive version of 'Fairy Tale Lullaby', crudely recorded at the Folk Barge. A catchy, childlike, achingly twee confection of mildly psychedelic dream imagery, 'Fairy Tale Lullaby', was Martyn's signature song. It spoke the language of the times enthusiastically, if not fluently, and gave voice to his more innocent, loving leanings. It was already entering the folk repertoire. Sandy Denny sung it that summer with her mentor, Alex Campbell, at his Glasgow home at 19 Rupert Street. Given that it had not yet been recorded or released by Martyn, she most likely heard it first at Richmond Road or the Folk Barge. 'A lot of people learned to play that song in an open D tuning,' says Brian Miller. 'I used to play in an ensemble with a woman called Miriam Backhouse. She did a lovely version of that.'

Whether it was one song or two, or the entire package, when Johnson brought Martyn to the attention of Blackwell, his interest was immediately piqued. 'I liked John, and really rated him,' says Blackwell. 'First of all, he had a beautiful voice. He hadn't developed that rough sound he developed later; it was just this pure, angelic voice. I didn't see him so much as a folk artist, I felt that he was really a jazz artist. I always saw him that way, I was very clear about that. I'd been in New York spending a lot of time with jazz musicians, so at that time my life was jazz and Jamaican music. I had an ear for it. It was before he started all the echoplex stuff, but he was already somebody who didn't follow the normal rules of music – four bars, eight bars, twelve bars. He would be playing seven, nine, eleven bars – it could be anything, you never knew where he was going. That's why I signed him.'

'In some ways for Chris, John was easier to access than the more folky stuff like Fairport,' says Richard Thompson, a founder member of Fairport Convention, the pioneering folk-rock band which signed to Island in 1968. 'Chris loved Jamaican music, and blues was more accessible [to him]. He really liked John, liked having him on the roster.'

Island at the time specialised in ska, reggae, soul, blues and jazz. The only other white acts Blackwell had been involved with were Alex Harvey and The Spencer Davis Group, artists he had signed but then leased to Fontana. Martyn was not an obvious fit, but then Blackwell was not anybody's idea of an obvious record company executive. 'Blackwell gambles on everything,' says Phill Brown, who worked closely with him as a producer and engineer at Island during the Seventies. 'Horses, everything. He's a fantastic gambler.' He gambled on people most of all, a trait evident in his later dealings with Bob Marley. Signing Martyn was in the end attributable to gut instinct. It paved the way for a flood of folk and roots acts to come through on the label in his wake.

Although Blackwell was interested early on, Ceelen is clear that he did not sign Martyn to Island before the recording of *London Conversation*. Instead, the session that resulted in his debut album was paid for upfront and independently. It was recorded in a single summer Saturday afternoon in Tony Pyke's home studio at 37 Dryburgh Road, Putney, on two-track tape, at a cost of £158 – the equivalent of about £2,500 today.

Ceelen recalls staking £100 of the budget. 'I thought Theo paid the other half! My work visa didn't allow for work other than for Saga Records, so there was no mention on the sleeve of me.[7] I probably thought [I'd be] getting some returns from the sales from the album, but we were not part of the deal, since John [eventually] signed directly with Island Records. I must have been naive. I must also add that, for the time I stayed at Theo's place, I never had to pay for the lodging. I think it's only fair to add that.'

Ceelen attended the session, along with Pyke, Johnson and the outstanding Trinidadian jazz flautist Harold McNair, who is not credited. Blackwell did not attend, though he allowed himself a credit on the sleeve for 'overseeing' the production. 'I remember going on the bus together with John while he was playing the sitar and writing his last song for the album,' says Ceelen. 'I thought it was funny, us sitting at the back row, barefooted and playing with the sitar.'

The twelve songs comprised a no-frills rendition of much of Martyn's live set. He played alone, except when McNair accompanied him on 'Rolling Home', the experimental sitar song Martyn had been polishing en route. Did he ever finish it? It's not entirely clear. McNair would play a far more significant role on Martyn's next record, *The Tumbler*. Ceelen recalls that the flute player was offered a cheque from Johnson for his contribution, 'but he wanted cash to buy bread'.[8] The entire process was typical of the hand-to-mouth, somewhat off-the-books approach to making records in the lower echelons of the music industry.

Once the album was recorded, Martyn's momentum momentarily stalled. He played no advertised shows in or around London between early July and early November. Looking back in 1974, he said that he had returned to Glasgow and worked on a building site for a few weeks, 'but couldn't hack it'.[9] It was a period of limbo, although presumably Theo Johnson was beavering away on the business side behind the scenes. 'We were left in the dark,' says Ceelen. 'John just disappeared. As we knew he came from Glasgow, we somehow managed to obtain an address and I wrote to him [to say] that if he wanted to be a well-known artist he had to be in London.' A few weeks later, Ceelen bumped into Martyn on Oxford Street, and 'he told me that he just signed a contract with Chris Blackwell for Island Records'.

Matters of the heart may have been behind his abrupt disappearance. His relationship with Linda Dunning had survived his abrupt exit from Glasgow in the spring. He travelled back and forth on the train, eager not to lose her. While in London, he had called her in Glasgow every night without fail from a telephone box. 'I [thought] it was lovely and romantic,' she says. 'But probably what it really was, was him making sure I was home.' His insecurity and the frequent time he and Dunning spent apart may have been one of the spurs for their engagement in the summer of 1967, over-commitment often being the child of uncertainty. They went to a little antique shop on Sauchiehall Street, to pick out a ring. She was twenty and he was nineteen. Her mother remained furious.

His possessiveness extended to male friends, says Donnie Barclay. 'He was frightened of losing people. He didn't even like me making friends. If I got too close to other guys, he didn't like it.' While back home, Martyn baked hash cakes for Davie MacFarlane, getting his friend stoned for the first time, and accompanied his father on his nightly trips to the Corunna Bar. Sometimes he brought his guitar along and played in the snug. 'His dad was great with him,' says Tommy Crocket. 'I think he was pretty proud, although his taste in music was a lot different.'

After months living an itinerant life, Martyn now had a home base in London, a room in a shared house at 21 Whittingstall Road, Parson's Green, in Fulham. He lived there with Barclay, who had moved down from Glasgow, and a revolving cast of fellow exiles, artists and mutual friends. The rent was four pounds and eleven shillings per week; thirteen guineas for the whole place. 'It was like Piccadilly Circus,' says Barclay. 'You never got any sleep. Andy Matthews, who ran Les Cousins, was never out of the place. Sandy

Denny would always be there. Roy Harper moved in when John moved out.'

Whatever he was doing while they were apart, when Linda Dunning came to visit, Martyn was straight. 'There was a lot of stuff going on at the house, and I wouldn't be around it,' she says. 'I wouldn't be around drugs. I wasn't cool at all, and on occasion I told them all what I thought.' The British singer-songwriter Al Stewart had met Martyn at Les Cousins and become a friend. He visited often and recalls a birthday party at his flat where 'someone was smoking dope in his bathroom and John got very upset and threw them out into the street'.[10]

Though he had a taste for alcohol, Martyn was not yet a habitual drinker. He may have been consciously steering clear of over-indulging, given his family history, but he was also aware that heavy drinking was regarded as rather contemptible within the counter-cultural circles in which he was beginning to move. 'In the flat we were in, it was really uncool to be a lush,' says Donnie Barclay. 'They didn't like it. We'd have a couple of pints, but if you went back to the flat pissed, they weren't very happy. He never smoked that much dope, either.'

Through their entire four years together, Martyn never took drugs or drank to excess in the presence of Dunning, nor did he display an aggressive or violent streak. 'It was a more innocent, gentler time in his life,' she says. 'When I learned about [his abusive behaviour] later, I was very surprised. I wouldn't have expected that, based on the time that I spent with him and loved him.'

In London, he and his friends would often visit his mother, who had gone through more life changes. Betty's marriage to Peter Donaldson had been dissolved, and she had recently started a second family with John Collins, a builder by trade, six years her junior. Martyn's half-brother, David Collins, was born in 1965, in Marlborough, Wiltshire, where Betty had until recently been running a pub with Donaldson. David was joined by Martyn's half-sister, Julie Ann, in the summer of 1969, when Betty was forty-four.

She and Collins quietly married between arrivals, in August 1968. They lived at 7 Crescent Court, a two-bedroom flat in a modern apartment block in Surbiton, where John Collins found work as the caretaker. For a time, when he had first arrived in London, Martyn was given the key to the communal boiler room and allowed to stay there for free, bedding down with a 'palliasse [straw mattress] and a blanket'.[11] 'Many is the party we had in the boiler room, I can tell you!' he told me, winking, years later. He enjoyed spending time with his baby half-brother – 'he was quite enamoured with him,' says Dunning – and saw his uncle Harold, aunt Ivy and grandmother Maud regularly, although his maternal grandfather was now dead.

His mother is hard to capture. Strong female characters from British television soap operas crop up more than once as points of reference. For Linda Dunning, Betty was an 'upmarket Elsie Tanner'; for Paul Wheeler, she was 'more Dot Cotton'.

'His mother was a lovely person,' says Dunning. 'I was very close to her and she was always lovely to me. She was a unique, interesting person. One of a kind. A musician, a singer, very independent. She did her own thing. She didn't mince her words, she told you how it was. I don't actually think she cared what other people thought, and [John] was the same way. He was very close to his mum. They were both highly intellectual; they would have conversations about things that were at that time way over my head. They were parallel souls, sharing a love of music and a refined intellect, each forging their own unique path against the tide, regardless of other's opinions.'

Paul Wheeler stayed at Betty's house with Martyn many times in the late Sixties. He observed a very real and present loving relationship, as well as a secondary dynamic as his friend's career began to take on a more professional footing. 'I felt she was very ambitious for him, in the way that mothers can be. She knew the score, she was in the business, and she was watching very carefully. I do remember her being not just ambitious for John but calculating about it. The classic controlling mother who was kind of living vicariously through her son. She seemed a hard-nosed woman who had been around the block, and a little world-weary with it. In the morning, she'd say things like, "It's no use talking to me until I've had my cigarettes."'

'He loved his mother,' says Donnie Barclay. 'I didn't see any animosity. He never spoke much about it or gave much away about how he was feeling. He could put a front on.'

In his writing, where Martyn was at his most unguarded, there are suggestions that he found aspects of his mother's lifestyle challenging. One of the more ambitious songs on *London Conversation*, 'Ballad Of An Elder Woman', read as a biting comment on her circumstances, depicting a lady and her younger male companion: '*your husband*', sings Martyn, eyebrows and hackles raised, '*or so you say*'.

In part, 'Elder Woman' – in common with many pieces Martyn wrote around this time – was influenced by the prevailing fashion in pop music for miniature domestic dramas, a style typified by The Beatles' 'She's Leaving Home'. His versions of the form, however, came with little sense of narrative detachment. Like many of their peers, he and Paul Wheeler would discuss the way in which the nuclear family had failed not only them, but their generation in general. Being raised by his grandmother, seeing his father struggle and the consequences of his mother's choices at close hand, fed into a withering view of post-war morality and the tatty veneer of maintaining 'respectable' appearances. Much of that disgust poured into 'Ballad Of An Elder Woman', from the stark imagery of a tree stripped bare of blossom, to its blunt dismissal of a matriarchal figure who has '*nothing to teach me*'.

Perhaps this is what Martyn meant when he later called the lyrics on his debut album 'acute, viciously accurate, and very personal'.[12] The description proves laughably misleading when applied to the tuneful but twee folderol of 'Golden Girl' and 'Fairy Tale Lullaby' – with its elves, pixies, goblins, magic purple seas and dancing woods – but makes sense applied to the more reflective material. 'Who's Grown Up Now' was convincingly autobiographical, a song of adult transformation and acute love-terror. The poetic title track betrayed the sadness and confusion of a young man a long way from home, while in 'Back To Stay' Martyn reflected on his romantic insecurities, writing the words after Linda Dunning had told him she was going to spend the summer working in Norway. 'I don't think he was too happy about that,' she says. 'The songs were about our life.'

Of the non-original material, 'Sandy Grey', by Robin Frederick, was a beautiful song written for Nick Drake, which cast him 'in the role of wandering, rootless, fatherless boy'.[13] At the time, Martyn didn't know it was about Drake, or indeed even who Drake was. Perhaps he saw something of himself in it. 'Cocaine' was a safe choice from the folk-blues canon, while his version of Bob Dylan's 'Don't Think Twice, It's All Right' was a gently undemanding sweetener. Davy Graham had already recorded the song, as well as the Irish traditional ballad 'She Moved Through The Fair', which Martyn cut at the same session but which was left off the album. It was discovered decades later on the flip side of the master tape, the sole outtake from a productive day's work.

Island released *London Conversation* in November 1967. In Glasgow, there was great excitement. 'It all happened quite quickly,' says Fiona McGeachy. 'We were awful proud of him, because he was making records. I would lie in bed and listen to his music at night on my gramophone.'

It was a modestly impressive start, if not especially distinctive, much in thrall to the school of Jansch and Graham, and the more impish fancies of The Incredible String Band. The swing and attack he brought to his live shows wasn't yet apparent, but there were flickers of real individualism. That the songs were full of dawns, the sun repeatedly breaking over a city morning, was fitting. *London Conversation* is the sound of a promising young artist waking and stretching, finding his feet and his voice, struggling to stand out among the legions of similarly gifted artists around him, but firmly on his way. He gave copies to his mother and father. Presents, perhaps, but pointed ones. At nineteeen he had achieved what they never had or would. His own LP was usually to be found tucked under his arm. 'I boasted about it everywhere but nothing changed in my life,' he said.[14]

'He never really seemed that excited about it,' says Donnie Barclay, yet it was a bold statement. He had moved to London, signed a recording contract and made an album in a matter of months. 'People were impressed simply because he was doing more than they were,' says Ewan McVicar.

Martyn first appeared at Les Cousins during an all-nighter in November 1967, billed as a 'contemporary Scottish songwriter' in *Melody Maker*. Cousins was a dingy basement club at 49 Greek Street in Soho, below a Greek restaurant owned by Loukas and Margaret Matheou. They had given their son Andros – his name was commonly anglicised by his friends as Andy Matthews – the run of the cellar. In time, Martyn and Matthews developed a friendship 'that was very deep and essential to John,' says Ralph McTell, his near contemporary at Cousins. 'Andy was the non-intellectual big brother.' The Matheou family lived nearby on Frith Street. Musicians would often repair there at the end of the night, in search of moussaka.

During the week, sessions at Cousins ran from 7.30 p.m. to 11 p.m. The weekend all-nighters lasted from midnight until 7 a.m. No alcohol, no food, no coffee. Just endless music, spilling out. Artists who weren't booked to play that week were usually watching. 'Everyone would go and hang out,' says Stefan Grossman, an American folk singer who started playing at Cousins at the same time as Martyn. 'All your contemporaries would show up if they weren't gigging. It was the hot spot.'

Martyn was attending to business. Theo Johnson had helped him get started but he was a hustler, zipping around town on his moped cutting deals. He offered Martyn a punitive management contract which would shear 45 per cent from his income for the next decade. Martyn refused in brusque terms, and shortly afterwards signed up with Sandy Glennon's agency.

It was at Cousins in 1968 that he began to make a name for himself. Between June and November, he enjoyed an almost unbroken string of weekly residencies in the early slot. In such a tight-knit scene, Martyn's arrival was closely observed.

'When I first saw him – he was nineteen, I was twenty-three – he was *enviable*,' says Ralph McTell. 'Angelic looks, a mass of curly hair, piercing dangerous eyes. He was a skinny kid in plimsolls and no socks and his music matched his personality, full of youth and vigour, sexy and fun, dangerous and mischievous. On the Glasgow folk scene where he started, they mixed in blues and country music, and John took what he wanted from that: he tuned the guitar every which way, but he always kept this steady, Big Bill Broonzy thump at the bottom end. Even when he was talking about deep subject matters, there was still this youthful, driving swing. It was a very physical way of playing.'

Richard Thompson first saw him play at an all-nighter at Cousins. 'He was impressive,' he says. 'The whole package was interesting: writer, singer, player. I remember thinking that this was a very talented person, someone with what I like to call musical intelligence, who thinks deeply about music, and as a result is able to create something that is original. He was an individual. He was definitely listening to all the old blues guitarists [but] I still feel as an acoustic guitar player he was absolutely unique.'

He was noteworthy not just as a player, but as a performer. He talked amusingly and at length between songs, sometimes for as long as a song itself, an apparently unfiltered spillage of competing voices, accents and attitudes. Many of those who looked closely at Martyn's on-stage demeanour sensed an attempt to prevent the deep vulnerability already apparent in the music from rising to the surface and becoming overly dominant. Some insecure people will do anything in their power to divert attention from themselves; others demand that everybody look their way as often as possible. Martyn chose the latter strategy. Why else wear sunglasses in a basement?

'I think a lot of what happens on stage comes from nerves, from an insecurity about how people are going to see you,' says Thompson. 'Talking on stage is born out of [that], then it becomes a habit, then you get comfortable with it. Maybe that's what happened with John. He was a lot of fun on stage. I used to enjoy that aspect of it.'

Ralph McTell felt the 'bravado, the mannerisms on stage, were disguising a very deep shyness'. For Jacqui McShee, Pentangle's vocalist, 'it was almost like a front, hiding some vulnerability, though he would never admit to it. He was in touch with his feminine side, creatively.'

The performative zeal of Martyn was an aspect many of his peers appreciated. Martin Carthy found the theatrics of 'Seven Black Roses' dynamic and fun. McTell recognised it for the cheap trick that it was, but thought it impressive and charming, nevertheless. 'It was a big jump to go from Scotland to London at nineteen and start doing his shtick in that way. It was musical exploration, and joy and enthusiasm. There was naivety, too. He was no London lad. He didn't have the London thing. He wasn't London cool. On the contrary, he was bubbly and full of fun. I always thought he was just in awe of the power of music.'

Not everybody warmed to Martyn. There were factions among the London club scene. On one side, a new crop of folk-influenced singer-songwriters, including Al Stewart, Roy Harper, John James, Stefan Grossman and Mike Chapman, with Martyn, the youngest, bringing up the rear. Set slightly apart was the more established crop of guitarists, less known for their songwriting. Chief among them were Bert Jansch, John Renbourn and Davy Graham. To some of the more serious-minded folk artists, Martyn was gauche, young, excitable, loud and something of a show-off. 'A lot of the older folkies were wary of him because he was the new kid on the block, but that didn't bother him,' says Donnie Barclay. 'He was very confident.' Grossman remembers that he could be 'very opinionated, pushy and a little obnoxious'.

The yin to Martyn's yang on the Soho beat was Jansch, who had made his first move to London early in 1963, forming a close bond with the extraordinary English folk singer Anne Briggs. A fixture on the scene, with several albums to his name, Jansch was introverted, taciturn, rather dour. Staunchly unstarry on stage, he was austere Edinburgh to Martyn's gallus Glasgow. 'Bert was the exact opposite of John,' says McTell. 'Bert was ultra-cool. Everything he did had deep significance, even when he said nothing. Where John would say a million words and rabbit along, twitching.'

The two men had a wary relationship, which at times degenerated into outright hostility. The roots of the problem were tangled. Martyn was given to jealousy, both personal and professional. Jansch was six years his senior and, at this stage, certainly, well ahead of him in terms of profile and reputation. Martyn would have regarded him as a potential scalp. Later, when Martyn started going out with the singer Beverley Kutner, who became his wife, the knowledge of her past romantic history with Jansch further fired his insecurities. In 1965 Kutner appeared as the mysterious dark-haired muse on the cover of Jansch's second album, *It Don't Bother Me.*

They could be cordial and convivial, and there was a genuine respect for the other's abilities. 'His guitar playing was a winner,' Jansch told me in 2009, two years before his death. 'It's a very lazy blues style, easy, not harsh or brittle. It was quite laid-back, actually. He had a definite style that could only be John, his singing as well. The whole thing came as a package.' Often, however, there was little love lost. Disagreements turned physical at least once. 'He was a very fiery person,' said Jansch. 'He didn't hold back when it came to his views and what he thought of people – me included. We had quite a few run-ins.'

Martyn enjoyed a similarly combustible relationship with the late John Renbourn who, according to Stefan Grossman, 'had very few good things to say about John Martyn'. That relationship also turned physical later in the Seventies. For Davy Graham, however, Martyn always retained a deep and sincere affection, as one might for a first love. Perhaps it was Graham's confrontational edge. 'Davy would play standing up, and he would really whack the guitar,' says the Welsh singer-songwriter John James, who released his debut album on Transatlantic in 1970. There may also have been a macho affiliation. Martyn once told me that Graham was 'the hardest guy I ever met'.

The sense of evolution and competition made for an enjoyably frenetic scene around Cousins. There was a gladiatorial aspect to it, and Martyn rose to the challenge. It was not in his character to back down.

He spoke his mind, but, while his views on other musicians were often blunt, his ears were wide open. He listened hard and borrowed promiscuously.

Martyn first met Paul Wheeler early in 1968, at an Incredible String Band show in Richmond. They quickly became close friends and remained so for decades. Wheeler loved him but recognised the calculation below the apparently devil-may-care surface. 'When we first met, my opening number at my gigs was always [Otis Spann's] "Jelly Roll Baker" – and John, without saying anything, just took it! He never asked or commented on it. I thought, if he could do that to me, he could do that to anybody. It was quite cold.' 'Jelly Roll Baker' became Martyn's new set-opener, and in time morphed into a partial revision titled 'The Easy Blues'.

He was light-fingered, but everything he took, he twisted. 'He hated formal tuition,' says John James, who was already experimenting with jazz stylings, piquing Martyn's interest. 'I showed him three or four jazz chords, but his guitar was in all these different tunings. He would listen to me, hear the notes and retune the guitar until he got something that sounded almost the same, but just slightly different. If he felt that I was giving him a formal tuning – "John, this is an A minor sixth chord" – he'd go, "No, no, no!" It had to be his way. Then the next day he would write it into a song.'

His dedication to unusual tunings was almost obsessive. It was about more than music. It was a statement of individuality: none can follow me here. He also liked the aesthetic appeal, his fingers splayed eccentrically all over the fretboard. 'Looks good, man,' he told James. 'Looks good!'

He practised religiously and prepared thoughtfully for each performance. He changed his guitar strings before almost every show. His pre-gig routine first involved gluing fake nails onto his playing hand. He progressed to procuring a pink resin used in dentistry to make templates for false teeth, building a thick layer onto the thumb and forefinger of his right hand to enable him to attack the strings. 'He made it look like he was just strolling in off the street with his guitar over his back, but it wasn't like that,' says Donnie Barclay. 'He was very particular about how he did things. Everything had to be perfect. He was very professional. In the early days, I never heard him playing badly. Every gig was perfect.'

His work ethic was that of the tightrope walker, rather than the draughtsman. A wayward perfectionism. The motivation was not to achieve crisp virtuosity, but to have the freedom at his disposal to fly free and make it different every time. 'He did a lot of the semi-blues repertoire that John Renbourn and Bert did – bits of Reverend Gary Davis and Jelly Roll Morton – but his take on it was always slightly off-centre,' says Martin Carthy. 'He played it as he heard it; there was never any attempt to be exact. That went right through his stuff. It always felt risky, with a big smile on his face all the time, making himself laugh. His improvising was gorgeous and so full-on.'

Visually, he made an immediate impact. His blond curls were getting longer now, and he dressed very deliberately to impress, in the crumpled boho chic of the time. A suit with a T-shirt and Dunlop Green Flash training shoes; a linen shirt with a tweed waistcoat. Advanced art student, dapper but consciously careless. The first time McShee laid eyes on him, during a floor spot at Cousins, he was wearing OshKosh denim dungarees, 'looking like an overgrown cherub, with this blond curly hair'. He was almost comically desperate to coax his fine, light covering of facial hair into a beard.

Socially, Soho was an adventure. Martyn went for late curries after shows with his contemporaries and savoured the acerbic bons mots flung around Muriel Belcher's infamous Colony Room drinking club on Dean Street in the company of Jeffrey Bernard and Francis Bacon. Between regular spots in Cousins, there were dates in the Horseshoe Arms on Tottenham Court Road, the de facto home base of Pentangle, and at the Hanging Lamp in Richmond, as well as trips back to Scotland and forays into the interior. Everyone bumped into everyone else, in town and on trains, in bus stations, clubs and living-room floors.

During this time Martyn shared bills with, among others, Ralph McTell, Davy Graham, Dr Strangely Strange, Mike Chapman, John James, Sammy Mitchell, Roy Harper, Stefan Grossman, Bridget

St John and Sandy Denny. On March 3, 1968 he opened for Pentangle at the Horseshoe Arms, very likely the first time he met Danny Thompson. On the middle weekend in June, he was at the Highcliffe Folk Festival in Sheffield, appearing alongside Clive Palmer, Hamish Imlach and Christy Moore, who recalls his performance as 'stunning'. He and Imlach stayed with Bridget St John and her flatmates at their student digs in Crook Street, where she was struck by their father–son bond.

Ron Geesin was on the same bill and recalls that Martyn 'turned up with a quantity of dried magic mushrooms neatly contained in a handkerchief and gave us all some. We were complementary spirits. I was interested in natural subconscious flow, and though John and I were never that close, we certainly spoke the same language.'

Tiring of the communal scene at Whittingstall Road, Martyn had by now moved, alone, to a garden flat in a Victorian terrace at 20 Beaufort Road in Surbiton – which he rebranded 'Suburbiton'. He was cleaving to the deep green dream of his childhood haunts, half a mile from his mother and just across the river from Hampton Court Park. 'I remember his mother's boyfriend decorating this place for John, and John being very touched that he should go to all this trouble,' says Paul Wheeler. 'He was taken aback. I think he almost wanted to feel resentment but couldn't, because this guy was being very nice.'

That summer, he worked as the sideman on a delivery van to augment his gig fees. He and Dunning planned to marry the following year, and she spent the summer with him, working at the local Woolworth's. They listened to Joni Mitchell's *Song Of A Seagull* and at the weekend caught the train to Camber Sands with Wheeler and his girlfriend Diana, where they swam and played music on the beach, fond memories which inspired the instrumental 'A Day At The Sea'.

'It was this thing of life and music and songs being utterly integrated,' says Wheeler. 'We would do something and that would immediately be put into a song. Life and art were just completely fused together.' Wheeler wrote the words to a beautiful new song called 'Fly For Home', which viewed Martyn's fragmented, long-distant relationship through the compassionate gaze of an empathetic observer. 'I felt for him in that situation, and I knew that feeling of someone close to you being taken away,' he says. 'I suppose you could get very psychotherapeutic about it.'

The flat at Beaufort Road was invariably full of music and people. 'I remember meeting him down in London on a bright morning,' says Ewan McVicar. 'John had an oud, a North African instrument. I showed him how the fingering went, and that impressed the hell out of him. He pointed out to me four guys sleeping on the floor. [One] was Jackson C. Frank. I think Al Stewart may have been another.'

Martyn and Stewart were spending so much time together the former invited the latter to produce his second album. Or Stewart offered. Later, they both seemed a little baffled by the fact of it, as did Chris Blackwell. 'It wasn't my choice,' says Blackwell. 'It wasn't my world, it wasn't my music.'

On July 11, 1968 they went into Regent Sound on Denmark Street to make *The Tumbler*. On several songs Martyn was accompanied by Wheeler on guitar and Harold McNair on flute. David Moses played a little double bass. Though the label says stereo, it was recorded in mono.

McNair was Martyn's first meaningful musical foil, whose early death from cancer in 1971 almost certainly prevented further, deeper collaboration. Al Stewart recalled how insistent Martyn was that McNair be on the record, in order to help make the music looser and more expansive. 'McNair opened my mind up a lot,' said Martyn. 'He was the first fully fledged jazzer that I had encountered... it was an inspiration to meet someone like that, it turned my head around.'[15]

His attempts to stretch the fabric of his songs are most apparent in the eccentric sucking sounds which punctuate 'Hello Train', created by running the tape backwards, and on the unsettling String Band oddness of 'The Gardeners', a song Martyn had learned from Ewan McVicar, who had picked it up from the Bostonian singer–songwriter Bill Lyons while spending time in Cambridge, Massachusetts.

'I came back and sang it at the Glasgow Folk Centre and John was really impressed, because he liked the unusual drop D tuning,' says

McVicar. 'He wanted the song, so I gave him the song, and it turned up on his second album, but credited to him by mistake! He was very apologetic. He said he had told [the record company] but they hadn't changed it.' McNair added wild, free-form patterns while Martyn played a scrambling, untidy guitar pattern and sang with sneering intensity. The result was his most experimental recording to date.

McNair's sweet, soaring flute hangs like an apparition over 'The River', one of Martyn's loveliest early compositions, which was, according to Wheeler, a diary-like snapshot of the period when he lived in his mother's flat, awakening in the morning to discover that she wasn't there. Both moving and melancholy, it ends with the young adult looking back to his childhood self, as the rain falls softly and '*wets the curly hair*'. On 'Dusty', he aligned himself to the circus freaks and colourful outsiders appearing at Hampton Court Fair.

There were two further covers among the nine originals. One was a spirited run at 'Winin' Boy Blues' by his beloved Jelly Roll Morton, a blues revival standard which on the album is mistitled 'Winding Boy'. The other was Henry Thomas's merry jug-band romp, 'Fishin' Blues', on which Wheeler also sang, a rare instance of Martyn harmonising with a male singer. Linda Dunning and Wheeler's girlfriend Diana also attended the session, roaring along on the deeply silly 'Knuckledy Crunch And Slippledee-Slee Song', Martyn's very own 'Laughing Gnome'. Along with 'Sing A Song Of Summer', these pieces cultivated an affected, saccharine and rather ingratiating strain of pastoral cuteness at which Martyn proved highly adept, but from which he would shortly turn away. He added a rather generic original slide blues titled 'Goin' Down To Memphis' and finally recorded his tone-shifting party piece, 'Seven Black Roses'.

The Tumbler shifted his career forwards, if only incrementally. Martyn was able to increase his gig fee, which mattered, and in the second half of 1968 he made the first of many appearances in session for John Peel, initially on his *Night Ride* show on BBC Radio 1, playing mostly songs from his new album. Sales were slow, however, and Chris Blackwell was niggled by the knowledge that he was not getting the most out of his artist. 'It was too early for us to be of any help for him,' he says. 'We [had done] the first record, and of course who would buy a record by a white kid who was jazz and folk, on a label that was only known for releasing Jamaican music? It was a huge disservice to John, because no one was looking at Island for a new folk artist. So it didn't do well for him at all. We had another go with *The Tumbler*.'

Commercially, at least, the results were much the same, but in many ways Martyn was fortunate to be left to his own devices. Many of his contemporaries discovered too late that their carefully wrought compositions would be subjected to gaudy arrangements in the studio in the hands of unsympathetic producers, resulting in what Leonard Cohen described, in the wry liner notes on the initial pressing of his 1967 debut album, as a 'blood feud... the arrangements wish to throw a party. The songs preferred to retreat behind a veil of satire.' Martyn's music was never subjected to such poorly conceived arranged marriages. When the time came for a controversial union, he made all the moves himself.

was a unique, interesting person. One of a
.' Martyn's mother, Betty, as a young woman.
rtesy Julie Purdey)

'He had a three-piece suit with short trousers and
a bow tie. That was his gran's influence.' Martyn
(bottom right) dressing to impress at Langside
Primary School. (Courtesy Brian Stanage)

as such an interesting house. A strange house.' The McGeachy family seat, 10 Tantallon Road, in more
nt times. (Graeme Thomson)

'It was first love, and a great time. He was very carefree.' Aged 18, with his fiancé Linda Dunning, in a b
in Charing Cross, Glasgow. *(Courtesy Linda Dunning)*

Aged 16, with Linda
Dunning in a photo bc
in Millport during the
September weekend,
1964.
(Courtesy Linda Dunn

was barefooted, playing the sitar and writing last song for the album.' One of a series of ts originally planned for Martyn's debut album, *don Conversation*, 1967. *(Courtesy Linda nning)*

'His rise was meteoric. He seemed to go from support slots in Scotland to headlining in Les Cousins in a short time.' On stage at Cousins, flanked by its owner and Martyn's 'non-intellectual big brother', Andy Matthews. *(Ray Stevenson/ Shutterstock)*

fell hard for Green England. An idealised country of riverbanks and willow trees, sleepy, sun-dappled serene.' Going down the river, London, 1968. *(Ray Stevenson/Shutterstock)*

Key influences and enablers, clockwise from top: Bert Jansch, Theo Johnson and Davy Graham.
(Popperfoto/Getty; Van Johnson; Brian Shuel/Redferns)

ends and foes, clockwise from top left: Chris Blackwell, Joe Boyd and Nick Drake. *(Brian Cooke/Redferns;* *chael Putland/Getty; Keith Morris/Redferns)*

'They were both extreme by nature. In one way they were the perfect match.' Martyn with his first wife, Beverley, shortly after their marriage in April 1969. *(Keith Morris/Redferns)*

Above and right: 'He could be sweet, gentle, boyish and beautiful, but then you had the other side...' Martyn at home in Hastings and (opposite page) with his stepson, Wesley Kutner. *(Brian Cooke/Redferns)*

'I thought I knew how people played guitar, but he was truly unbelievable.' Martyn in full flow at the tim
of *Solid Air*, 1973. *(Gems/Redferns)*

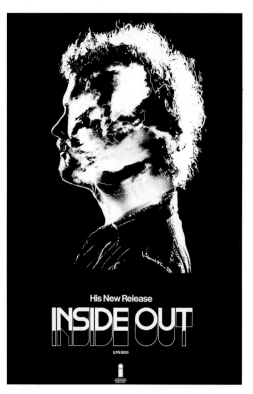

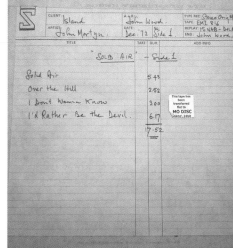

Left: 'Probably the purest album I've made
musically.' Island promotes Martyn's extraordinar
Inside Out, October 1973. *(Brian Cooke/Redferns)*

Above right: 'An incredible album, beautifully dor
The master tapes for *Solid Air*.
(Courtesy John Hillarby)

4

By the time *The Tumbler* was released, in October 1968, Martyn had met the woman who would become his wife and sometime musical partner for the next decade. 'She took me so much by surprise,' he recalled forty years later. 'She took me by surprise every day.'[1]

Maureen Beverley Kutner was twenty-one, a singer, songwriter and drama school graduate who had grown up in Coventry, one of five children. Her parents were Jewish refugees from Poland. She had a difficult relationship with her father, whom she remembered as a cold, distant man who was violent towards her mother (an allegation which has been disputed by at least one of her siblings).

Kutner left Coventry for London in 1962, aged fifteen, and immersed herself in the folk scene. Dark-haired, dark-eyed and dark-voiced, she was a beautiful thrift-shop bohemian who harboured creative ambitions more substantial than fulfilling the role of muse to her boyfriend Bert Jansch.

Already a distinctive singer, she began learning the guitar and writing songs. Her jug band The Levee Breakers released a single, 'Babe, I'm Leaving You', on Parlophone, before Kutner signed as a solo artist to Deram Records in 1966. Her agent and producer Denny Cordell attempted reverse alchemy by turning her raw, bluesy edge into pop cheese. 'He did my songs in a really over-the-top Europop style,' she recalled. 'I might have been one of the first [female] singer-songwriters in those days – there weren't many. It was a whole new thing for a woman to be in the business. It was a man's world, and the attitude was, "What are we going to dress you up in?" Denny even wrote my interviews for me.'

Kutner released less than a handful of singles on Deram in 1966 and 1967, and, although nothing quite stuck, she was well regarded. Jimmy Page, Nicky Hopkins and John Paul Jones played on her songs. Donovan was a fan – indeed, an admirer. She performed on bills with The Nice and Jimi Hendrix. Paul Simon, with whom she was having 'an on-off relationship', invited her to the States. While Martyn was recording *London Conversation*, Kutner appeared alongside The Who, Otis Redding and Hendrix as the guest of Simon & Garfunkel at the Monterey Pop Festival in June 1967. She was billed as 'Beverly' and performed three songs, though the memory is 'a blur. I was bricking it and trying desperately not to show it. I shouldn't even have been there, I didn't have a Green Card. Paul did say, "If you marry me you can get a Green Card," and I thought, Well, that's not very romantic.' Her set was not included in D. A. Pennebaker's film of the festival, *Monterey Pop*.

On returning to England, Kutner's life hit several bumps in the road. In quick succession, she parted ways with Deram, her mother died of cancer and she became pregnant. Her son was born on May 13, 1968, and named Wesley, blending his father's surname and mother's first name. The father was Jonathan Weston, who worked for Denny Cordell at Essex Music and managed Procol Harum for a brief time. In 1969 he produced a session for David Bowie. When it became clear that Weston did not embrace the responsibilities of fatherhood, Kutner found a room in a home for unmarried mothers. Such were the limits of the enlightened Sixties.

While pregnant, in February 1968 Kutner joined Witchseason, the production and management company set up by two Americans, Joe Boyd and Tod Lloyd. She also signed to their publishing offshoot, Warlock. 'I had known her before on the folk scene,' says Lloyd. 'She was hanging around with Bert Jansch and The Young Tradition. I was very taken with her. She had a good amount of talent, a nice sense of rhythm. She used to play really simple guitar and sing to it in this dark voice.' Boyd also rated her. They decided Lloyd would produce some sessions, with Boyd supervising.

Witchseason paid her a retainer of £15 a week, which had to go a long way. 'What I remember principally is that, after Wesley was born, she spent a really, really hard time as a single mom and was very depressed,' says Lloyd. 'She was living on subsistence money from Witchseason. It was coming out of that [that] she and John got together.'

When Wesley was a few months old, Kutner came into John Wood's Sound Techniques studio to record a set of demos, with a band which included the brilliant Ghanaian Afro-rock drummer Remi Kabaka, and Greg Ridley, the bass player from Spooky Tooth. The demos included three of four originals, says Lloyd, and a 'truly moving' cover of Bob Dylan's 'Like A Rolling Stone'. There was no record deal in place. The plan was to work on more songs with a view to recording an album in America. Then everything changed. 'A couple of weeks later, Beverley announced that she had fallen in love with John Martyn,' says Joe Boyd. 'They were going to get together and live together and make music together.'

Martyn met Beverley late in 1968, at the Chelsea College of Art. He was playing a show, and she was in attendance with their mutual friend Jackson C. Frank. She brought her guitar and sang a song during the floor spots, but Martyn was more interested in her physical attributes. He saw a strikingly sexual woman dressed in second-hand velvet clothes, with a palpable aura of mystery and magic. The mutual attraction was immediate and powerful. Kutner was 'knocked sideways'[2] by his looks, his air of danger, his youthful energy and quicksilver talent.

They quickly became an item. On their first date, Martyn took her to a bistro in Chelsea and ordered in French. He visited her at home with armfuls of muesli, cheese and honey, cooked her curries and stews. The singer-songwriter Steve Tilston first met Martyn at his local folk club, the Volunteer in Loughborough, early in 1969. He was impressed by his elephant cords, his fur coat and the fact that he bought a Chinese meal for everyone afterwards and paid for it with a twenty-pound note. He was most impressed, however, by his devotion to his new girlfriend. 'He came back to our place and we stayed up virtually all night, rolling joints. He was going on about how much in love with Bev he was. Talking about her non-stop.'

Their connection opened him up emotionally as a writer, led him to places he may not otherwise have been able to access. When she left, the doors to those rooms closed again, at least partially. Where the sentiments on his first two albums had been heartfelt but largely callow, Martyn would henceforth prove more daring in his attempts to plumb his feelings and dredge up the joy, vulnerability and blind rage which his love for her, and hers for him, brought out of him.

It was a passionate, deeply felt love affair. It was also a catastrophically ill-matched union, one which cruelly curtailed Kutner's career and ultimately wrought an immense amount of damage and destruction. Its legacy amounted to two children, a pair of fascinating albums, some wonderful songs and a long, painful spiral of abuse, addiction, depression, anxiety and retribution which has yet to fully play out. 'It seemed right at the time,' Martyn told me of the marriage, 'But fuck me, what a mistake.'

'They were both extreme by nature,' says Vari McGeachy. 'In one way they were a perfect match, in another way they kind of deserved each other because they were both so complex and difficult. Dad always said to me that when he met Mum all he wanted to do was go off into the sunset and live happily ever after – and in many ways they did. All the elements were there, but circumstances just didn't allow it… What was a shame was the magnitude of it. They were both extreme individuals, so the fallout was extreme, too.'

There were several layers to the attraction. Kutner admits she did not always make the best choices when it came to men, being too eager to see the good and often blind to the bad. She had a poor relationship with her own father, and no relationship with the father of her child, whom she felt was weak in ways in which Martyn was demonstrably not. Martyn, meanwhile, harboured complicated feelings about his mother and extended family. 'He took me on, I had a child, and he [thought], "She's got a kid and she's kept him,'" says Beverley. 'That must have been the first thing that he found attractive about me.'

'He was all over this thing that this was a meeting of minds as well as bodies, and how important that was,' says Paul Wheeler. 'He was very militant about the head and the heart. It was part of the John and Yoko thing, it was a new move. Men respect women! The idea of marrying someone who already had a child was already part of the agenda.'

Wesley Kutner was still less than a year old. Martyn did not officially adopt Beverley's son but raised him as his own for the next decade. Here it all was, at just twenty: a ready-made family. 'He fell for her, and she was gorgeous,' says Linda Thompson. 'But he wouldn't have considered, "Oh my goodness, I have to take on this parental role." No, no, no! That wasn't his job at all.'

There was an obvious complication in Martyn getting together with Beverley Kutner. He had fallen for her before ending his relationship with Linda Dunning. They were due to marry after she completed her teaching qualifications and moved to London in the summer. They had discussed children, and decided they wanted four. 'We had even talked about names,' she says. 'These are things you do when you are young and in love.'

Deep down, she already knew the relationship wasn't going to work. 'He had said he didn't want me to be a teacher, because we wouldn't see one another, because I'd be working during the day and he would be working at night. I thought to myself, I didn't go to college all these years to be your groupie.' Even before meeting Kutner, he was already serially unfaithful. There was no shortage of female company for an up-and-coming troubadour, even when he did not go chasing it. Martyn had both motive and opportunity. His chat-up line – 'Can I buy you an ice cream?' – was often superfluous.

When Dunning came to stay at Beaufort Road before Christmas in 1968, she learned the truth about his affair with Beverley in circuitous fashion. Martyn had gone out shopping, and while tidying the bedroom she discovered a letter from a woman, 'who had obviously been living there. She said she missed him, and her little boy missed him. I had left at the end of the summer, and apparently someone else moved in.'

The twist was that the letter was not from Beverley Kutner, but from another woman with a young child, who Dunning believes was an ex-girlfriend of Mike Heron. Martyn came home to find Dunning 'freaking out'. Instead of confessing to one liaison, he instead told her about another.

'He was sitting cross-legged, and he said he had met this musician, Beverley, she was so cool, and how he really needed to explore this – and what he thought would be great would be if he lived with her until I came back in June and then we would get married. He was serious! That was it, over and done. It was pretty horrendous.'

Martyn left, and Dunning ran to his mother's house nearby. 'I was hysterical, and she straightened me around, gave me a shot of whisky, and told me, "You're too good for my son."' Over the past eighteen months, as part of their shared life, Dunning had brought many of her own possessions down to London, including baking utensils belonging to her grandfather. Stiffening her resolve, and perhaps drawing from her own past experiences, Betty told her, 'I want you to go back around there in the morning and find anything you can that is of value, take any money that is lying around, and take your pie funnels, and go.'

Dunning returned to Glasgow heartbroken, but aware that 'we would have gone our separate ways anyway. He was moving into a different world.' The news was greeted with bunting in Newton Mearns, but with genuine sadness in Tantallon Road. When it ended, says Fiona McGeachy, 'I remember my granny being awfully disappointed.' Years later, when Dunning – now married, and pregnant with her third child – bumped into Tommy McGeachy in Shawlands, he hugged her and said, perhaps rather theatrically, 'I mourned you, my dear.'

Martyn did, too, at least in the place where he always dumped his innermost feelings – his music. He commemorated their relationship in 'Would You Believe Me?', a new song which made an immediate impression on his friends. Both Steve Tilston and John James recall him playing it in clubs, bent almost double over the guitar, strumming the strings with a plectrum, which he never normally used. 'Boom!' says James. 'What's this? That was a turning point. That's where he left all that "Fairy Tale Lullaby" stuff behind.'

It is, says Tilston, a 'song of regret' in which Martyn alluded to their planned marriage and stated that, although he hadn't wanted to lose her, he had had to '*bruise*' her. 'I heard that song and I couldn't believe it,' says Dunning. '[Especially] that line about keeping the wolf from the door for four long years.' Paul Wheeler's girlfriend hated that particular lyric with a fury, deeply resenting the depiction of a woman as a mere prop whose only use was to salve the soul of the tortured male artist.

Dunning got on with her life, moving to America, marrying, working, raising children. She had no further contact with Martyn until 2006, when she attended his show at the Royal Concert Hall in Glasgow. Backstage, she met him for the first time in nearly forty years. 'It was kind of surreal,' she says. 'He was on something, very mellow. He remembered that I used to lay my hair on the ironing board and iron it. What a thing to remember…' Her mother, now in her eighties, had driven Dunning to the concert. Before dropping her at the concert hall, she told her daughter in no uncertain terms not to go out dancing after the show with Ian McGeachy.

Both Joe Boyd and Tod Lloyd were wary of the potentially explosive impact Martyn might have on their artist's life. 'My memory is that Beverley was someone to whom things happen, rather than someone who makes things happen,' says Tod Lloyd. 'There was, I guess, a string of people who weren't very nice to her. In the hands of somebody like John, it probably wasn't the best possible outcome.'

'My feeling about him from the beginning was there was a lot of pent-up anger here,' says Boyd. 'A lot of insecurity and a lot of jealousy at the surface. The music is not wishy-washy. Even when it's one man and an acoustic guitar, it's intense. In retrospect the idea that the John and Beverley pairing could ever work as a combination of personal and professional was unlikely.'

Boyd and Martyn never got on, although stories of explicit enmity tend to be exaggerated. A tale of Martyn confronting Boyd with a hatchet has grown with the legend. 'That's a fantasy he might have wanted, but I don't think so,' says Boyd. Had it happened, one presumes he would remember. The problem arose after a mutual friend expressed the opinion that Boyd harboured a soft spot for Beverley, news that apparently prompted Martyn to pick up a weapon to challenge him, before being talked down.

Relations were cool but largely cordial. The reasons behind any difficulties are not hard to discern. Boyd recognised Martyn's gifts but was not a particular fan of his music. He had first seen him perform, at a location he no longer recalls, on a bill in south Glasgow in 1966, while on a northern reconnaissance mission linked to his relationship with The Incredible String Band.

'John was clearly a young talented part of that Scottish school of Davy Graham acolytes,' he says. 'There's a whole generation of them. I thought it was pretty good, but I was never that enamoured. I liked Davy Graham. I was never a huge Bert Jansch fan. Coming from America, where there are so many hot guitar licks being played all the time, I was drawn mostly to Robin Williamson's more Middle Eastern and North African take on Davy's approach.' Martyn felt that Boyd had 'a different conception of what British music should be'.[3]

In 1968 Witchseason had cut a confidence-and-supply deal with Chris Blackwell which meant Island would bankroll Witchseason, while in return two Witchseason artists, Nick Drake and Fairport Convention, would join the label. Later that year, after Martyn's first two albums had failed to do any serious business, Blackwell had asked Boyd to formally take on Martyn under the Witchseason banner, believing he would benefit from a much more bespoke, hands-on service than Blackwell felt able to offer. Boyd politely declined.

'I went back and had a listen, or maybe I'd already had a pretty close listen, to those first two albums, and basically I said to Chris, "No thanks. No, he's good, but he's just not my cup of tea." I've never known whether this conversation got back to John, whether Chris had said to him, "Hey, I've got an idea, let's put you in with Joe Boyd," [and then I'd said no].'

They were also temperamentally ill-suited. Boyd was, and remains, urbane, forthright, a cool strong breeze. Martyn, in the words of his friend in the late Sixties, Jo Watson, was more akin to a 'little whirlwind'. What they shared was a desire to be the top dog in any room. It's not hard to see where friction points may have occurred.

'Sometimes guys have that sort of struggling, confrontational way of dealing with each other,' says Boyd. 'To try and show who is the bigger cock of the walk. I think there was a little bit of that in my relationship with John, on his side and on mine.' In general, they rubbed along, but it was never easy. Given that Boyd was pivotal to the idea of he and Beverley working together, it was a rocky foundation from which to build.

Martyn and Beverley married on April 22, 1969, at Chelsea Registry Office. Boyd and Nick Drake came, as did Betty and John Collins. His mother commented that the whole affair was 'like a strange play'.[4] Martyn wore a tweed suit, no socks and an artfully rumpled shirt. The reception was a free-for-all in the couple's new flat in Hampstead, where they ate chicken curry, drank champagne and smoked joints.

It was not bliss, but between the spring of 1969 and the spring of 1971 Martyn and Beverley enjoyed long spells of domestic happiness in Hampstead. 'They were like puppies living together,' says Jo Watson. 'Playmates.' Martyn called Wesley 'Wezzles' and would swing him around until his arms nearly flew off. 'They seemed very happy for a while,' says Linda Thompson.

They were young – barely out of their teens – with little money but a world of freedom. Their first home together was at Pilgrim's Place, a dog-leg tucked away off Hampstead High Street. They moved a few hundred yards to Denning Road, a pleasant street of red-brick villas near the heath and the pond. Keats country. Hampstead was middle-class creative cosmopolitan. The great satirist Peter Cook lived only a short hop away.

The basement flat at 40a Denning Road was decked out in the required style. There was a hammock in the living room, patterned rugs and throws strewn around, cushions on the floor and scarves draped over lamps. The record player took pride of place, with LPs scattered around without their sleeves. Their trendy Trimphone was always going missing, hidden under a pile of clothes or a carelessly tossed guitar, necessitating a mad scramble whenever it rang. Martyn was never particularly reverential towards his instruments. He playfully poked fun at artists who gave their guitars women's names and caressed them like long-lost lovers. For Martyn, a guitar was a tool. He stripped the lacquer from their bodies, stuck tape all over them, wired them up, bashed them about. Anything to rough them up.

It was the beginning of a decade of uninhibited family living, eccentric, self-absorbed and often extreme, a post-hippie de-construction of the domestic ideal conducted with little regard for the long-term welfare of their children. 'I don't think there was ever much in the way of conventional family life, or things you keep from the children,' says Vari McGeachy. 'We were privy to everything. It was a lifestyle. It was how they rolled. We were born into that environment, and like any dysfunctional environment, it is normalised for you. Things were always crazy, they just got progressively so – and dangerous in the end.'

Martyn was the accelerated heartbeat of the house. 'He was so explosive,' says John James. 'Beverley was calm. She was not aggressive at all, very placid.' If he suddenly took a notion to play slide guitar, he would rush outside, smash an empty wine bottle, and use the glass neck. 'There was always great enthusiasm and movement,' says Jo Watson. 'He had a great urge to paint the place. You'd go around and there would be half-painted roller marks up the wall. He was very twitchy. Edgy, nervy, and kind of exhausting. Great fun, but, "bloody hell, I'm knackered!"'

Their social circle was drawn largely from the Witchseason and Island stable, which offered a familial, nurturing camaraderie. Martyn's friend from Glasgow, Linda Peters, was now stepping out with her future husband Richard Thompson. The couple were living together in Hampstead within walking distance of Denning Road and were frequent visitors. Nick Drake often dropped in. Andy Matthews came with his wife Diane. Other regulars included Paul Wheeler, Joe Boyd, John James and his girlfriend Jo Watson.* Bridget St John was among the many friends who would babysit Wesley. Ed Carter and Mike Kowalski, members of fellow Witchseason signings The New Nadir, were regular guests. Martyn's Glasgow friends Tommy Crocket and Donnie Barclay would visit, and he kept in touch with his family, including his aunt Agnes and her children Janet and Marion, who were now living in Orpington, Kent.

The nights passed in a happy blur of alcohol, dope, music, food and poker. They played the jewels of their record collections to each other. Martyn tended to leap from enthusiasm to enthusiasm. At one point he was obsessed with Mississippi Fred McDowell. Then there was a soul compilation called *The Sue Story!* which he played to death.† 'You'd go around there and he would be raving on Marvin Gaye,' says John James. 'He'd be dancing around the living room to *That's The Way Love Is*; he liked the groove. He would rave about people. I remember when he saw Dudu Pukwana, he was jumping around the flat: "Dudu, man! Dudu, man!" For a day he would want to be him, then it would be someone else.' Throughout his life, he displayed a pronounced bias towards black and American musicians, whom he felt were far superior in terms of feel, the delivery of that intangible *something*, compared to their British counterparts.

---

* The Martyns were witnesses when the couple married at Brixton Registry Office on January 9, 1970, the day after Martyn had played Kingston Polytechnic. He brought a bottle of champagne, which he opened in the registry office, where it fizzed all over the leather-top desk. In the taxi he produced glasses from a bag, which he duly smashed.

† Released in 1965 on Sue Records, an offshoot of Island Records, *The Sue Story!* was a compilation featuring sixteen soul cuts from the likes of James Brown, Ike and Tina Turner, Otis Redding and Irma Thomas.

Martyn, Drake and Richard Thompson would play in each other's company, but almost always individually rather than interacting with one another. 'I never remember them jamming together,' says Linda Thompson. 'They were all brilliant guitarists, very different and stylised, so you couldn't just jump in. They were careful not to tread on each other's toes. They were all quite wary of each other. It's a dick thing; they all wanted to be better than each other. Never heard them sing together, either.'

The drug scene was mild. The Thompsons didn't smoke pot, but everyone else did, and there was plenty of alcohol. 'Richard could drink anyone under the table – he had hollow legs,' says Linda Thompson. At this time, and in this company, Martyn did not seem more extreme than anyone else. 'He was great fun, and at that point he seemed like a loving person,' says Richard Thompson. 'I always saw that side of him at that time. It got darker later. It was almost like there were two Johns: the Glaswegian thug and the loving hippie. Certainly in the time that I knew him, the hippie was winning the battle. Wesley was sweet, a really lovely little kid, and at the time that I knew John he was a good, very present parent. I think he took it seriously.'

A highlight of the social scene was poker nights at the house of Bob Squires, a 'small-time crim', according to Thompson, employed by Witchseason to run errands, supply drugs and chauffeur Martyn around when the need arose. At one point they went off to Wales together. The Witchseason corps would often convene in Squires's kitchen for competitive games of poker and Liar's Dice. While Nick Drake was a dark horse at the latter, 'John was famous for cheating,' says Richard Thompson. 'Just famous for it. It would be blatant but no one would say anything. Everyone would just shrug their shoulders.'

'I have a memory one night that we were playing poker, and John was doing very well,' says Tod Lloyd. 'And all of a sudden, we discovered a hand of cards had been put to one side. Someone had just, you know, *forgotten* to throw it back into the pile. We talked John into giving everybody their money back. It was good for me, because I was losing.'

During this period Martyn became very close to Nick Drake. In 2005 Martyn told me, 'Nicky was one of my favourite human beings in the world.' They had first met a year before the release of Drake's debut album, *Five Leaves Left*, introduced at a party by their mutual friend Paul Wheeler, who had studied with Drake at Cambridge. 'My impression of Nick's reaction to John on first meeting was that Nick found John very entertaining and amusing,' says Wheeler. 'He laughed a lot at John's perceptive and witty comments. Those were qualities which John used to win over live audiences... I think John was impressed by Nick's "cool".'

Throughout his life, Martyn's friendships with other men could be intense: tactile, tempestuous, thoughtful and surprisingly gentle, with lots of kisses and hugs. There are several songs in his catalogue where he expresses without any bashfulness his love for another man. 'John was different from other people in Glasgow; he was very free,' says Linda Thompson. 'He wasn't at all uncomfortable or frightened of loving a man – not in a physical way – which was quite unusual in those days. Nick and John loved one another. It was quite Greek, without the sex.'

Drake was living in Haverstock Hill in Belsize Park. The Martyns were a single stop down the Northern Line in Hampstead. Half a mile apart. Drake was accustomed to being looked after – it had been that way at home, at school and at university – and the pattern continued among his friends. His drug dealer, Bob Squires, even bought him a car. 'Whatever Nick had, we were all helpless in front of it,' says Linda Thompson. 'He had this messiah thing, which he did not try to cultivate at all, which made it all the more powerful. He truly didn't care if you were there or not.'

Although he was by nature introverted, at this point Drake could be a lucid conversationalist among the right people. He enjoyed company 'as long as he could choose to come and go,' says Wheeler. 'He was like one of those cats which turn up at many households, all of which are under the impression that they have a unique role in providing food, shelter and company for him.'

At Denning Road, 'he became one of the family, really,' says Beverley Martyn. 'He would come around and babysit sometimes. He smelled the food cooking. I don't think he had money to eat. He wore his father's cast-off suits and his shirt was fraying at the edges.'

When the Martyns went on holiday to Hastings, staying in the house they would eventually buy in the old town, Drake would sometimes come with them, sitting on the beach in his shabby suit, gazing out to sea. 'He was the most introverted character I've ever met,' says Beverley, whose love for Drake was powerfully maternal. She would feed him, wash his socks, provide a safe haven. 'I was very protective. I realised how sensitive he was, and John was very good with him, very gentle. Nick was no threat, so John looked after him. He was the only person John allowed, apart from Art Garfunkel, to visit me when he was away. We'd make jokes, take the piss and try to make him laugh. We'd open the door and go, "Oh no, not Nick Drag again!"'

On the surface, Drake and Martyn were poles apart. 'Nick was a bit of a fragile lad,' says Danny Thompson. 'He was the kind of performer who would come on stage and stare at the floorboards during his whole set, then walk off without saying anything. I couldn't really understand that; it made me feel a bit uncomfortable. John was completely the opposite.'

Posthumously, Drake has been almost deified, artfully moulded into the platonic ideal of a tortured artist, a beautiful young man too sensitive for the cut and thrust of the music industry or, indeed, the modern world in general. Some of that is true, and some of it is a feat of retrospective branding which has little romanticism about it. The resurrection of Drake in the Nineties as the quintessential cult artist was driven by a hard-headed marketing decision by PolyGram. Having bought Island Records, the company were keen to recoup losses on artists who had never sold any records.

Drake was gentle and withdrawn and enigmatic, certainly, but the reverence around him obscures part of the picture. Paul Wheeler maintains that he and Martyn were not quite so far apart as the mythos suggests. 'I was in the middle of Nick and John, and I had a close relationship with both of them,' says Wheeler. 'They are often cast as opposites – upper-class versus working-class and all that – but none of those things are actually true. It depends what bit you look at. In terms of sensitivity they were quite close, and Nick could get very angry indeed. He would have seen that as a question of honour and integrity. John also had some of that, although sometimes it was just a case of him losing his temper.'

If Danny Thompson became Martyn's wildly extrovert alter ego, his sharp, bright, full-beamed reflection, then Drake was his dark shadow, something like a conscience: a hazy likeness of the more vulnerable, private and guarded part of his nature, the one revealed in song but rarely in person. 'I think John's spirit related to Nick's spirit,' says Bridget St John. 'He might have been outwardly different, but inwardly he and Nick were very, very similar. They both could tap into the really deep beauty in things.'

Drake sold so few records in his lifetime he scarcely presented any professional threat, but his blank immunity to approval and his unshowy refusal to compromise presented a form of unspoken challenge to Martyn, who affected not to care about such things but probably in the end cared too much.

Sitting by the window in Denning Road, Martyn would see Drake descending the steps down to the basement and immediately rearrange his demeanour. If he and a friend were exchanging ideas on the guitar, that would stop. Drake would usually go into the kitchen first to talk quietly with Beverley. Martyn would twitch and mutter impatiently until Drake loped through to the living room. Early on, he made attempts to persuade his notoriously performance-averse friend to gig more frequently, phoning Andy Matthews at Cousins to book dates and arranging support slots on the rare occasion when he and Beverley played headlining shows. When Drake released *Five Leaves Left* in the summer of 1969, Martyn played the record in the company of friends, skipping impatiently from track to track: 'What do you think of that? What do you think of that?'

He was naturally competitive, but he was also attracted to Drake's talent and the manner in which it contrasted with his own. 'He just couldn't believe Nick's technique,' says Joe Boyd. 'John was a spectacular guitar player but with a rough edge; there was a lot of approximation going on. That was John. He was always reaching beyond, [whereas] Nick would sit there for hours and work out a part and then play it absolutely impeccably and perfectly every single time. All those tunings were more sophisticated and complicated than what John was doing. So I think there was a fascination.'

There were less lofty connections. 'They did mountains of drugs together,' says Linda Thompson. There is also the suspicion that, however superficial, Drake's artfully faded officer-class credentials appealed to Martyn, who was not averse to concocting a heavily mythologised personal biography, in much the same way that Bob Dylan had a few years previously. In Martyn's case, his imagined CV betrayed a surprising degree of intellectual insecurity.

A public schoolboy and son of a managing director, whose family home in Tamworth-in-Arden was sufficiently grand to come with a name attached – Far Leys – Drake had access to a social cachet that could neither be bought nor earned. Martyn very obviously appropriated parts of his backstory, as well as that of Paul Wheeler, telling several friends at the time that he had also attended Cambridge University, 'which was certainly bollocks,' says Wheeler. As late as the Nineties, Martyn told his keyboard player, Spencer Cozens, that he had studied Comparative Religion at Cambridge for a term before going on the road.

There were other bold fictions. He invented a stint – followed by a rebellious expulsion – at the Glasgow School of Art after leaving Shawlands Academy. While living in Woodstock in 1969, he told his neighbour Rod McLeod that 'he'd been in some sort of monastery studying martial arts in Scotland'. He told Wheeler when they first met that he had recently competed in the Tour de France. Clive Palmer accompanied Martyn on a series of short tours around Scotland and the North of England, but Martyn's memory that they lived together in the Lake District was fanciful. He also talked of a teenage trip he had taken to Morocco, on his own, 'following the hash trail' to Fez in Davy Graham's footsteps.[5] 'He didn't go to Morocco when I was with him,' says Linda Dunning. It's doubtful he went at all. 'He could bullshit, that's absolutely true,' says Richard Thompson.

He was inventing himself in the image which he desired. There was, perhaps, no great harm in it. His next adventure, at least, though it had the feel of a dream, turned out to be true.

5

Six days before his wedding, on April 16, 1969, Martyn and his bride-to-be recorded demos of four new songs with Joe Boyd and John Wood at Sound Techniques. Two months later, as a belated busman's honeymoon gifted from the music industry fates, he jetted off to play the hippie princeling in Woodstock, in upstate New York.

After meeting Kutner, Martyn experienced a rapid promotion within the Witchseason roster. He started out as the guitar-playing new boyfriend of the main artist, before graduating to potential co-writer and finally co-headliner. There is a well-versed theory that he had accompanied his wife to Woodstock primarily to support her, only to push himself into the centre of the picture once there. It was unlikely to have been so nakedly calculating. More plausibly, he sensed an opportunity beckoning and simply walked towards it. 'I was signed originally to be her back-up guitar player on a few sessions she was going to do in America, but it eventually seemed obvious to go as John and Beverley Martyn and to make an album together.'[1]

The Sound Techniques demos, later included on the reissue of *Stormbringer!*, suggest the decision for them to work in tandem was taken many weeks before they travelled to the States. 'Joe and I had been recording Beverley in England, and it had never really clicked,' says John Wood. 'It was Joe's original intention just to work with Beverley in America, that was how it was planned. Then Beverley and John got married, and at that point it became a joint project.'

'I guess I felt that there was so much potential here,' says Boyd. 'There was definitely a honeymoon period where I was enthusiastic about it.' Chris Blackwell was also pleased, partly because it meant that, following two relatively unsuccessful solo albums, and via the scenic route, he had finally achieved his wish for Boyd to oversee Martyn's music. Beverley was not necessarily averse to the idea at the time, either, although there is no doubt that his role expanded into something more substantial than she first imagined. 'John's contribution got bigger and bigger and the music we were making was so good it seemed the right direction to go in,' she said.[2] They looked fantastic together, and perhaps the potential which hadn't yet been fulfilled in their respective solo careers could be sparked into life through the positive friction of close collaboration. And, in any case, as Martyn pointed out, 'I had my own contract with Island anyway. I wasn't a passenger.'[3]

The demos convinced Island that their next move would be more marketable as a double act. They were recorded with unfussy solo acoustic guitar and precious little interaction. The bluesy 'One Of Those Days' was the sole track given over to Beverley, who sings it with what sounds like her own guitar accompaniment, with a cracked intensity reminiscent of Marianne Faithfull. Martyn sings the other three songs. He performs 'I Don't Know' alone, while on 'John The Baptist' and 'Traffic-Light Lady' Beverley harmonises on the chorus. Otherwise, it could be two separate artists performing in two separate rooms. There was little obvious creative chemistry, and vocally it made for an uncertain blend.

Boyd was nevertheless excited by the potential. 'I suggested, "Why don't we internationalise this and go for something really cool?"' he says. 'Not commercial in a crass way, but something that has real international potential.' Within two months they were on their way to Woodstock.

A year later, Joni Mitchell's 'Woodstock' memorialised the transformation of a sleepy hamlet two hours north of New York into a mecca for the counterculture, even if the coordinates were fuzzy. Never mind that the music festival, held over three days in August

1969, took place in Bethel, some forty miles from Woodstock itself, or that Mitchell had never even been to the town. The myth of magical Woodstock has remained potent ever since.

A historically important site for Native Americans, Buddhists, artists and artisans, between the mid-Sixties and early Seventies this 'bucolic do-nothing town'[4] enacted a powerful gravitational pull. The Sixties scene centred around Bob Dylan, who at the behest of his manager Albert Grossman had been coming to Woodstock since 1963, buying a house there in 1965. His backing band The Hawks had followed suit, changing their name in the process to The Band. By 1969, the town was also home to the 'skittish' Van Morrison, Tim Hardin, Richie Hawkins, Jimi Hendrix and scores more musicians, who settled in the serene communal isolation of the Catskill mountains.[5] Landmark records like Dylan's *John Wesley Harding* and *The Basement Tapes*, Morrison's *Moondance* and The Band's first two albums were either written or recorded there. George Harrison and Eric Clapton dropped by to soak up the atmosphere and bestow their blessings.

Beneath the soft, sentimental cover story of a dappled artistic paradise lay a hard reality of drug and alcohol abuse, bent business deals, gossip, claustrophobia and serial bed-hopping. Van Morrison later remembered Woodstock as a 'fucking horrible place'.[6] Far from a communal idyll, it was an often fragmented and paranoid scene, and after the brief boom came the inevitable bust. Spooked by the popularity of the Woodstock Festival and the influx of gawkers breaking into his house and even his bed, Dylan left for New York with his family. Morrison headed west, while The Band succumbed to heroin and alcoholism in the backwoods.

The hangover was yet to kick in when the Martyns arrived. In the summer of 1969, immediately prior to the festival nearby, Woodstock was still just about acquainted with its innocence. In the wider timeline of the town, he and Beverley were bit-part players with walk-on parts, but while living there they tapped enthusiastically into the spirit of the place. The amplified, roughly rhythmic semi-acoustic music of *Stormbringer!* leaned heavily on the influence of The Band, one of the few contemporary rock groups Martyn really loved. 'They were the first band I ever felt close to,' he said much later. 'The best I'd ever heard.'[7]

They spent a couple of months in town, between June and August. Following a brief stopover at the Chelsea Hotel in New York, they headed north, moving into a quaint two-storey frame house with a front porch on Lower Byrdcliffe Road, recently vacated by the folk artist Happy Traum and his wife Jane. Saxophonist David Sanborn lived just up the street. Dylan was nearby on Ohayo Mountain Road, on the other side of Tinker Street, though devilishly hard to spot. Van Morrison had recently moved to the top of the same track, on Spencer Road. The Band's erstwhile HQ, Big Pink, was just out of town on Stoll Road.

'I lived next door to Hendrix for a while in Woodstock,' Martyn told me, with a pinch of poetic licence. Hendrix's manager Michael Jeffery owned a substantial property on Lower Byrdcliffe Road; Hendrix later bought a house a few miles away in Traver Hollow. 'Every Thursday he would appear in a purple helicopter. It was fucking surreal. I'd come straight from a basement flat in Hampstead and there I am, with Hendrix dropping out of the sky every week. I had a couple of beers with him, a couple of spliffs. He was a very quiet little fella. He didn't give a fuck.'

Their nearest neighbour was an Italian Mafia type who ran the local hamburger joint, where he repeat-played a recording of himself on the jukebox singing a self-written tear-jerker. Another neighbour was Pam Feeley, who twenty years previously had been the childhood sweetheart of the actor Lee Marvin. She lived with her children next door, in the ground floor of 'a rambling old house... its doors all rimmed with sweet honeysuckle vines'.[8] Shortly after the Martyns left the scene, Marvin returned, every inch the hero from some celluloid cowboy romance, to reclaim his first love, sweeping Feeley and her children away to a new life in Malibu and Arizona. They married and remained together until the actor's death in 1987. Who can say where a meeting between Martyn and Marvin might have led but, alas, their wandering stars did not align.

For now, Feeley was dating a New Orleans trumpet player, another small cog in the vast, ever-churning Woodstock music mill. Her eighteen-year-old son, Rod McLeod, played guitar and bonded with his new neighbours. 'My recollection is that John was just the most talented person I've ever known as a musician,' says McLeod. 'He heard something in his head, and if he couldn't play it, he retuned his guitar until he could. I'd never seen anything like it before. I found that an amazing talent.'

In some ways Woodstock was an idyll. Martyn wrote 'Woodstock' while living there, a decidedly minor addition to the canon of songs commemorating the spirit of the town and its environs, a list which includes Mitchell's 'Woodstock', Bobby Charles's 'Small Town Talk' and Van Morrison's 'Old, Old, Woodstock'. Pandering to the more mawkish leanings of his creative mind, it is a litany of homespun attractions sung in his most affected Anglo-folk voice, and included a passing nod to The Band, '*play[ing] country cool and sweet*'.

At times, life imitated art. They swam in the rivers and picnicked in the woods. Martyn fished. Their old friend from the London folk scene, Jackson C. Frank, was also living in Woodstock, and on occasion he drove them into the surrounding countryside. There were forays into the Kaaterskill Wild Forest near Palenville, where Martyn scudded down the creek in a rubber tyre, plunging into the swimming hole while his wife sat on the bank with Wesley pondering the possibility of a permanent alternative life in the wilderness, at the same time wondering where her husband's devil-may-care streak might lead.

They socialised with the local musicians, picked and sang. 'We had them over at least once or twice for dinner and had a friendly time with them,' says Happy Traum. 'Jane remembers John sitting on the steps of the house, playing his guitar, and I came over, and we played together at Lower Byrdcliffe. I remember them at that point being a lovely couple, and very, very together.'

'It was a very special time,' says McLeod. 'We all smoked a little and drank some, [but] I don't remember any big party scene. He doesn't stand out as being wild with his drug or alcohol use. We all drank a lot.

He went around town and it was a family. He had that little boy, he was very loving, and it was pretty healthy.' On July 20 they attended the Newport Folk Festival, held each year in Rhode Island, a couple of hours east of the town. Pentangle played, as did Happy Traum.

There were tensions, however, including a flare-up between Jackson C. Frank and Martyn, who later told the writer Mat Snow that he distrusted artistic communities. There were misgivings on both sides. Martyn wore his enthusiasms and insecurities a little too much in plain sight for the low-key mellowness of Woodstock, while being surrounded by so much heavyweight competition fed his neuroses. According to John Wood, Martyn never quite shook off the uncomfortable awareness that he had only gained an entrée into this world courtesy of his wife's contacts. 'There was no question that John did have problems of security on that album, because of the situation,' says Wood. 'It was originally Bev's record.' It was a view shared by Martyn's peers back home. 'I think amongst musicians the thought was that Beverley was going to be really famous and he'd somehow managed to get himself a leg-up by being with her,' says Steve Tilston.

It was in Woodstock that the physical and psychological abuse which Beverley Martyn suffered throughout the marriage first surfaced. Beneath his upbeat, energetic, loving exterior, those close to Martyn were already aware that his was a hair-trigger personality which could switch in a flash. 'I saw flashes of temper one time,' says McLeod. 'He had a rough quality about him, even with the golden hair and beauty.'

Martyn performed once in Woodstock, at the town Playhouse on the Fourth of July, at a benefit in aid of Pete Seeger's Hudson River Sloop Clearwater project, held to raise funds to aid a clean-up operation on the river. The bill also featured Happy Traum and his brother Artie. Martyn played a solo set, which included a version of Bob Dylan's 'Don't Think Twice, It's All Right'. According to Beverley, he 'didn't want me to do much singing,'[9] but she joined her husband for one song, a performance of 'Jelly Roll Baker'.

Afterwards they encountered Dylan in the flesh. Over the years, Martyn chiselled away at this meeting until all that remained was a brief, bright anecdote which said practically nothing about how he really felt about coming into contact with someone he so admired. 'I played with Bob Dylan,' he told me, which was not quite true. 'It was just weird. I was tongue-tied. He was very quiet, very small. Polite. He had white socks on and the rest of him was all in black.'

In the Playhouse foyer that night, Dylan in fact seemed to gravitate towards Beverley, who was star-struck. 'Meeting Dylan was a big deal for me,' she says. 'He was my dad figure as a fifteen-year-old girl, or the brother I never had. Bob would tell you what it was about; you'd think he was talking to you. I adored his work, his poetry, his music and his voice. And I thought he was cute. I thought he was Bucky Goldberg, my Jewish cowboy! So to meet him was really something. He said, "I'm really pleased to meet you," and I said, "You can't possibly know what it's like to meet you," and we laughed.'

Physically, Beverley Martyn was very much Dylan's type: dark-haired, sad-eyed, voluptuous, radiating a certain mystical spirituality. The mildly flirtatious attention he paid her did not sit well with Martyn. Back at the Byrdcliffe house 'he went berserk,' she recalled, shouting and throwing objects at her, including a fork which hit her under the eye and left a bruise.[10] Moments later, Martyn was on his knees, sobbing, begging his wife not to leave.

The key personality regarding the album they were here to make was Paul Harris, the American boyfriend of Joe Boyd's friend from Cambridge, Susie Campbell. She and Harris had met in England but were now living together in a loft in New York. Harris was a gifted piano player, classically trained, as well as a fine arranger. He had recently made a magnificent contribution to 'Time Has Told Me', the opening track on Nick Drake's debut album, *Five Leaves Left*, released that summer on Island while Martyn was in Woodstock.

Harris and Campbell travelled upstate to Woodstock most weekends during the summer, staying in a log cabin and working on the arrangements. Harvey Brooks, who had played bass on *Highway 61 Revisited* and performed live with Bob Dylan in 1966, also visited, tempted to the woods by the quality of the smoked salmon, though he brought his own supply of bagels. 'I was brought in for that New York folk-rock explosion sound,' says Brooks. 'They were fun to work with, though I was totally unfamiliar with what they did. Paul Harris was pretty much directing it. He was the arranger that put it together around them.'

When it was time to record, Boyd and Wood flew in from London, the Martyns came down from Woodstock, and they convened in studio one at A&R in New York, chosen for its European mixing desk. Wood had never recorded in an American studio before.

They worked at a clip: a handful of days for the tracks, two more to mix. Boyd was brisk and businesslike, while the level of musicianship on display was a quantum leap for Martyn. As well as Brooks, the cast included John Simon, who played harpsichord on the slightly feeble 'Tomorrow Time' and had produced The Band, Leonard Cohen and Simon & Garfunkel. Harris's keyboard parts, particularly on the title track, were rapturous, reminiscent of his work with Drake. The trio of drummers, meanwhile, were gold standard. Fresh from The Mothers of Invention and Rhinoceros, Billy Mundi played on 'Go Out And Get It', The Band's Levon Helm contributed to 'Sweet Honesty' and 'John The Baptist', and Herbie Lovell played punctuative percussion on the title track and 'Would You Believe Me?'

'We didn't have a drummer on the first day,' Wood recalls. 'Joe said to Paul, "We need drums." Paul said he would see who was in town. The first night he gets Billy Mundi, then Levon Helm turns up – these guys could just sit down and wallop it out. The third night we did have to resort to getting a session drummer, and we get Herbie Lovell, who had played on all the great Atlantic hits of the Sixties. He was incredible. All these guys just sat down with the beat-up studio kit and sounded incredible. From a recording engineer's point of view, that record was a doddle. I just had to sit there and watch them do it.'

Beverley added acoustic rhythm guitar, but Martyn played the vast bulk of the parts. It was the first time he had used electric guitar on a record, and he took the opportunity to showcase his versatility. On 'Would You Believe Me?' he not only peeled off a string of lilting country-rock licks, he used a Watkins Copicat echo machine for the first time. An attempt to replicate the strange swirling texture of Garth Hudson's organ playing in The Band, the swell and sob was perfectly attuned to the sentiment of the song.

Martyn ended up writing and singing six songs to his wife's four, as well as taking charge of the musical direction. 'It was a positive session,' says Brooks. 'When people know what they're doing, it's easy to find your place. They were pleasant to work with and musically intelligent. My observation was that [John] was the director. Somebody's got to do that. It seems that they were harmonious in those respective roles.'

Joe Boyd was 'very excited' about the results. 'We took the tape back to England and Paul wrote some string charts and we recorded them in London at Sound Techniques.'

Everyone was excited about the potential of *Stormbringer!* In October 1969, Boyd was courted by Bob Crewe, the writer, producer and impresario behind the success of The Walker Brothers and The Four Seasons, among others. Crewe was an old-school New York Brill Building character who heard *Stormbringer!* by chance while it was being mastered at Sterling Sound in New York. 'He was going, "What the fuck is this? It's fantastic,"' says Boyd. 'He called me and said he wanted to release it [on his CGC label] in America. I said okay. Because Island didn't have an outlet in America, we did deals artist by artist.'

Boyd was flown to New York and courted by Crewe, but 'it was like worlds colliding. He was slick and full of hype, saying, "I'll give you an advance, we'll pay for a tour..." In some ways, I regret that I didn't actually do the deal, but I just could not imagine, somehow, John dealing with Bob Crewe.' Instead, Boyd sent an acetate of the record to Joe Smith at Warner Bros., who put out *Stormbringer!* in the States.

The album released in February 1970 was a lavish affair, graced with a wonderful cover designed by Nigel Waymouth and dominated by an extraordinary image taken by Japanese photographer Hiroshi. It depicted Martyn and Beverley huddled together on Hampstead Heath, floating on a raft of cold, sharp light, she all in white like a Narnian queen; he, her shaggy, bare-ankled protector, surrounded by a sea of darkness and a foreboding sky. They looked like they could conquer the world.

'We really thought, Wow, this is great – we've got a great cover and we've got a great record,' says Boyd. 'It was a legitimate swing for the fences, as they say in baseball.' In other words, *Stormbringer!* was a calculated risk. 'Joe knew how to spend money making records and worry about paying for them afterwards,' says John Wood.

'*Stormbringer!* cost a lot of money,' Boyd confirms. 'Living in Woodstock, paying Levon Helm double scale, hiring a string orchestra in London under the direction of Paul Harris. I had discovered mastering at Sterling Sound in New York. I didn't fly over to supervise, but I sent the tapes to Sterling to be mastered because I really liked this one engineer there. We definitely were acting as if there was plenty of money, and John couldn't have been more enthusiastic about it at the time. He loved all of that.'

Such largesse would have significant repercussions further down the line. For now, the album of 'funky folk' was an appreciable leap forward for Martyn, not only in terms of musical expansiveness but in relation to his songwriting and his singing, both of which had become richer, fuller, more revealing.

'Would You Believe Me?', his agonised farewell to Linda Dunning, was one of several songs referencing Martyn's recent life choices. The sense on *Stormbringer!* was frequently that of a couple talking to one another. On 'Traffic-Light Lady', Martyn addressed Beverley directly and the covert beginnings of a relationship which was '*a secret*' shared only between the two of them, imploring her to open up to him about her life and her child.

The feisty 'John The Baptist' played on the biblical story of Salome, daughter of Herod, who, according to one of numerous interpretations, demanded the head of the prophet on a platter. Casting himself in the title role and his new wife as supporting actress, it laid bare Martyn's terror of commitment in light of his new-found status as a husband and stepfather. She doesn't just want his heart; she wants his head, too. Marriage not just as emasculation, but decapitation. A very literal death.

The lyric touches pointedly on the power balance in their professional relationship – 'She never sings too soon' – and includes Martyn's first serious piece of self-mythologising. He portrays himself as the existential outlaw who has been, at least temporarily, tamed into domesticity, framed in a 'Wanted' poster on the nursery wall, a hefty price hanging on his head. On the slow, tranced roll of 'Sweet Honesty', Beverley Martyn counters with her own conflicted feelings about taking on this man who uses words to cut her down to size, and never takes the time to 'treat a woman kind'.

With its tender strings, Harris's lyrical piano playing and words depicting a departing woman who refuses to look back at what she is leaving behind, the title track is perhaps the most beautiful piece Martyn had recorded up to that point. So much so, it takes some time to realise that his wife doesn't feature on it.★

Martyn would later remark that 'a lot of things came from those sessions. Nobody had really thought of combining acoustic instruments with drums before then. It sounds a little conceited to say that, but I think that the album was rather ahead of its time.'[11]

The review in *Melody Maker* cautiously agreed, declaring *Stormbringer!* their folk album of the month while at the same time noting Martyn's trajectory away from defined notions of genre. 'Ahead of its time? Who knows – time loses all meaning and relevance when *Stormbringer!* is on the turntable... [It] has not been conceived in the folk idiom nor does it bear much resemblance to anything John has done in the past.'[12]

The album was 'deceptive', wrote an uncredited reviewer in *Beat Instrumental*. 'Relaxed it may be, but the more you listen to it, the

---

★ In 1969 a pre-fame Elton John recorded publishing demos of 'Stormbringer', 'Sweet Honesty' and 'Go Out And Get It', as well as several songs by Nick Drake, for Joe Boyd's Warlock Music. A grey-market CD, *Prologue*, was later released, copied from the original vinyl demo disc. Linda Thompson sings four tracks.

more its muscles are revealed, the deeper you can go... the whole thing hangs together beautifully.'[13]

Does *Stormbringer!* hang together beautifully? In many ways, yes. The sound was fat and full, the textures appreciably organic, the rhythm convincing, the songs strong. It was a world away from anything happening in the embryonic folk-rock scene in Britain in 1969. Martyn had already developed a finely honed aversion to the growing trend for putting a 4/4 rock beat over traditional British folk music. 'It's like a cross between a swan and a duck – the rhythm section being the duck,' he said many years later. 'As soon as you put that bass and drums on it, it coarsens it and changes the nature of the music and makes it into something quite unacceptable to me.'[14]

'I remember hearing *Stormbringer!* – John Wood played it to me – and realising I had such a long way to go in terms of being a rhythm section player,' says Dave Mattacks, at that time the drummer in Fairport Convention. 'It scared the life out of me. I had a conversation many years later with John. He made a comment which I thought was unfair and negative. We were talking about the English folk music thing, and he said, very simply, that it doesn't swing. I was put back on my heels, but I now have a deeper appreciation of where he was heading. I think he was saying there was a lack of bounce in some of the more inherent four-square fills that Fairport and some of its contemporaries had come up with, and I realised I was guilty of contributing to that. He was working with players who had an inherent swing in there. I don't mean swing as in a strict tempo, I mean a certain amount of grease and feel in the groove.'

Any album featuring Levon Helm, Billy Mundi and Herbie Lovell could not help but have grease in the groove, yet something was missing. The centre did not hold. 'The only shadow on the whole thing for me at the time was that they didn't really sing together,' says Boyd. '[It] ended up with John having his songs and Beverley having her songs, and they didn't really work together that much. It's not really integrated in that sense.'

The two albums Martyn and Beverley made together contain some beautiful songs and performances, but there is rarely a sense of two artists working in unison. Each would sing the songs they wrote, with the other usually, but by no means always, chiming in on the chorus or middle eight. It's a methodology which lends not only the records but the entire concept of their partnership an oddly disconnected feel.

There were moments when the possibilities shone. On the beautiful 'Traffic-Light Lady', the listener gained a sense of some deeper connection; one could imagine the couple sitting at home late at night, playing for fun, finding joy in each other's presence and wishing to share in it. Such glimpses were few and far between, perhaps because the songs were, in the end, written independently and so utterly bound up in their own emotions. 'I wasn't convinced,' says Wood. 'It seemed to be either her songs or his songs; there didn't seem to be that much of a partnership. *Stormbringer!* is basically two solo artists brought together.'

It may have mattered less if not for the fact that, for all the money laid out, the album did not pay its way. Its lack of success was a blow to all concerned and coincided with a downturn in Witchseason's fortunes. 'I wasn't rich,' says Boyd. 'I hadn't succeeded monetarily, but I felt like everything I had done [so far] had worked well. I spotted this little folk duo in Scotland and, the next thing you know, they're at the Woodstock Festival and filling the Albert Hall and the Lincoln Center and selling hundreds of thousands of copies. Fairport is going from strength to strength, artistically. It was all going the way I thought it should go. Then Nick's record comes out, which I think is a fantastic record, and *Stormbringer!* comes out, which I think is a fantastic record, and they don't sell. That was a big shock for me. And for Nick, and for John and Beverley.'

Upon returning to Britain, Martyn had rolled back into the usual routine: solo gigs at Cousins, one-night stands at colleges, folk clubs and blues festivals. He came back 'full of how he'd been to the States,' says Steve Tilston. 'At that time we were all listening to The Band, and he said, "Well, I've been recording with Levon Helm!"'

On September 24 he and Beverley supported Fairport Convention at the Royal Festival Hall in London, alongside Nick Drake, who was on the bill again for the official launch of *Stormbringer!* at the Queen Elizabeth Hall at the Southbank Centre on February 21, 1970. In an attempt to recreate the album, they assembled an ad hoc approximation of the New York session band, with Spooky Tooth's Mike Kellie playing drums, The New Nadir's Ed Carter on guitar and Mike Kowalski on bass, although his first instrument was drums. Carter and Kowalski played on Drake's second album, *Bryter Layter*, and were also members of The Beach Boys' touring group.

They were all excellent musicians, and they rehearsed for two days before the show. At the Queen Elizabeth Hall, Martyn and Beverley performed together, and apart, before being joined by the band for half a dozen songs. The experience did more, perhaps, than any other to push Martyn on his own path. He called it 'the most humiliating musical experience of my career'.[15]

'That gig didn't happen because there was a lack of empathy,' Martyn said later that year. 'The musicians were really excellent but they were drawn from different scenes. The guitar and bass player were heavily into Latin music and the drummer was very heavy. It's really a drag making a good musician play the sort of music he doesn't feel. It's purely a matter of emotion. You just have to be very careful with a band... Even if one member of a band is a bit unsure why he's there, then it fucks the whole thing up.'[16]

At the time, Kowalski had 'no idea that John wasn't quite happy. After the gig we would still go around to his flat, and he didn't mention anything. We had a great rehearsal. He was pretty persistent in what he wanted: simplicity. He didn't want anyone to overplay.' As for the show itself, 'I don't think there were too many clams in there.'

The issue was a wider one. Virtuosity wasn't enough. As a musician who worked off his moods and emotions, Martyn couldn't tolerate having to limit the parameters of a performance in order to accommodate what he felt were the unsympathetic creative instincts of other players. There was also a suspicion that his wife was cramping his style, on and off stage. 'What happens backstage is that after the gig, let's say there are twenty people there,' says Tod Lloyd, who observed the aftermath of the show. 'Then a half hour later, there's probably fifteen people there, and forty-five minutes later, there's probably ten. People peel off. I can remember Beverley really wanting everybody to peel off, so that they could go and do whatever it was that they were going to do. John, I didn't get that feeling from.'

It didn't augur particularly well for the next duo album, *The Road To Ruin*, which followed in short order. The cast list included many of the musicians who had originally been earmarked to appear on Beverley's solo album, including Alan Spenner, Dudu Pukwana and Dave Pegg. Paul Harris returned, and Mike Kowalski appeared – on drums rather than bass this time – on the strafing, stoned blues-rock of 'Auntie Aviator', one of the record's highlights.

The album was made in the face of a headwind. Joe Boyd, struggling under the weight of financial and creative pressures, was already planning an exit strategy. His relationship with Martyn became even more a battle of wills, with Boyd bowing out of a confrontation. He retreated to the control room, read his newspaper and allowed Martyn to lead. 'John said play this and we played it,' says Kowalski. 'If he didn't like it, he would tell us.'

In place of the rootsy American orientation of *Stormbringer!* came a homegrown jazz feel, a rather polite form of dishevelment, courtesy of session men such as Lyn Dobson and Ray Warleigh. They were fine musicians but, in the eyes of Martyn, who had a knee-jerk aversion to all but a few British players, not quite what was required. The musicians came and went, adding and layering. 'That record wasn't a spontaneous thing, unlike the others,' Martyn said. 'It was a question of: "We'll do an overdub", "Can we do it now?", "No, do it next week." And so we just went back and forth and back and forth.'[17]

It was somehow laboured, yet also hurried. 'We rushed to get it done before I left [for America],' says Boyd. 'I think it actually sounds like a more integrated record; it has more of a unity to it and they actually sing together.' If anything, there was even less of an obvious connection this time. The album featured three co-writes, four tracks by Martyn and a charming cover of Paul Wheeler's sweet signature song 'Give Us A Ring', recorded as 'a measure of our friendship,' says Wheeler. 'As a thank-you present, with a play on the words of the title, John gave me his wedding ring in a spontaneous gesture; I still have it.' Beverley Martyn wrote one song alone.

The Road To Ruin was released in November 1970, in a dark, disquieting and commercially unappealing cover featuring a black-and-white image by Max Ernst, taken from his 1933 book of recontextualised Victorian illustrations, *Une Semaine de Bonté* (*A Week of Kindness*). It was a beguiling but sometimes confusing listen in which the competing styles did not often convincingly converge. The songs bumped awkwardly into one another. Martyn and his wife shared vocals on only two of the nine tracks. 'I'd go to the studio a few times and John really didn't want Beverley to sing,' says Linda Thompson. 'It was a joke. It wasn't right, and it was hard for Beverley.'

It is easy to hear the fault lines between two differing sensibilities. The skipping jazz-pop of 'Primrose Hill', an ode to the bohemian whirl of North London, was written by Beverley and sung by her alone. Similarly, the gear change was far from seamless between 'Sorry To Be So Long', a busy, piano-heavy, conga carnival with Martyn contributing mean blues harmonica, and the soft, hazy tones of 'Tree Green'. 'Say What You Can', with its obtrusive sax overdubs and rather tepid groove, barrels inelegantly into the opening minutes of the title track, a haunting meditation in which Martyn, for the first time, began to blur the edges of his Ss into sibilant Zs, against a quivering, tensile backing track. It's a mesmerising moment. The extended instrumental coda which follows feels, aptly, as though it belongs to another song, another artist.

An interview with Jerry Gilbert in *Melody Maker*, ostensibly to promote the new album, revealed the strain. Martyn seemed 'permanently on the edge of a holocaust' as he dismissed folk clubs, revealed he had lots of new solo songs he wanted to record, and claimed that 'I don't think a lot of people would know what I'm aiming at.'[18]

The writer also picked up on his tendency to dominate the conversation and to speak on behalf of his wife. 'Beverley is a lot more into pop,' he said. '[Her] tastes are much more jazzy than mine. Her harmonies and mine are very different. She would use tunes I wouldn't even consider.'[19] Just to emphasise the point, he stated that they would not be playing any more gigs together any time soon. If the muddled runes of *The Road To Ruin* had not sent a clear enough signal, then here was blunt clarification.

'Beverley was a sweet person, I liked her a lot,' says Richard Thompson. 'She was talented, a good writer and singer. I never really thought about what her and John's relationship was like behind closed doors. You never really know what goes on with couples [but] it seemed to me that John could be controlling... John obviously liked to feel that he was in the driving seat, and that if it was a partnership, that he was the dominant partner. You got that feeling after a while.'

By the time they had finished *The Road To Ruin*, Joe Boyd 'had the feeling that John's heart was not in having Beverley on stage with him. I don't think he ever fancied the idea of sharing the spotlight.'

The two records they made together can be construed, depending on one's view, as a gesture of supreme generosity from a young wife, or a hostile takeover on the part of her forceful new husband. Perhaps a little of each of those impulses played out, alongside love, undoubtedly, and willingness and goodwill on both sides towards the idea of sharing a meaningful creative experience. In the end, their collaboration was an act of optimism and opportunity rather than one of musical good sense. One could see how and why it happened, and also why it hadn't quite worked.

Crucially, it was never seriously taken forward where it mattered – on stage. The duo-plus-band experiment at the Queen Elizabeth Hall would not be repeated. After the release of *The Road To Ruin*, the couple only ever played a handful more shows together, most notably a run of three dates in November 1972, in Manchester, Brighton and London. Beverley sang a little on some of her husband's solo albums, strummed a guitar here and there, but she was entering a long, slow, deeply painful fade-out. It would be hard to argue that going it alone was not the correct creative decision for Martyn – the evidence of his next run of records speaks for itself – but it came at a price.

'I never stopped making music,' Beverley Martyn told me. 'I did the odd gig with John for three or four years, and one or two on my own, with Ralph McTell and the String Band. [But] my career was over by then. I had no future: there was no record deal for me – it was all lies. What started out to be my album ended up in his control. I think John wanted to be Nick Drake, and that's what he did. He got Danny Thompson together and they went free-form.'

6

In 1971 Danny Thompson entered Martyn's orbit as foil, wingman, bad influence, sparring partner, myth-maker and blood brother. Martyn's music would never be the same again.

They were not quite strangers. Martyn had supported Thompson's pioneering folk–jazz band Pentangle once or twice, and Thompson had played string bass on 'New Day' on *The Road To Ruin*, but these occasions had not brought about a close connection. 'I knew him before, on the road,' Danny Thompson told me. 'We did Newport Folk Festival [with Pentangle, in 1969] and he was there. He used to phone me up when I didn't know him and say, "Do you fancy doing a gig?", [but] I was on the road.'

That changed with Thompson's involvement on *Bless The Weather*. Martyn's third solo record was the true beginning of an epic, tempestuous love affair, just about platonic, punctuated with cuddles and kisses, haymakers and headbutts, and an unspoken musical understanding which bordered on telepathy. 'To an extent it was a romance,' says Linda Thompson.

'When we got together, it was like love at first sight,' says Danny Thompson. 'Bosh. This beautiful, handsome, curly-haired boy, ten years younger than me, with all that attitude and energy and honesty.'

Born in Devon on March 4, 1939, Thompson was raised in South London. He was a big, burly presence, a handy footballer in his youth, a useful boxer and a hard drinker, with a head for money but a poetic soul. Adept on several instruments but a master of the upright bass, Thompson possessed an intuitive understanding of jazz, in particular. He began his professional career after completing national service, playing on numerous sessions, including Cliff Richard's 'Congratulations', before joining up with Alexis Korner. In 1967 Thompson formed Pentangle with John Renbourn and Bert Jansch, alongside vocalist Jacqui McShee and drummer Tony Cox.

By the time of his association with Martyn, Pentangle was in its final throes. They would release one further album, *Solomon's Seal*, before splitting at the beginning of 1973. In contrast to life with the band, which had become stifling and hamstrung by internal personal conflict, Thompson's engagement with Martyn felt fresh and energising. 'I'd had five years on the road, and music had become like a recipe for success,' he says. 'I thought, This isn't what it's all about. It's supposed to be like when we were fifteen, practising in the garage with your mates. That's what it was like with John.'

Over the years their exploits have been wildly exaggerated, their complicated friendship presented as something less tidal than it was in reality, but it would be hard to overstate the potency of the music they made together. The loose-limbed interplay between Thompson's empathetic, time-shifting bass and Martyn's voice and guitar unlocked his songs from notions of regular rhythm and structure, opening up entire new vistas in his music. It formed the backbone of Martyn's greatest period of creativity and much of his best live work.

They tore through towns, behaving extremely badly, until 1978, when Thompson stopped drinking and their paths diverged, only occasionally to entwine again. The details until then are hazy. Thompson regards the music they made together as one long song, an improvised dialogue with no beginning and no end, a circular movement, as natural as breathing, of almost continuous creativity.

'My entire association with John, bless him, all those years, it's all one thing,' he says. 'I could make up some romantic tale – "he came in and lit up the room" – but no. We'd get together, have a few drinks and play in the front room, like two naughty boys enjoying ourselves. It wasn't like a job. He'd say, "This is the kind of stuff we're going to do," he'd run through the song, then I'd play and say, "So, something like that then, John?" He'd say, "No, *exactly* like that!" There was nobody sitting there saying, "No, no, no, not like that, more like this." We didn't have all that. It was just us, and very trusting.'

The bond extended beyond music. Thompson never knew his father, who had been declared missing in action during the war. His upbringing had been lonely, tough and wounding. 'We had a great deal in common, the same insecurities,' Martyn recalled. 'Mine was my parents being divorced, his was being orphaned. He was brought up by wicked nuns in a convent and bore the scars all his life.'[1]

As one significant character arrived in Martyn's life, another departed. Having become increasingly stretched by the complications of putting out sixteen albums in a year and singularly failing to make them pay, Joe Boyd left the UK in January 1971 to take over a role at Warner Bros. in Los Angeles. Before doing so, he sold his Witchseason stable and Warlock publishing company, both in a perilous financial state, to Chris Blackwell at Island Records. 'It left him with a stable of artists in turmoil, all poised at crucial points in their careers,' Boyd recalled in his memoir, *White Bicycles*.[2]

None better fitted that description than John and Beverley Martyn, who were pondering a personal and professional crossroads. They were now, at least in theory, both Island artists and, according to Martyn, the initial agreement in the handover from Witchseason was that they would record individual solo albums for the label. That was not how it worked out. Only Martyn emerged at the other end with a contract. Sometimes he blamed Boyd, alleging that he had mishandled the Witchseason sale. At other times, he claimed that Island simply reneged on the deal. He said that Muff Winwood, their A&R man, told him, 'We'll have you but we can't have Bev... She sings flat.'[3]

'He came home and woke me up at 3 a.m. to tell me that they didn't want another album from me, they only wanted one from him,' Beverley later wrote. 'It broke my heart.'[4] Whatever the circumstances, she always suspected her husband didn't put up much of a fight. He was the one dealing directly with the record company.

'After he died, I found out a lot of stuff,' she says. 'Like the fact that there was no contract with me – he signed contracts for John and Beverley Martyn as he was my husband. The royalties all went to him, and even when the contracts were renegotiated, they didn't tell me about it so it just carried on going to him.' According to Beverley, 75 per cent of the royalties were assigned to Martyn, and 25 per cent to her.

A print advert publicising the release of *Bless The Weather* explained away her absence, claiming that Martyn's new solo record had originally been planned as a third duo album, but that Beverley had got pregnant – thereby, presumably, rendering her incapable of singing.

Mhairi Katherine Tulah McGeachy was born on February 15, 1971 at Queen Mary's Hospital in Hampstead. Katherine was for Martyn's aunt Kitty, the Gaelic forename Mhairi (which nowadays she writes as it is pronounced, Vari) in honour of Hamish Imlach's daughter Vhari.

They had talked about moving away from London even before the baby arrived. Martyn found the energy of the city increasingly sapping and unhealthy. In spring 1970 the proposed destination was Hampshire. By the end of the year it was Scotland. Not long after Mhairi was born, they finally left for Hastings, renting a house they had previously used for holidays, at 10 Cobourg Place in the Old Town. They later bought the property for £7,000. It was near the station, and when working in London Martyn would catch the train home – sometimes the last service of the day, often the first of the next morning. At other times, on a whim, he would hail a taxi for the seventy-five-mile journey and charge the fare to Island.

A historic seaside town on the Sussex coast, with a shingle beach, a pier and amusement arcades, Hastings offered faded Victorian grandeur on the one hand and the smuggler's romance of the Old Town on the other. During the time Martyn lived there, the combination of a vibrant grassroots music culture and the local fishing industry created a lively nightlife fringed with a heavy drug scene. Their five years living in the town 'were some of the happiest times and some of the worst as well,' says Vari McGeachy. 'We were a family, we were together. Hastings had its appeal for kids – beaches, rock, hillocks. It was good fun to explore.'

The house at Cobourg Place was not family-friendly. Neither Martyn nor Beverley drove and the Old Town was a maze of tight streets and sharp bends. There was no garden and, situated at the top of the cliff with steep steps descending to the town, the ferrying of shopping and small children were particularly arduous tasks. Two doors down from number 10 stood Harpsichord House, where the writer, mystic, magician and 'wickedest man in the world', Aleister Crowley, had first lived when he moved to Hastings in advanced age, and where the occultist Rollo Ahmed later resided. Martyn was one of a number of musicians, notably Jimmy Page, but also David Bowie, who harboured a fascination with Crowley and his Thelemic ethical code: 'Do what thou wilt shall be the whole of the law.'

While Martyn was following his true path, his wife often felt sidelined and isolated. Martyn could be a loving father when the mood took him, warm, fun and tactile, but he was often absent. Few men in 1971 changed nappies or pushed prams. Martyn was assuredly not one of them.

The combination of her husband's apparent indifference to her own music, having a second child to look after and moving out of the city effectively killed off Beverley's career. Martyn was not oblivious to the ramifications. 'That destroyed her somewhat and might have contributed to the deleterious relationship between us,' he later conceded.[5]

There were other reasons. In Hastings, the volatility of the marriage steadily escalated. As the decade wore on, the rough diamond and lovable roustabout who acted out in bars, hotels and on stages all over the world became something far more combustible behind closed doors. Martyn displayed classic patterns of coercive behaviour – controlling, manipulative, mercurial. Quick to emotional and sometimes physical violence when drunk, drugged or simply enraged, he fostered paranoia and panic even when he was being nice. Such was the suddenness and extremity of his changes, it was impossible to know which version of the man to expect from day to day, hour to hour. Living with him, wrote Beverley, was 'like you were on an adrenaline rush all the time'.[6]

There were moments of calm, however, particularly when they played music together at home late at night. The magnificent 'Don't Want To Know' emerged from one such session. Beverley hit on the song's repeating refrain and Martyn ran with it, yet when he recorded the song for *Solid Air* the writing credit was his alone. As Van Morrison's ex-wife once noted about the role of muse, 'it's a thankless job and the pay is lousy'.[7]

Back on the road, Martyn relished the swash and the buckle of cutting through the country, a one-man operation. 'I had a knife in my pocket, a Fender amp in one hand, the two pedals, the fuzz and the wah-wah, three leads and a guitar,' he said, much later, clearly still enraptured by the romance of it all. 'I loved it. It was cool just running around. No one came with me – it was a fresh time. I used to get on a train or a plane and roll joints on that old waxy toilet paper and just sit on the toilet and get high.'[8]

He was itching to move forward. Clarifying his contractual situation with Island had been a protracted affair, and by the point where he was ready to make his next album, he was disillusioned with folk clubs and the insularity of the scene, the limits of the performative expectations and the parameters of the music. On *Bless The Weather*, he hit upon a mix of songs and stylings which broke new ground for him. Beverley sang backing vocals and played guitar on two tracks.

The album was recorded at Sound Techniques. The co-producer was John Wood, engineer on the two joint albums. 'Joe asked if I could produce a solo record with John, and do it for £2,000,' Wood remembers. Martyn later recalled that he was paid an advance of £6,000 from Island for the record, which would chime with Richard Thompson's memory that 'John was on a budget. He wanted to save money and record very cheaply and keep the change from the record advance.'

It was the first of Martyn's records to properly capitalise on Wood's extraordinary ability to shape the sound of the music being played in a room. 'John trained in classical music, and he was really good at miking acoustic instruments, particularly,' says Thompson, who contributed to the album. 'Somehow, he'd always get a better sound than another engineer. He knew the position in the room, the right mikes to use; just a great, great engineer. He did not like bullshit, he did not suffer fools. If something wasn't right, he'd let you know, but he was fair, and his approach led to some fantastic results.'

The album took three days. 'A lot of stuff, like "Sugar Lump", was one take,' says Thompson. 'John might have run through it once, perhaps not even the whole song – "twelve-bar, goes like this" – okay, bang.' Aside from a brief, jaunty finale of 'Singin' In The Rain', this bawdy blues was the album's sole moment of levity.

At times, the haste was apparent. Some songs sounded half finished, which they effectively were, much of the material being written on the hoof and recorded the same day they were composed. Other tracks simply ran out of road and drifted to a close. Whether any of them would have benefited from a more attentive approach is a moot point. The spark and spontaneity is part of their beauty.

The instrumental interaction was frequently dazzling. Martyn had heard pianist Ian Whiteman at a Sandy Denny session and invited him along. Whiteman suggested he bring Roger Powell, his regular drumming partner. According to John Wood, hiring Danny Thompson had been his suggestion. Whoever's idea it was, it was a masterstroke, worth the trouble for the last two minutes of 'Head And Heart' alone, quite apart from the funky push-me, pull-me flow of the title track.

Thompson shared the session with Tony Reeves, who played bass on the first two Davy Graham albums and was impressed with Martyn's desire to explore. 'He was into jazz and I was a jazzer,' says Reeves. 'He liked messing around with sound, fuzz-boxes and pedals, and so did I. He was taking liberties, and I liked doing that. I may even have used a wah-wah pedal on double bass.'

In terms of sonic experimentation, the preeminent track on *Bless The Weather* was 'Glistening Glyndebourne', a free-form instrumental running to six and a half minutes. It stands apart as the first sustained example of Martyn messing with form, moving away from song into sound. An impressionistic evocation of a dream-like scene he had witnessed on the night train to Hastings, of glad-ragged operagoers from Glyndebourne embarking the carriage in the summer rain, he framed the piece as a rebellious statement against 'straight' music, although those of a romantic disposition might hear in the reflective opening passage a pang for the refined musical life his mother and father were never quite allowed to fulfil.

It is an outstanding ensemble performance. Powell builds up an urgent, click-clacking rhythm. Whiteman's impressionistic piano is elemental, exquisitely empathetic. After two minutes, Martyn's viciously manipulated vortex of guitars scud across the landscape, adding scattered rhythmic patterns, loosing off notes like artillery fire. This was no longer folk, but what was it?

Martyn had been experimenting with delay, echo and repetition for a couple of years. 'Glistening Glyndebourne' was where his ambitions finally took flight. His mind had been turned by Pharoah Sanders' *Karma*, recorded in February 1969 and released later that year. Martyn first heard it while visiting Ed Carter and Mike Kowalski in Chilham, Kent, where Kowalski and his wife lived in one of his parents' farm cottages. 'I turned him on to *Karma*,' says Kowalski. 'It's a very outsider album. John loved it. We'd listen to it and get high. He loved American bebop.'

Sanders was a tenor saxophonist who had played in John Coltrane's ensemble, appearing on his mid-Sixties albums *Ascension* and *Meditations*. They influenced each other. Along with Coltrane and his wife Alice, Sanders was a trailblazer in spiritual jazz, *Karma* being a landmark example of the genre. Comprising two tracks, the album is dominated by 'The Creator Has A Master Plan', a 32-minute epic featuring wave upon wave of free-jazz exploration. Firestorms of Sanders' saxophones and Leon Thomas's yelping vocals combine with flutes and Oriental and African percussion. The piece repeatedly breaks down into extended extemporised instrumental parts, notably in the third section, where Sanders creates a unique soundscape using split-reed technique, overblowing and screeching polyphony.*

Martyn's first reaction to *Karma* was a determination to learn the saxophone. He tried, but realised that he could not make the desired strides quickly enough. Instead, he resolved to do more with the tools already at his disposal. He was, after all, a one-man band, and his foremost preoccupation was to develop ideas which he could execute himself on stage.

Post exposure to *Karma*, his interest turned to polyrhythms and modal music, with tight harmonic frequencies, travelling back and forth in dizzying patterns within relatively narrow apertures. His approach to his voice and his lyrics also changed perceptibly. The shift can be traced back to 'Road To Ruin', but the deconstruction begins in earnest on *Bless The Weather*. The slurred vowels, the elision of words, the swoops from sweet high alto to breathy bass – all are testament to the fact that Martyn began to think of his voice as an instrument rather than simply a conventional tool for communicating melody and meaning.

By *Solid Air*, recorded in 1972, 'his voice was almost like a horn,' says John 'Rabbit' Bundrick, the keyboard player who performed on the record. 'He would smooth in his entries like a saxophone. It was almost like an actor's voice.' In time, the relationship became symbiotic: voice and music fed on each other, one almost becoming the other, with words deployed as simply one more texture as Martyn strove to pare down his lyric writing. 'I gave up trying to be poetic,' he said. 'I like words to have two or three meanings.'[9] Of roughly contemporary singers, perhaps only Tim Buckley and Tom Waits were so radical in their manipulation of what came out of their mouths.

Following exposure to Sanders, he also began exploring ways in which he could expand the reach of his guitar playing. As dexterous

---

* In the last year of Martyn's life, the fates were aligning to bring about a collaboration with Sanders; sadly, he died before it ever happened, although one can't help thinking such a meeting would have been far more productive three or four decades previously.

and facile as he was, he only had two hands and ten fingers. The solution he reached was to manipulate the sound through tape-delay effects boxes. On *Bless The Weather*, he used the WEM Copicat, which allowed the selection of various delay times by activating one of five different playback heads. Adjusting the heads altered the length of the delay, meaning Martyn could effectively 'play' the machine as he played the guitar. Used in combination, as Martyn was often wont to do, multiple heads produced complex echo effects. Exploring these textures at home in Hampstead, 'he was just like a child at Christmas,' Jo Watson remembers.

Later, he turned to the Maestro Echoplex, which worked by recording on a looped tape what was being played, then feeding back the sound almost instantaneously via a variety of sonic treatments. This 'rectangular chrome box had a loop of tape fitted on top, and a sliding system of record and playback heads altered the delay in real time. Sustain and volume could be controlled separately, and… there was an additional effect labelled wet/dry mix.'[10]

'What happens is that the note comes out of the pickup on the guitar and goes into the fuzz-box which I use now and again, and then it goes into a combination of volume and wah-wah pedal which I use a fair bit,' Martyn explained. 'It comes out of that and goes into an echoplex which repeats the note so you chop in between rhythms, and you can choose your own timings because it's completely elastic. You can set the number of repeats. I just like the idea of making a machine human in that way, and I like impressing the humanness of yourself onto a machine rather than the other way around, which is what happens in a lot of cases.'[11]

Since the Fifties these machines had been used to create wicked slapback and reverb. The great rock 'n' roll guitarists Chet Atkins, Scotty Moore and Carl Perkins all used echoplex. They were also utilised widely in post-war contemporary classical and ambient music, by Stockhausen and Terry Riley. Miles Davis used it to manipulate the texture of his trumpet. It was not new, but Martyn was one of the first to explore its effect on an acoustic guitar. 'I don't think anyone had used an echoplex in exactly the way that John used it, so it was innovative,' says Richard Thompson. 'The way John used it, and in the duo with Danny, was a very interesting, individualistic sound.'

He took it to the margins, applying extreme delay to very fast arpeggiated riffs, setting the time pattern against the rhythm he was playing. The results were spectacular and hugely distinctive. By 1970 he was already experimenting with it on stage. John James travelled with him the first time he performed with a pedal and an amplifier, and recalls that, before the show, 'he was so on edge'. Andrew Means, reviewing Martyn's February 13 show at Les Cousins for *Melody Maker*, claimed: 'John Martyn has developed one of the most incredible sounds I have ever heard from an electronically-aided instrument... I can find nothing readily available with which to compare his guitar... the music leaves one with few of the familiar foundations with which we come to terms with organised sound. It was apt to distort space and time.'[12]

This was precisely the effect Martyn desired. It moved him away not just from the folk world, but from any easy or common reference points. 'It was like each effect had its own colour,' says Bundrick. 'It was like watching a rainbow of sound floating around his head. It was brilliant; things were bouncing off of everywhere. He did a lot of double hitting on the strings, tapping them twice, setting off delays to double himself. It was fucking awesome.' It quickly became his signature sound.

So much for the fireworks. At the heart of *Bless The Weather* is some of the most exposed writing of Martyn's life, wrapped in perhaps his most blissful and beguiling set of songs. The title track was a mesmerising but disquieting barometric reading of a love affair which swings between impossible extremes. The curse he places upon the man that '*takes you away*' can be read straight, as the jealous threat of a possessive lover, which is certainly plausible. It can also be heard as punishing self-analysis, an acknowledgement that the rages Martyn unleashed upon his wife would ultimately drive her from him. 'I think he was worried that Beverley was going to leave him, because his mother left him,' says Wesley Kutner. 'It was a self-fulfilling prophecy, really. He was afraid of losing the catalyst for his creativity.'

Though the subject of the chorus is 'you', the song is equally concerned with the singer's inability to navigate two competing impulses, leaving him at the mercy of the elements within him. The mood is woozy, ominous, building to a storm.

Bobbing serenely on dazzling pearl-strings of acoustic guitar and Thompson's lyrical double bass, 'Head And Heart' goes further in outlining the precise shape of Martyn's insecurities. The need to be loved '*like a child*' is nakedly devastating, but equally revealing admissions follow, measuring the distance between the seeming and the being, a man fearful of '*looking tall*' yet '*feeling small*'.

'Walk To The Water' tells of a quasi-mystical spirit woman, her power positively tidal, lighting up a seaside town. Everyone involved is clearly relishing riding the spring-heeled groove, so much so they are reluctant to stop, particularly Smiley de Jonnes, whose cheerfully improvised steel drums begin as a pleasingly fresh texture but end up rather outliving their effectiveness.

The album is stacked with ravishing melodies and scattered with declarations of freedom. 'Go Easy' prefigures the loving universalism he would expand upon six years later on 'One World', but there is also a firm resolution to follow one's chosen path in order to do '*whatever you want to do*'. The song is the lucky charm of the self-defined wastrel, a drowsy acknowledgement of the non-conforming life he has chosen, '*raving*' through the night, '*sleeping away*' the day; and also, of course, a little something to numb the pain, even if self-medicating was at a minimum during the sessions.

'I don't remember any [stimulants] in the studio,' says Richard Thompson. 'There wasn't a lot of experimenting with substances to create a certain mood, or anything like that – a lot of that stuff is bullshit, anyway. All that, "I need to smoke a joint to create the right mood, I need to have a bottle of vodka before I can perform." It's mostly just excuses for not actually playing. On that record I don't remember any of that at all; it was very businesslike.'

'Just Now' makes peace with Martyn's itinerant lifestyle, always in motion, picking up new friends and letting good people drift away. On 'Let The Good Things Come', the ghost-like, papery guitar and

Beverley Martyn's thin, shimmering backing vocals pull the song just out of focus. It's a strange little hymn, a string of wishes to break through the obstacles keeping him grounded. On 'Down By The River', he is engaged simply in trying to be himself.

It is a formative album. We hear Martyn, a husband and father of two at twenty-three, '*turning the wheel*' to become a man. If the record as a whole suffers by an infinitesimal degree from a certain conformity of pace and mood, the limited dynamic range is something he would address in subsequent records. It stands as a magnificent testament to the gentler side of John Martyn – loving hedonist, humanist, free spirit, doubter, lost child, river-dweller.

Bless The Weather was released in November 1971 to positive reviews. In a sizeable critique in *Rolling Stone*, Stephen Holden classed Martyn alongside Joni Mitchell and Jackson Browne, in matters of quality if not style. 'His tunes have a fluidity and grace that few of today's composers can match. The most beautiful of them also have a melancholy fervour that is often accentuated by Martyn's heavily aired acoustical strumming of major seventh chords.'[13] While noting his previous work, Holden called the album 'an impressive debut', a phrase which captured the sense of *Bless The Weather* as a new beginning.

Martyn toured in January and February. For much of the Seventies he maintained a haphazard concert schedule. There was little delineation between dates, and scarcely any sense of him explicitly promoting an album. The earliest years in the decade were a blur of folk clubs, university rectories and canteens, municipal halls, small theatres and rooms upstairs.

The solo dates in early 1972 were part of a three-act bill which also featured Bronco and Claire Hamill, both Island label mates. A solo singer-songwriter from the North East of England, Hamill was only sixteen when she signed her record deal. In the autumn of 1971, she recorded her debut, *One House Left Standing*, at Basing Street; Martyn played guitar on the first two tracks.

During the tour, when Hamill was seventeen, he embarked on an affair with her which continued off and on for several years. 'I found him very mesmerising, very magnetic,' says Hamill. 'He never ever drained me in any way, quite the opposite. I found him stimulating, I loved being around him. We were great friends. I can just see him striding about the place, [with] all these funny mannerisms. The way he chose to flick his fingers and flick his nose and draw air through his teeth.'

With her, he talked a little of his early domestic upheavals. Hamill was also the product of what in those times was still referred to as a 'broken home'. Her father had left her mother and their children to start a new life in Canada. 'Sometimes he talked… about his fractured family life. I also came from a fractured family, and John and I recognised that about each other. I was very naive when I met John – about everything. I was so very young [but] I did recognise that in him because he was so flamboyant, and so larger than life, and sometimes that covers up something. He'd touch on it but not in any great depth. John was very much a man's man. He was never at home with that soft side of his personality. Not in public. Just in the music. He had this tortured part of himself, which made his music so much deeper.'

Martyn was not generally minded to discuss his feelings or insecurities. He went under duress to one counselling session later in the Seventies, at the insistence of his wife. According to Beverley, he was told that his creativity would be adversely affected if he started trying to change his behaviour. According to Martyn, the therapist 'said I was perfectly rational, perfectly sane, and that was that. She wouldn't take any money. So I went back and told Beverley there was absolutely nothing wrong with me and she had to accept that.'[14]

Hamill wrote 'Speedbreaker' about Martyn, a lively character study released in 1973 on her second album, *October*. 'He was bold and could be quite brusque,' she says. 'I don't think he was ever brutish, but he was feisty. He was almost like a bomb that was going to go off, if you weren't careful, because he had this fiery, passionate nature. He could be so incredibly charming as well.'

115

Later that year, on September 6, Martyn shared the bill with Sandy Denny at the Queen Elizabeth Hall. He toured as her support act, billed as 'My Friend, John Martyn', on and off until the end of the year. While doing so, he grappled with his next record.

Solid Air got off to several false starts, the first dating back to a session at Basing Street a year earlier, in September 1971, during which he had first recorded 'May You Never', Martyn's most popular and enduring composition. 'You could put it into a hymn book,' says Richard Thompson. 'It's a beautiful song.'

The most common thesis is that he wrote it for his friend Andy Matthews, who ran Les Cousins. 'He and Andy had a bond and a recognition beyond the ordinary,' recalled Matthews' wife, Diana. 'It was that which John initially wrote about in "May You Never". One summer day he bounded into the Frith Street flat with the DJ Jeff Dexter and told us, "I've written a song for you." He and Andy spent loads of time together.'[15] Then again, Ewan McVicar has met 'three people who told me who that song was written about. A guy I met once on a plane told me it was about his son, someone John was knocking about with.' Others theorise that it was written about his own children.

Paul Wheeler refutes the idea that it is about, or for, any person in particular. 'As I remember, he wrote it very much as a signature song. It was a very calculated thing.' Wheeler recollects that the line about love being a lesson *'we learn in our time'* was loosely appropriated from Lesley Duncan's 'Love Song'.

Such utility is the great value of 'May You Never'. It feels usable, relatable. We all know someone about whom it could or should have been written. It is a series of very secular prayers for a wayward sibling-cum-soulmate to keep his woman close, his temper in check, and to always have a warm place to lay his head. That these pitfalls were all directly pertinent to Martyn's personal hang-ups and weaknesses lends weight to the interpretation that he was, at least partly, singing to himself. Though it remains his most famous song, covered by superstars and bar-stool amateurs alike, he never quite saw what the fuss was about, and at times resented the dominance it came to demand in his catalogue. When I raised this with him, he shrugged and called it a 'lollipop', a sweet, simple and insubstantial diversion.

He first recorded 'May You Never' with a band in September 1971. Released as a stand-alone single in November – oddly, the same month *Bless The Weather* came out – the group version is an overly polite folk-rock hybrid with uncertain intent and a plodding rhythm. Martyn claimed that Free guitarist Paul Kossoff played on the single; if so, you can't hear him, while the saxophone is rote, with none of the guile and nuance you might expect from a man who had recently had his musical mind expanded by Pharoah Sanders.

The single was culled from a longer jam session which featured Kossoff, his Free band mate Simon Kirke on drums and future Free bassist Tetsu Yamauchi, and which marked the messy origins of his next record. When it came to the album sessions proper, begun at Sound Techniques in the summer of 1972, 'John had wanted to hire a completely different set of musos,' says John Wood. 'I think there may even have been one or more previous attempts before my involvement. We did one or two sessions, then I fell down some steps and [hurt] my ankle, and we had to call it off.' When Wood had recovered and the sessions reconvened, 'the bass player we had hired, who I didn't think was much good, actually, was not available, so we got Danny back.' Prudently, perhaps, Wood no longer remembers the original cast list.

By the time Martyn recorded an early version of 'Go Down Easy' on July 23, Danny Thompson was in situ on upright acoustic bass. They recorded thirteen versions of the songs that day, adding and subtracting slide guitar, organ and electric guitar as they experimented with different arrangements. There were further exploratory sessions in September, sketching out versions of 'I'd Rather Be The Devil' and 'Solid Air', but everything on the album was recorded at Basing Street much later in the year, rushed through during gaps between shows in London and the North of England in late November and the first week of December, to be readied for release before Martyn's first US tour early in 1973.

The core band comprised Martyn, Danny Thompson and Free keyboard player John 'Rabbit' Bundrick. Where drums or electric bass were required, they were supplied by Dave Pegg and Dave Mattacks, the rhythm section of Fairport Convention. Two former Fairport guitarists, Richard Thompson and Simon Nicol, also had cameos, playing mandolin and autoharp respectively on 'Over The Hill'. Tristan Fry and Tony Coe overdubbed vibes and saxophone parts later at Sound Techniques.

It was an expansive line-up designed to push Martyn to his limits. 'Certainly, "Rabbit" and Danny, because of their musicality, put him on his mettle more than the people he'd originally wanted to work with did,' says Wood. Despite its halting progress, in the end it was an exercise in spontaneous music making. 'It took a couple of weeks,' says Wood. 'All the tracks went down pretty much live. *Solid Air* didn't cost more than about £7,500.'

Where there were repeated takes, they were not in the pursuit of perfection but rather to allow the musicians an opportunity to bed in and feel the music, to try a new approach or mood. The blend was largely intuitive. There was little analysis or instruction.

'John's sessions were like really long and extensive jams... then the engineer would put it all together,' says Bundrick. 'When I was in Free, we would learn the track before we would record. With John, everybody would get to their instruments and we'd start playing, we'd just all join in, until all this stuff just started to gel. He didn't ask anyone to play a certain thing.' Dave Mattacks remembers it fondly as the 'first time I had been asked to play a little bit free'.

Martyn was a genial bandleader, smiling with encouragement when he heard a riff or a lick that he liked, relying on the musicians to pick up on the mood and find their place in the music. 'He never discussed the emotions of the songs,' says Bundrick. 'Everybody just got the emotion when he started playing, nobody questioned it.'

The title track was written for Nick Drake, who in February had released what turned out to be his last album, the mordantly beautiful *Pink Moon*, also produced by John Wood. 'I remember him going to see Nick,' says Paul Wheeler. 'The day he got back, he rang me and sang "Solid Air" to me over the phone, unaccompanied.'

By now, Drake was increasingly withdrawn and taking anti-depressants. His friends shuttled between exasperation and despair. 'I tried everything to wake Nick up,' says Danny Thompson. 'Being nasty to him, being kind to him, inviting him to my home in Suffolk – and John did the same. Maybe "Solid Air" was meant as a kick up the bum, but it was very difficult. As John says in the song, there was a lot going on in Nick's mind.'

Martyn said the song was 'done for a friend of mine, and it was done right, with very clear motives'.[16] Triangulating between murmuring empathy, frustration and foreboding, he divines not only Drake's quietly devastating emptiness, but the maddening impossibility of reaching him. There are declarations of unconditional love and solidarity, and the solemn promise to '*follow you anywhere*', wherever it might lead.

'I think "Solid Air" was written at an early stage of Nick's withdrawal into disillusionment and depression, moods which were shared by many of those who had invested heavily in the ideals of 1967 and watched those ideals decay, as chronicled by John Lennon in particular,' says Paul Wheeler. 'At that stage, I think John Martyn took the line that friendship was a panacea. The "you" in "Solid Air" was a projection of how John would wish to be treated, as an extrovert who always wanted company; for an introvert like Nick, who valued solitude, I think it would be perceived as intrusive that somebody should "*follow you anywhere...*"'

In the decades since Drake's death in November 1974, the song has become a kind of requiem. At the time, it was something more complicated, a necessary release of things that could not be expressed face to face, left floating in the ether. 'I've no idea if Nick was aware [that "Solid Air" was about him],' says Danny Thompson. 'John would not be the kind of person to phone up Nick and say, "I've written this about you." But the song allows the listener the freedom to hear how he feels about it. It's very astute and tender. All John's stuff is very personal. He didn't make up fanciful stories; it was from the heart.'

Attempted several times in the studio, the final cut is a work of almost casual brilliance. Session saxophonist Tony Coe has no recollection of even doing the session. The overdub of Tristan Fry's glorious vibraphone part was beset by technical problems, played on an instrument with a faulty sustain pedal and a broken motor. In the end he resorted to 'finger-damping', where 'you play one note and it rings off, then when you play the next note you have to stop the previous note with your hand, otherwise it rings in. It was quite complicated. Then at the same time I was turning the wheel, because the electricity wasn't working. You needed about four hands.'

The end result is fragile, unanchored, barely in motion. The influence of Pharoah Sanders' 1971 album *Thembi* can be heard throughout *Solid Air*, but it is especially evident on the title track, which shares its airy, unhurried mood and much of its sound palette with the album's opening track, 'Astral Traveling'.

Elsewhere on the album, deep struggles rise up to the surface. The hypnotic 'Don't Want To Know' possesses a terrible karmic power. It is a prayer for the dawn of a loving new world which nonetheless wishes to see the old one, with its obsession with money, materialism and mendacity, violently razed to the ground. It is one of Martyn's most beautiful yet pitiless songs, and one which resonates powerfully still: aeroplanes tumble from the skies, towns and cities crumble, dust settles and sinners crawl.

The unease which runs through 'Over The Hill' belies the breezy hop and skip in the music, with its twinkly conjuring of caravans and campfires. It is a song of conflict, between the open road and the four walls of hearth and home. The title phrase, of course, can also refer to someone who is past their best. The journey Martyn describes is a homecoming – the run into Hastings on the train rolled through rising countryside before the line dipped down to reveal the town – but also a more ambiguous internal one. Martyn often spoke about domesticity equating the death of creativity. He was a subscriber to the Cyril Connolly school of cliché that the pram in the hallway is the solemn enemy of good art, yet he also yearned for his family, its wholesome comforts and simple certainties. In 'Over The Hill', he is worried about '*my babies*' and '*my wife*'; worried, too, about what they are doing to him, and he to them. In the coolly clicking 'The Man In The Station', another man – more likely, the same man – is catching the same train home. This time he possesses a heart that is aching to flee and a face, glimpsed in the mirror, that is '*showing the strain*'. On 'Dreams By The Sea', a domestic fairy tale decomposes into a turbid nightmare of infidelity and drug paranoia.

'I never thought that John was conflicted,' says Claire Hamill. 'I think he definitely [recognised] his family responsibilities, he cared about his family deeply, but John was a very complex character. He had different compartments of his life. Being away from home, being away from his family, it must have hurt him, but I never saw that part of him. He was just in the moment. He was all about the gig, and the music. He was obviously a hedonist. No doubt about it. The sexual part of him was part of that, as well.' Yet the sexual urge expressed in 'Go Down Easy' is neither abandoned nor predatory, but deeply sensual, the connection of mind as well as body evoked in the tender teasing out between Martyn and Danny Thompson.

'Over The Hill' makes mention of '*sweet cocaine*' (coyly edited to '*dry champagne*' for the radio version) and 'Mary Jane'. The references were not careless. Hard drugs, notably cocaine, were now part of Martyn's life, and though they accentuated his mood swings, particularly when combined with alcohol, they had not yet impinged on his working practices. 'I remember him being fun to be around, but he was pretty focused,' says Dave Mattacks. 'This was before substances and drink really became such a huge part of him and his music making.'

The echoplex was given free rein on a wild, unruly whirl through Skip James's 'Devil Take My Woman', retitled 'I'd Rather Be The Devil'. Martyn's instruction to drummer Mattacks – 'just think free-form Elvin [Jones]' – gave some indication as to where he was heading. 'Because of what he was doing on the guitar, I didn't have to keep conventional rock-rhythm time,' says Mattacks. 'I could play some things around it, which is what I tried to do.'

Bundrick jammed clavinet on the track, its squelchy bottom end dovetailing with Martyn's corkscrew guitar. Indeed, Bundrick may well be the album's secret weapon. His electronic Rhodes piano tears through the dark, oscillating jazz-funk of 'Dreams By The Sea', which falls somewhere between Isaac Hayes' 'Theme From Shaft' and The Temptations' 'Papa Was A Rollin' Stone'. His rippling organ flights on 'Don't Want To Know' raise the song up to a new level, from where it rises further as Martyn, unusually, layers multiple voices into a full chorus. 'John influenced me in the experimental state,' says Bundrick. 'I started doing things on my keyboard like he was doing on his guitar and using some of those effects myself. He influenced me to use the wah-wah pedal on *Catch A Fire*.★ I heard how his blend of effects was working.'

When 'The Easy Blues', a frantically finger-picked rewrite of 'Jelly Roll Baker', glides into the brief 'Gentle Blues', the album's mix of the organic and the synthetic reaches a natural state of coalescence, rolling piano set against buzzing electronics.

The instrumental parts were recorded more or less seamlessly. The vocal tracks were more difficult. John Wood recalls they spent 'two pretty difficult evenings doing vocals, because John was quite uptight about the way he sang. He needed quite a lot of encouragement and support. It was hard work. Working with John *was* hard work. Make no mistake about it, it was not easy. I saw my role as a sort of facilitator. You are trying to get the best performance from the best people you can put around them, but you do every now and then pull them up sharp and let them know when they are being their own worst enemy. I probably had to do that more with John than with anybody else. Sometimes he would respond, sometimes he wouldn't.'

The final piece of business was a solo recording of 'May You Never', a definitive version of which had so far proved elusive. 'We literally were mixing the album on the Friday night, and I was flying on the Saturday morning to get the album mastered in New York,' says Wood. 'He had this version of "May You Never" that he was

---

★ Bundrick played extensive overdubs on Bob Marley & The Wailers' first album for Island Records, released in April 1973.

122

muttering and moaning about, a version that he didn't like. In the end I said, "For Christ's sake, just go down there with a guitar into the studio and do it." That was literally eleven or twelve hours before I went off with the tapes.'

Solid Air deepened the empathy between Martyn and Danny Thompson. 'He influenced me greatly,' said Martyn. 'He taught me more about music than probably anyone else I know.'[17] Thompson could run with anyone, and Martyn thrived on their growing connection.

Something strange happened to him around Thompson. If Witchseason's resident gangster Bob Squires had been Martyn's entrée into the world of charming Cockney ne'er-do-wells, Thompson was his graduation ticket. Such was the bass player's charisma, and such was the force of their musical connection, Martyn quickly fell under the spell. Though he regarded himself as 'pure Scottish, there's no getting out of that', he carefully cultivated the English elements of his upbringing, with an accent to match. As the pair grew closer, 'he did turn into Danny Thompson at one point,' says Richard Thompson. 'It was scary.'

'If he was close to someone, he would start absorbing their personality and being them,' says Martin Carthy. 'He did that with Danny, who would say, "I can't believe it, he's actually stealing who I am. He's becoming me!" All that wallop-dollop Cockney stuff. Danny was beside himself. It was very odd.'

What started as a bit of a game gradually gave seed to a new persona. The gentler side of Martyn never disappeared, but in time he turned into a far tougher proposition. 'He was like the many faces of Eve,' says Linda Thompson. 'He had different personalities for different things. It seems normal to me, because I do it too. Shrinks tend to find it very interesting.' The more aggressive aspect of his personality which began to take hold at this time was partly exacerbated by an escalation in drink and drugs, but it also became another means of distancing himself from the cosy consensus of the folk world. He began to nurture the hard edges of the rock star. It was a form of protection, which had the effect of throwing a circle of fire around him. 'For a while I had the reputation of a real bad boy: this man was going to punch you out, shoot you or fuck you,' he said years later. 'I deliberately cultivated it, because it kept people away from me. I want people away from me, basically...'[18]

Solid Air was released on the first day of February 1973, evidence for some reviewers that Martyn was 'one of the most important innovators we've got'.[19] Song for song, *Bless The Weather* is arguably a more downright beautiful compositional work, but *Solid Air* is replete with an elusive and intoxicating atmosphere which makes for a deeper listening experience. It remains the John Martyn album which people who aren't particularly big fans of John Martyn are most likely to own, while 'May You Never' has transcended boundaries, becoming part of the communal songbook. Plenty of performers fostered in the folk scene were content simply to bring their stage show into the studio. Martyn's ambitions travelled far beyond that. He understood what it took for music to come alive in the studio and to make enduring records.

Reviews of *Solid Air* were positive but relatively scarce. It was up against stiff competition in its own field. While it is always dubious to talk about a golden age in any medium – the glow in which retrospective critical analysis comes to bask rarely leads to a clear-eyed view of what was actually happening at the time – it is the case that the corps of roots-orientated artists with folk origins assembled on Island Records in the early Seventies created a body of work which is in retrospect of an uncommonly fine quality. Music of taste and invention, as deep, dark and disposable as life itself, poetic in an unself-conscious, very human way, the flaws and frailties left unexcised.

Among the highlights are: *I Want To See The Bright Lights Tonight* and *Pour Down Like Silver* by Richard and Linda Thompson; *Full House* by Fairport Convention; *Bryter Layter* and *Pink Moon* by Nick Drake; *The North Star Grassman And The Ravens* by Sandy Denny; and *The*

Low Spark Of High Heeled Boys by Traffic. It is testament to the quality of *Bless The Weather* and *Solid Air* that they shine in such company.★

If Chris Blackwell did one thing better than almost any other music mogul, it was to allow his artists their head. It seems almost churlish to add that, Traffic aside, they enjoyed very little commercial traction. That was hardly the aim. In the era of glam, Philly soul and progressive rock, of the early stirring of disco and stadium rock, they spoke to a healthy but bespoke audience; Martyn was selling 30,000 to 40,000 copies of his records. Their modest successes enabled their creators to continue to play, and to make more records, and to continue to play – and that self-sustaining cycle was enough. It is how a stratified music industry used to operate. The irony, of course, is that they sold more copies than almost any record in the charts today.

Martyn had little to do with the mechanics of promotion. He would meet the team at Island in the Cross Keys pub on St Peter's Square to talk through cover concepts and press releases, but he was not hands-on. 'In the first five years I think I was in the office twice,' he said. 'It was never something that interested me.'[20] He could generally rely on interview and review coverage in *Melody Maker*, *Sounds* and *New Musical Express*, and a handful of less mainstream publications, where he was as a rule bracingly candid. 'He was very open, he was unguarded, and journalists loved that,' says Brian Blevins, Island's press officer. 'John touched so many different genres and combined them so inventively that he could appeal to almost any writer, no matter what their interests.'

Opinion divides on whether *Solid Air* was viewed by Island as anything particularly extraordinary at the time. Blackwell describes it as 'an incredible album, beautifully done', but John Wood says, 'I never got the impression that Island thought the record was that great, frankly. I thought *Solid Air* was a really good record. I had a lot more faith in it getting some notice than *Pink Moon*, but no bugger at Island ever said to me, "What a great record!" Including Blackwell, who could have done.'

★ At this time, Island was also releasing landmark records by King Crimson, Roxy Music, Free, Cat Stevens and the world's finest reggae artists.

According to Blevins, 'We saw it as a major event, and the artistry and the mastery was clearly evident. We really got behind it a lot in every aspect. In broadcast promotions, certainly in press and advertising.' It was nothing so gauche as a hit record, and there was no single release attached to it, but it raised Martyn's profile appreciably, particularly among a certain subset of switched-on listeners – as well as his peers. 'I remember seeing him playing stuff from *Solid Air* on *The Old Grey Whistle Test* and running down to my local record shop in Putney the next day,' says Ralph McTell. 'The bloke said, "Oh, so you saw *Whistle Test* last night, too? Well, we ain't got none. Sold out."'

For some, seeing Martyn sing 'I'd Rather Be The Devil' and 'May You Never' on *The Old Grey Whistle Test* on March 13, 1973, waistcoated, curly-haired, elfishly bearded, hunched over a pulsating guitar, breathing slow fire into a microphone, was as substantial a game-changer as seeing David Bowie sing 'Starman' on *Top of the Pops* nine months earlier. For the committed smokers, hipsters and modern jazz hounds, the surfers of outré sonic wavelengths, he was the kind of artist you wanted to hang out with, befriend at parties, seek approval from for your impeccable taste.

His shows were intimate gatherings of like-minded souls. He would joust, joke, swear, react in the moment. Fans would throw spliffs for him while he was on stage, pass up bottles. 'People thought, He's one of us,' says John James. 'He had a following, like a football team.' Martyn was the hedonist with a heart who women felt understood them and men longed to be. 'He always saw himself as the lone pilgrim,' says Mark Cooper, a lifelong Martyn fan who first saw him play in Les Cousins. Cooper subsequently created *Later… with Jools Holland* and became BBC Head of Music for over twenty years. 'He was our idea of a Kerouac or a Woody Guthrie. He felt free and unrestrained, with this open-hearted music and wild guitar style. It was very inspiring to me and many others.'

Solid Air sealed this pact, forging a deep connection with his fan base which remains today. It's a pity he didn't like the album more. 'John always moaned about *Solid Air*,' says Wood. 'He never gave me the impression he liked the record much.' Indeed, in the immediate aftermath he publicly expressed his disappointment. 'I'm not as pleased with it as I have been with previous ones, although vocally it was a step forward,' he said, shortly after it was released. 'I've never sung as good as on that record, but at the time I made it I was capable of singing even better – and playing better. It was all too rushed.'[21]

'He actively hated it,' says Jim Imlach. 'I could tell you a dozen times where he said he hated that album, hated the songs. I think it was because of "May You Never". He hated the whole acoustic thing. It was part of his journey, but he didn't want it to define him. He wanted to be innovative. He was a stubborn sod.'

Martyn may have been protesting a little too much. 'The truth is, I don't know any serious artist who can say they are happy with their album,' says Danny Thompson. 'They are always unhappy. That's normal.' Perhaps when the album in question attracts more attention than any of the others, the dissatisfaction simply grows exponentially.

He spent January and February in the United States, opening for Traffic and Free, the first of three major support tours he undertook there in the Seventies. Traffic were the main attraction. Given the size of the venues – often between 10,000 and 20,000 capacity – his 30-minute opening slot focused on his 'electric' repertoire, rather than anything more intimate. It was a tough assignment, though it won him small pockets of new admirers, some more prestigious than others.

'During that tour I took Bob Marley backstage,' Chris Blackwell recalls. 'I told him, "You've got to see this guy." I stood him back behind so he didn't see anything at first, then I moved him forward and he saw that all the sound that was happening was coming from this one guy. He couldn't believe it. "Where are the others?" He was totally blown away. John had mastered the echoplex.'

The Pittsburgh Press, which reviewed the show on February 1, made mention of his 'worthwhile mood music... Martyn is a skilled guitarist and he utilized some sophisticated new echo equipment. He has a background of blues and folk singing and the solid training helps bring added dimension to his performance.' Martyn never broke through commercially in North America, but he found a dedicated audience, primarily in the North East and Canada, where he was able to fill clubs throughout his career.

'He was always well received. I never saw him have a bad day,' says John 'Rabbit' Bundrick, who was touring as part of Free and often roomed next door to Martyn. 'He was a great, fun guy. In one of the hotels they had swords up on the walls in the room. John took them down and marched around the hotel with them, making everybody laugh. He was like a kid, a hyperactive kid: he had to either damage something or at least play with it. If there was something on the wall, it was going to come off.'

The tour involved thirty-five shows in thirty-nine days. It was Martyn's first experience of touring America, his first exposure to red-eye flights, faceless hotels, loneliness and disorientation. He came home briefly to play some British shows in March, after which he was back Stateside in April for more dates. He became ill, suffering from boils and infections, and by the end of it all he felt that he'd lived 'three years in two months'.[22] He used cocaine and alcohol increasingly as a crutch to keep himself going. If there was a tipping point where Martyn's appetites went from being essentially recreational to something more compulsive, it probably occurred during this period.

'At first, I drank because I was nervous performing, then the lifestyle got hold of me,' he told me. 'You have a drink before the gig to set you up, then you have a drink to celebrate, then you have a drink in the morning to liven up, then you have a drink on the plane… it's all soundchecks and aeroplanes and hotels. There's literally nothing else to do. You can read the paper, but that loses its charm after a while.'[23]

7

'I'm not really a great joiner,' Martyn told me in 2005. 'I prefer being on the fringe.'

If one were searching for evidence of Martyn as a serial member of the Groucho Club, an instinctive non-team player, a man who bolts at the first sign of consensus or acceptance, in short, a contrarian of the first rank, *Inside Out* would be the place to start.

He spent July 1973 at Island Studios in Basing Street and its nearby sister studio, Fallout, recording his fifth solo album. Not merely recording it; conceiving, imagining, dreaming it. For all its light-headedness, its drifting refusal to be anchored, *Inside Out* is a remarkably lucid record in one respect: it was an album designed to set the modest industry gains Martyn had achieved through *Solid Air* firmly into reverse: to fox the hounds and send them off the scent.

It is a jazz-minded improvisation created almost entirely in the studio, a fuzzy miniature taken from a larger canvas stitched together from a series of unruly, unmapped performances. It is beautiful and maddening; indulgent and deeply and entirely inimitable. The splendidly of-its-time cosmic cover art, depicting the artist's inner thoughts as a fury of lightning bolts and thunderclouds, visualises the ultimate guiding principle of Martyn's music. Creation as the ultimate catalytic converter, spinning a ton of messy psychological shit into sunshine – and vice versa. Inside. Out. Outside. In.

As a deep dive into a storm-tossed subconscious, it reveals a lot about Martyn. In later years he would claim it was the only one of his records that he could stomach. 'I still like *Inside Out* best.' Why? 'I didn't want to be stuck into being straight.'[1]

Inside Out is straight like a boomerang, a flight through curved air. It was as though Martyn's reward for the more streamlined magnificence of *Solid Air* was the permission to cut loose and truly soar, an instinct that captures, in so many ways, not only his essential spirit, but the quintessence of Island Records.

'My policy was a policy that could only work when somebody owns the company; you wouldn't be able to defend it to a corporation,' says Chris Blackwell. 'My policy was that if there was somebody I wanted to sign, it was because I thought that they were a real talent, somebody really special and, ideally, unique – which initially makes them less poppish, which makes them less likely to make money, in commercial terms. When one is making an arrangement like that, there no is way I can help them be them. I am there to help them if they ask me, of course. I can give advice, but frankly that didn't even happen that much with John. That was my policy. I was not on top of artists at all – only if I were producing a record, where I would have some involvement in the running order and the mix and things like that.'

'Chris Blackwell let his artists breathe and develop through their formative period,' says Danny Thompson. 'I know for a fact Chris was not seeing his money recouped from his investment in people like John, and many others in Island Records. Later he was rewarded for loving these people so much. He allowed them to breathe and to become successful.'

Inside Out is the sound of Martyn breathing deep and long. 'I dived in completely and created within very intense surroundings,' he said. 'There was no distance, no self-consciousness. It's probably the purest album I've made musically.'[2]

He went into the studio with Richard Digby Smith, who had joined Island in 1970 and had risen through the ranks from tea boy to tape op to engineer. Digby Smith was de facto co-producer on the album, although he is not credited as such. There would be no outside producer this time, no disciplinarian influence in the shape of John Wood. 'After *Solid Air*, I didn't work with John,' says Wood. 'That was his choice. I don't quite know what happened. Blackwell seemed to want to take him under his wing.'

An album that frequently cuts loose from the moorings of conventional songwriting drops a significant clue regarding its intentions in the opening seconds. Martyn comments that whichever sounds the musicians had been creating prior to the listener's arrival had felt 'natural', before he slides sleepily into the opening track, 'Fine Lines'. From the start, we are alerted to the fact that what we're hearing is merely an excerpt, edited highlights of a larger whole.

Its 8-minute centrepiece, 'Outside In', is the richest seam within the area of Martyn's work which includes 'Glistening Glyndebourne', 'Call Me Crazy' and 'Small Hours', in which he seems to spiral into inner space and play around with the construct of time. As it picks up pace and begins to spin, the influence Martyn exerted on the reverb-heavy guitar style of The Edge from U2, not to mention less high-profile bands such as A Certain Ratio and Bristol's Blue Aeroplanes, is overt.★

'Outside In' was rooted in extemporised performance, but it required a dense tapestry of treated and layered guitars to find its shape. 'He had an idea in his head,' says Digby Smith. 'He was really into his guitar going through delay pedals, the Mu-tron [phaser] and the echoplex and recording the guitar with effects on it. He would overdub wild, crazy, avant-garde, random phrases on guitar, and think nothing of doing four or five takes of that. Then I'd say, "You and Danny go and have a pint, and I'll sift through these takes and pick out the best bits and make a compilation." What you hear has a certain amount of manipulation, some comping, which he was always happy to let me do.' The Rolling Stones' in-house saxophonist, Bobby Keys, added horn to its later, becalmed passages. He 'just staggered into the

---

★ U2 signed to Island in 1979, making them label mates with Martyn. It's not inconceivable that Chris Blackwell instigated an introduction to Martyn's music. One of their early singles, 'A Day Without Me', played on the title of Martyn's 'One Day Without You'. They also recorded a B-side called 'Walk To The Water'.

studio after doing some overdubs with the Stones and said, "Can I blow?", and we said sure.'[3] His playing evokes a beach firework display rendered in slow motion.

Once again, Martyn drew from a remarkable pool of musicians, most of whom were readily available to him on his doorstep at Island. Fallout Shelter, the label's second studio, was housed in the basement at 22 St Peter's Square. If you threw a rock, you'd hit a rock star. 'Steve Winwood would have been around all the time,' says Digby Smith. 'You would grab these people, put a bit of Hammond on the track. Remi Kabaka would play on anyone's music, he always had his congas in the back of the car. Chris Wood would walk around with the sax strap around his neck, ready to go into action at any moment. It was almost like one giant band of all the Island artists. Everybody would play on everybody else's record, you only had to ask.'

Inside Out was the album on which Martyn brought his outside appetites into the studio. The shape of the sessions was often dictated by the strictly rationed licensing laws Britain inflicted upon itself in 1973. Access to the Cross Keys pub across the road was considered sacrosanct, for lunchtime drinks and further liveners before closing time. The session off-cuts include twenty straight takes of 'The Glory Of Love', during which Martyn gets progressively and audibly more inebriated. At other times, the players broke from almost spiritual levels of creative interaction to throw beer bottles across the studio.

'There was a considerable amount of chemical assistance required throughout, and John was very generous,' says Digby Smith. 'It was a plastic bag of white powder, several ounces of the stuff. We used to keep it in one of the two-inch tape boxes, and it was the first thing you would do on arrival, lines of coke the length of the desk. It was epic. It fills me with fear and dread thinking about it now.'

Digby Smith recalls one session which lasted from Friday evening until Monday lunchtime. 'I can't remember whether I got into a cab or an ambulance. We worked on one song, the same song, for three and a half days. It was such a ball. Mind you, we did spend about twenty-nine hours of that period in the Cross Keys. We were all young, incredibly fit, and as mad as a bag of spanners.'

'You see, I don't work like that!' says John Wood. 'I was older, and I came up through a very disciplined background, learning my craft at Decca studios. I couldn't – and still can't – hack undisciplined messing about in a studio. I will not do it. It unfocuses the project. If you don't keep knowing what you're going to do at each point, it just becomes a mess. And John was not a disciplined worker, that's for sure, which is probably why he didn't like working with me.'

Digby Smith is at pains to emphasise that 'it wasn't just a mad, drug-crazed romp. We were working, we were completely in the zone with John's music. He was absolutely serious about the heart of the music, and pretty clued up technically about how he wanted it to sound. He had an assortment of pedals; there was lots of technical stuff to keep you on your toes. It was such fun. Danny and John were just such a comedic duo. It never turned nasty. Even in the most epic and unnatural circumstances, I cannot recall a single moment of unpleasantness or uneasiness.'

The lack of focus, at least in the traditional sense, was partly the point of *Inside Out*. Martyn wanted it to be 'heavier... with more blowing'.[4] Aside from 'Outside In', the album's journeys into experimental exoticism include the instrumental 'Eibhli Ghail Chiuin Ni Chearbhail'. A pretty Irish air dating back to the early 1800s and recorded by The Chieftains in 1971, the Gaelic title broadly translates as 'The Fair And Gentle Eily Carroll'. Martyn took a sharp axe to all that tradition, very likely with glee, deploying a wickedly fuzz-toned guitar on the melody line and a churning drone for the bottom end. The result is a warped Celtic death dirge, forlorn and ominous, which sounds as though it is powered via a crank handle.

The barely structured 'Ain't No Saint', with its hot-potato scatting and fluttering dynamics, resolved itself in the sharp clack of Kabaka's arrhythmic congas and some wonderful Arabesque guitar figures. Spanish and North African inflections featured again on the instrumental 'Beverley', a sad, soft, disquieting blend of Thompson's sawed string bass, Liam Genockey's splashy cymbals and the cries of Martyn's treated guitar.

'Look In' was all jazz-funk grunt and grind, a pre-echo of the music Martyn would go on to make in the Eighties. Like 'Outside In', it became a playground for extended forays into improvisation in Martyn's subsequent live shows.

Inside Out was not short of such voyaging, guided by surf and stars rather than map and compass, yet there were wonderful songs, too. 'Fine Lines' is one of his very best, as tender a song of friendship as 'May You Never', except that here the love extends beyond a brother to a brotherhood of the '*finest folk in town*'. It reeks of woozy late-night gatherings, the 5 a.m. pre-dawn reckoning when the music settles to a faint pulse, the bright edge of the chemicals begin to soften and blur the senses, and the awareness of a universal human bond is a matter of peaceful certitude.

'Fine Lines' cuts deeper than the drunken arm slung around the shoulder, travelling through skin and bone to the soul, via the deeply felt connections forged in smoke-filled rooms and over smeared glasses, in the warm communion of bodies slumped platonically on sofas. Loneliness is there, too, whispering at the window, the exquisite sadness that comes from knowing that good times are ending even as they are happening. The fragility is so profound one can hear the air shake around the strings, feel the cadences of all those empty spaces.

'Ways To Cry' picks up where 'Fine Lines' seems to stop. Martyn offers a slurred susurration, vowels strung together like worry beads. It is so seductive, it takes a while to realise he is offering baleful excuses for his infidelities. If he ever took another woman, he pleads, it was '*in my need for you*'. While he was away on tour, women Martyn had met on the road would telephone Cobourg Place and ask for him. He also continued seeing Claire Hamill off and on through much of the early Seventies. Regarding his numerous flings with other women – some of whom were close to her – Beverley Martyn says, 'There were rumours about what he was up to on tour, but I thought, Well, I've got these children…'

The album ends with 'So Much In Love With You', a late-night jazz noir, with lascivious saxophone from Bobby Keys, gumshoe piano tinkles from Steve Winwood, rim-crack syncopations and sharp blues licks from Martyn. One can almost imagine him shucking his cuffs and clicking his fingers.

The theme is surprisingly coherent. *Inside Out* was perhaps the closest Martyn ever got to a concept album. The breezy version of Billy Hill's 'The Glory Of Love', first made famous by Benny Goodman in 1936 and a standard thereafter, is no throwaway – *Inside Out* is a love theme for the wilderness, over and over again clinging to its lifeline amid stormy seas. 'The only politics that work is the politics of love,' he pronounced while at the same time acknowledging that conforming to such an ideology was always going to be something of a stretch.[5] 'Love is something I like to foster in the family but at the same time I'm very loud, quite mad and can be an exceptionally nasty person.'[6] 'Make No Mistake' might be his deepest dive into the agonies of love and the duality of the feelings it laid bare. Throughout, Martyn returns to the opposites contained in the album title. He might seem fine outside, but inside '*I had to look again*'; he is laughing '*from the inside out*'. Look out! Look in! Look all about!

If Martyn's music generally seems to exist beyond the constraints of time and the reach of musical trends, during this period he drifted further away than ever from the currents of fashion. He appeared to be creating in a vacuum. He claimed to ignore the music press, to listen only to 'jazz imports', and exhibited a swashbuckling disregard for the zeitgeist. David Bowie was 'a poseur'[7], and as for new bands, 'I'll listen to a group just once to make sure I was right the first time I dismissed them'.[8] The great guitar heroes of the age – from Jimmy Page to Mike Bloomfield – left him cold. When he did deign to declare his tastes, he did so with a vague air of showboating superiority: Billie Holiday, Pharoah Sanders, John and Alice Coltrane, Spanish cellist Pablo Casals, oboist Léon Goossens and Indian classical sitar player Vilayat Khan were among those who made the cut. 'Oh, he could be pretentious, John,' says Richard Thompson.

Regarding the work of those who were covering a broadly similar waterfront, such as John McLaughlin, Tim Buckley and even Santana, he heard plenty of head, but very little heart. Too much outside; not enough inside. 'It's a whole other scene to lay your heart on people,' he said. 'I want to be able to take my clothes off in front of everybody and say: "See? I'm just like you."'[9]

He was rarely so naked again as he appeared on *Inside Out*. Released on October 1, 1973, the album was a bewildering and frequently brilliant foray into the furthest reaches of his musical mind, an experiment in tone, form, texture, pace and placement. He later expressed satisfaction at its intentions, if not always its execution. 'I would have liked to have attacked it with more technical ability,' he said. 'What you get is a kind of vision of what I would have liked to have been playing.'[10]

Ian MacDonald's review in *NME* astutely recognised that Martyn 'has reached his long-promised fruition whilst simultaneously forfeiting most of his commercial potential'.[11] It was a hard sell for the suits, even suits as dressed down as those at Island Records. 'I remember it being not the right record after *Solid Air*,' says Chris Blackwell. 'Maybe it would have been better a couple of records later. I think people wanted another *Solid Air*, or an evolution somewhat from *Solid Air*. *Inside Out* had a whole different feel to it, it was like a different band.'

'It wasn't what was required!' Martyn laughed in 2005. 'I have no regrets about that. I'd rather have the respect of my peers. I'm very happy there.'

Martyn and Danny Thompson toured the album around the UK through the autumn. Pentangle had split earlier in the year, leaving Thompson free to take their musical understanding out of the studio and onto the road. In the following years they played many wild and wonderfully innovative shows, and some that careered in the opposite direction. Whichever way the dial swung on a given night, it was rarely boring.

Thompson gave Martyn a licence no other musician could offer. 'I'm trying to get freer and less structured, and Danny's the only cat I've found so far who can follow,' he told Ian MacDonald. 'I tend to play lead and rhythm and bass all together because of my background of solo experience in folk clubs, and musicians seem to find that hard to get into. Danny does it like second nature and it's been a gas to work with him.'[12]

'We were young, and we didn't have a rulebook,' says Thompson. 'We were totally free. We were like two lunatics on the road, drinking and really enjoying ourselves, but he totally and completely [took the music seriously]. Otherwise, we'd all be kidding ourselves.'

'It was a great combination, a great image and a great sound, but I think, for both of them, they encouraged the worst sides of each other,' says Joe Boyd. There was an element of one-upmanship in their relationship, a constant desire to raise the stakes, whether that involved music, drinking, money or violence. Tales of their escapades on tour are legion, the hard kernel of truth polished over time into legend.

'There are millions of stories,' says Thompson. 'Here's one. We had just done a duo concert at the Birmingham Town Hall [on May 22, 1975]. There was this fantastic curry house called Rajdoot, and we were really looking forward to going there after the gig.'

Shortly after Martyn and Thompson sat down to dine, a man at the table next to them shouted a racially offensive term at a waiter. Martyn, who had his back to the table, raised his head in disgust, his antennae twitching.

'John didn't even look around,' says Thompson. 'He just looked at me and said, "I'm not having that." I said, "Have a look first, John, before you steam in. There's twelve of them." He said, "Are you with me?" "Of course." So he stood up and poked the bloke in the back and said, "You." As the bloke raised his knees to get up to fight, John nutted him and knocked him spark unconscious. The bloke next to him jumped up and John did the same to him. There were two bodies lying there. I said to the other guys, "Don't even begin. I taught him!" and they just stopped. That's the man who was on the stage an hour before singing about curling around you like a fern in spring.'

Equally well versed is the famous occasion when Thompson nailed a comatose Martyn under the hotel carpet for some drunken indiscretion. The following morning he ordered and ate a full room-service breakfast five feet away from where a brutally dehydrated Martyn, still pinned to the floor, ranted and raved.

These are not verifiable accounts. Indeed, the second story closely resembles a tale Willie Nelson told about his first wife. What is certainly true is that for the discarded photo shoot intended for the cover of *Live At Leeds*, the pair stripped down to their satin shorts and knocked seven bells out of each other at the Thomas A Becket boxing gym on the Old Kent Road. Both drew blood and seemed to relish a further thickening of their bond.

On the road, to free up the finances for other pursuits, they often shared a room, like a pair of fresh-faced barrack-room recruits. 'We were kind of inseparable in that way,' says Thompson. 'I don't want to make out that it was very mumsy. We used to have serious fights as well. I've been nutted by him. He was a very tough bloke.'

Whenever they crossed the border back into Scotland, which was often, Martyn would let out a whoop and they would point the car towards 10 Tantallon Road, which became home base for a few days of playing and carousing. 'We'd wake up early,' Thompson recalls. 'Breakfast was porridge, prepared by his wonderful, much-loved gran. Then off in a black cab for a ride out to a country spot, where we jumped over the drystone wall, then across the fields to a shallow stream. He flicked his bamboo fishing stick until six brown trout lay on the bank. He was a completely avid fly fisherman.'

After the fishing trip ended, it was 'back across the fields and into the nearest pub, two pints, and a return cab to number 10. "Hello, Gran, trout for tea." A bit of banter, then off to the local bowling green. We'd play and gamble with serious competitiveness, we'd almost come to blows. It was the same with snooker. Then we'd ride into Glasgow and enjoy the Scotia, or the Victoria Bar. We'd have a play and get completely pissed and share the oxygen with [our] best friend.'

In London, Thompson would take Martyn to his East End haunts, to the Thomas A Becket, once frequented by the Kray Twins, where the former British heavyweight champion Henry Cooper used to spar. Or to the Fellmongers Arms in Bermondsey, run by 'Nasty' Neville Axford, a former boxer. 'John used to get a bit outrageous, trying to be with the villains,' says Jacqui McShee. 'They said to Danny, "Don't bring him down here again," because he wasn't a proper East End Bermondsey boy. I think John loved the danger of it, and he did surround himself with some pretty unpleasant characters, hangers-on and worse.'

Martyn felt an open, almost innocent attraction to the criminal fraternity. He harboured a theory that villains and musicians had much in common. From the mid-Seventies onwards, he cultivated around him a loose affiliation of small-time felons, bank robbers, hard nuts and loose cannons, often employing one or more to drive him around, or 'manage' him.★ 'I spent a long time being fascinated by gangsters and lowlifes,' Martyn admitted shortly before he died. 'Just interested, what makes them tick and how they organise their lives, and there are some great things about them. I don't mind villains at all, to be honest.'[13] His daughter Vari attributed it to a simple romantic allure.

Not everyone warmed to the Martyn–Thompson double act. It was the kind of behaviour which was often more amusing when reported second-hand or viewed from afar than witnessed up close. 'When the two of them were together, they were a loud, hard drinking force,' says Richard Thompson. 'You got pinned to the walls when they entered the room, it was so high energy. They were so inebriated, full of aggression. During that era, I used to avoid the two of them because it was too much to handle.'

'Very big and very wilful, we were,' Martyn admitted. 'We behaved as if the spotlight was on us all the time and we were the only people in the world. Danny would go into a place and say, "This is for the damage." They'd say, "There is no damage." He'd say, "There fucking will be."'[14]

'They were two huge personalities and two big egos,' says McShee. 'I remember coming to a venue a week after they had been, and we couldn't use the dressing room because it was full of broken chairs.'

Al Stewart bumped into Martyn while they were both staying at the same Holiday Inn. 'I was dropping my stuff off and I saw John Martyn

---

★   One contributor to this book emailed a few days after our interview to request that he was not quoted regarding one particular individual, because he might still be 'at large' and was, in his estimation, a genuinely dangerous person.

and Danny Thompson at the bar… and decided to go up. John was standing there and his eyes were red; this was one o'clock in the afternoon and he was completely drunk and hostile. I'd made a record called *Nostradamus*, which everyone was making a big fuss about, and he looked at me and said, "Oh… it's you! Is Nostradamus still coming to get us then?" Not playful, he looked very angry and very drunk.'[15]

It was loud, stupid behaviour, intimidating and graceless. Underlying it all, however, was a warped kind of *Boys' Own* innocence, a mischievous desire to suck up all that life was offering. 'Those were the early years,' says Danny Thompson fondly. 'Be under no doubt at all that these were the happiest days of my life.'

Thompson couldn't always come out to play. For Martyn, the end of 1973 and much of 1974 was spent in America, performing solo. Following a week of warm-up dates at the Troubadour in Los Angeles, in February and March he opened for Yes on a series of huge shows in support of their double concept album, *Tales From Topographic Oceans*. Released in December, it was already a number one record in the UK.

Playing to audiences routinely exceeding 10,000, the Yes shows featured an elaborate Roger Dean set design, with much mechanical palaver and many moving parts, a hi-tech high-wire act which partly inspired Derek Smalls' malfunctioning pod catastrophe in the spoof rock documentary *This Is Spinal Tap*.

Martyn entered the baseball stadiums, basketball hangars and draughty coliseums with some scepticism, a one-man band armed only with a guitar and a box of tricks. Not just one man with a guitar – one man with a guitar who *loathed* Yes with a passion. 'He had this thing about Yes,' recalls Claire Hamill, who was friendly with the group. 'It was really, really weird how much he hated Yes. I just thought it was so funny.' 'I hated that band,' he said thirty-five years later. 'They were snotty, horrible people who thought they were intellectuals.'[16]

Arriving on stage at 7.30 p.m. to play a half-hour slot, Martyn soon discovered that, while individual members of the audience may have appreciated what he was doing and found themselves wondering, as

Bob Marley had previously, where the other guitar player was hiding, as a solid mass the crowd were dismissive most nights, sometimes outright hostile.

Depending on his mood, he would variously try to convert them, ignore them or bait them. A review of this 'accomplished if fairly obscure folksinger' from the show at Cornell University on February 24 appeared to catch him in a contrary mood. 'What the hell he thought he was doing Sunday night, I just don't know,' Bill Henk wrote in *The Ithacan*. 'Relying basically on electronic effects of echo and reverb and an amplified acoustic guitar, Martyn managed to alienate an entire audience who likely would have enjoyed his dominantly acoustic repertoire... He played three songs and got off.'

Then again, the *Billboard* review of the shows in Toronto and Montreal reckoned 'most of the fans probably didn't need an acoustic folkie to set them up for the Grand Rock they had paid for'. Every which way you lose. In Baltimore, Martyn shouted and swore at the audience. In Roanoke, he suggested they fuck each other for distraction. On the final night of the tour, in Chicago on March 6, 1974, he reportedly walked on stage and then promptly walked straight off again.

'That tour was a nightmare, a fucking nightmare!' he said. 'They didn't give a fuck about me, they didn't listen or care about what I was doing. It was very disheartening. With Free it was fun, but with Yes it was terrible, murderous. If you played your ass off you might win two or three of them over, but it was brutal.'[17]

The memory of Yes lead singer Jon Anderson that Martyn held 10,000 people 'spellbound' each night therefore seems somewhat rose-tinted, but his recollection does offer a corrective to the idea that Martyn's stint as an opening act was a complete bust. 'People have got to find their seats and get their popcorn and all that crap, but he really created such an energy in all the gigs we did,' says Anderson. 'It was wonderful to have him opening up; it was very new, very fresh, one guy filling the concert halls and arenas with that incredible sound. I never forgot it. It was extraordinary to hear him.'

What it did not do was what it was designed to do, which was increase Martyn's reach in the States. He made the most of it, nonetheless. He filled the days between Yes shows with small club dates, which apparently paid more than those 'tight-fisted mother-fuckers' did, and which offered the intimacy and audience appreciation he craved.[18] He settled his scores backstage by drinking the band's rider, stealing their food and making off with any available women.

In the late summer he returned to Basing Street to make *Sunday's Child*, the rather more well-behaved follow-up to *Inside Out*. Richard Digby Smith facilitated the technical side, while Martyn recorded with a core trio consisting of himself, Danny Thompson on bass and Liam Genockey on drums. 'It's much calmer, relatively speaking, after the madness of the previous record,' says Digby Smith. '[But] he would never articulate that. There were no road maps or preconceptions.'

Speaking about this period of his life a decade later, Martyn claimed to be 'blissfully happy... I was oblivious to the rest of the world.'[19] There are obvious and glaring caveats to that statement, yet *Sunday's Child* radiates a warm, domesticated glow. At its heart are love songs sung for his wife and to his children, born and unborn. It's as though he is trying to will another way of life into being through the power of music. Doubling down on the theme of contentment, he turned his hand to the zen-country standard, 'Satisfied Mind'.

'My Baby Girl' is a touching tune for Mhairi, his '*number one girl*', who implores her father to sing and play for her when he comes home. His daughter was, as she readily concedes, the apple of his eye. Beverley joined on backing vocals. The verses of the brisk Scottish folk standard 'Mairi's Wedding', which Martyn interpolated into 'The Message', were also pointedly chosen. 'You Can Discover' is a tender plea to his wife not to let their shared afflictions of '*madness*' and '*sadness*' divert them from continuing to explore their deep connection.

On an album where the tapping of folk sources was more overt than usual, the highlight is 'Spencer The Rover', a venerable traditional song with its provenance in East Sussex and Yorkshire, and which Martyn learned from one of the latter county's many fine folk singers, Robin Dransfield. Martyn was particularly enamoured with it. The following spring, the song gave its name to his second child, christened Spenser Thomas McGeachy.

'He initially asked me to sing on "Spencer The Rover",' says Martin Carthy. 'Nothing came of it, in the end. Don't know why. It tells you a lot about him that he loved that song so much. It spoke to him. It's a very grown-up song. I never understood it when I was twenty; when I was forty I did. The results were very true to the song, but very John. It was odd that he liked the most English of English songs. It's remarkable that there isn't a Scots song that did that to him.'

He sang it with rapturous tenderness on *Sunday's Child*, and many times more on stage in the years thereafter. Though he did not write the words, in his hands they read like wishful autobiography. In its empathetic depiction of a man who has been '*much reduced*' and '*caused great confusion*', one can hear a romanticised echo of Martyn's own transgressive wanderings.

In the song, Spencer has abandoned his family and embarked on a troubled, aimless ramble around the countryside. In Yorkshire, he beds down for the night in a forest. After a restless sleep, punctuated by dream-sent voices imploring him to go home, he returns to the family fold, a near-stranger welcomed lovingly back into their arms. Spencer is thereafter resolved to a future filled with nothing more taxing than taking his children upon his knee and listening to their '*prittle-prattling stories*'. It is a song about setting aside youthful appetites and wild schemes to instead settle for the simplest and most enriching rewards. For Martyn, such home comforts were fleeting and rare. Though they were similarly cherished, at least in theory, they offered only temporary respite.

The song smooths out the edges of his cavalier ways. Perhaps that is why he cradles it like precious cargo. It offers a glimpse of another path, impossible to follow but close enough to touch. He could never have written the song, but he sings it as a sacred text. Perhaps the performance is so profoundly powerful because it offers the happy ending his own actions denied him. In the studio, Martyn played acoustic guitar through the rotating Leslie speaker from the Hammond organ, as well as miking it acoustically, lending the track a spinning, beautifully out-of-focus sound.

Something else marks out the recording. The words to 'Spencer The Rover' tell a story. They move from A to B and on again, reaching a profoundly satisfying conclusion. There are few other pieces in Martyn's mature catalogue which do the same. His lyrics more often are thematic daubs which establish a mood or impression and go on simply to offer variations of colour and emphasis. They circle dreamily, they roll down the river, a single thought fluttering in the wind. Written down, they can appear slight, almost unfinished, which in truth they often were. He chopped enough timber to build a framework, but beyond honouring the atmosphere of the track, giving the emotion a place to reside, words were not where his passion lay. A hugely eloquent and far-reaching conversationalist, he was not an overly literary writer. He seemed to distrust linguistic certainties. Instead, he mined moods and ambiguities rather than tangled with narrative. Another reason that Martyn aligns more closely to a jazz sensibility than a folk one.

The domestic scene painted by *Sunday's Child* was a dream, but a dream with a flickering reflection in reality. At home, Martyn could be loving, tactile and affectionate with his wife and children. There were periods of joy and contentment: playing music late at night with Beverley, going to the beach with the children, taking them out into the countryside to fish and shoot, adding spice to the domestic routine. 'He would come back from travelling with exotic ingredients,' says Wesley Kutner, who as an adult worked as a chef for twenty years. 'It inspired me to be a cook. I was exposed to all these different flavours, and I used to play around and experiment.'

Martyn was on the road more than he was at home, and his arrivals in Cobourg Place were invariably noisy, exciting and dramatic. 'I remember things being relatively dull and peaceful while he was away, and then quite loud and chaotic while he was around, with a combination of everything: music, madness and people,' says Vari

McGeachy. 'I was always very excited to see my dad, plus I was his baby girl. He was excited, it was jolly; there was lots of tickling and laughing and jokes and merriment and music to be made. I always looked forward to it, but it could quickly turn into a not so pleasant experience, and you would be happy once he'd walked out the door again. Then you'd be missing him and be excited to see him again, and then you'd want him to go. That was the cycle.'

'You know, we had laughs,' says Beverley Martyn. 'He could be sweet, gentle, boyish and beautiful, but then you had the other side, which was manic and angry and totally helpless. You never knew where you were, or when he was going to turn. He was terribly paranoid.'

When his mood turned, he would demand to be fed at all hours, send his wife to bed, choose her clothes. He'd criticise her make-up, tell her to shut up when she spoke. He hurled objects at the walls, broke furniture. There were vicious shouting matches, threats, slaps and punches, which resulted over the years, says his ex-wife, in broken and fractured bones. 'I was literally terrified,' she says. 'I was frightened of him and he could see that I was frightened of him, and once you let a person see that you are frightened of them, they've got you.' There are things Martyn did to his wife which, says her son Wesley, are 'unmentionable, actually. You have no idea. I did go into the room often and see stuff, and I was very worried. He would beat the crap out of her because his shirts weren't ironed. I remember that. I remember it every time I iron a shirt.'

The trigger points for his rages were varied, often trivial: a family member wearing something which displeased him; the house being empty when he came home, or altered in some way; the wrong look, an ill-chosen word. 'Control was a lot of it, especially when he had been away for a long time,' says Vari. Often it was directly related to the comedown from drink and drugs. 'He could just wake up terribly, terribly, terribly grumpy and angry for no apparent reason.'

The children were all affected by the fallout, each in different ways. The family had a complicated internal dynamic. Wesley Kutner says he did not fully realise that Martyn wasn't his real father until after the marriage was over, in the early Eighties. He was told shortly before he met his biological father, Jonathan Weston, for the first time, at the age of thirteen. 'It was a life-changing moment,' he says. 'Such a fucking relief! I always wanted to feel like John was my father, but there was something different about the way he treated me compared to my brother and sister.'

Vari McGeachy agrees that Wesley was treated differently, but 'it could just have been as basic as, "You're a boy, you're a girl." John was very, very macho and quite old-fashioned.' She recalls as a very small child making a 'mean and wicked' comment about the fact that she and Wesley did not share the same father, 'but I suppose your consciousness of that kind of thing takes a while to kick in… all our experiences and memories differ. I was worried and concerned about what was happening between my parents – God, yeah – but what could you do? You are children, and helpless to some degree. I was lucky with Dad, I could defuse things, more so than the boys. Spenser was too young, and Wesley had a very different dynamic with John.

'Most of the time we would see and hear it and just hope for the best, and it would pass, like a bad storm. John was hugely loud. Dramatic. Sometimes it could sound worse than it was, other times… I know Beverley did get hurt. Dad's anger and rage was more chaotic and psychological. Shouting and screaming and hurling, rather than fisticuffs fights. He was a man of moods, and he would use his moods to dominate and get what he wanted – when he was angry. When he was not angry, he was great fun.'

The memories of her stepbrother contain less light, more shade. Wesley remembers a childhood where 'I wasn't allowed to be a child, I had to be hypervigilant for myself and for my mother. He made a lot of threats. I saw *The Shining* when I was an older kid, and to see that face of Jack Nicholson trying to get through the door with an axe – as a metaphor, that would sum up my childhood vision of John. I lived in total fear of that man. I thought my life hung on a thread.'

It was a time when domestic abuse was largely ignored, by society and by the authorities. Likewise, a time when alcohol, drug addiction and mental health issues were not afforded the same scrutiny and compassion as today. The trauma which affected them all played out behind closed doors. The family finances were another area in which Martyn liked to exert control. 'Mother didn't have enough money to keep things together; he held the purse strings,' says Wesley Kutner. 'We were like paupers when he wasn't there. It was rags to riches every three months. He was working, working, working. It was a sparse life, no luxuries. Whatever he was making, he was spending on the road.'

Away from home, there were random and sometimes shocking acts of violence. The saxophone player for the Average White Band, Malcolm 'Molly' Duncan, told a story in private of meeting Martyn on a train from Glasgow to London. He witnessed a soldier laugh at Martyn and call him 'a poofter', whereupon Martyn 'threw him off the train', causing serious injury. Throughout his life there were other incidents, some severe, where the police became involved.

The mood at Cobourg Place darkened further on the morning of November 25, 1974, when Nick Drake died at his family home in Tamworth-in-Arden from an overdose of antidepressants, a death deemed to be suicide by the coroner, though the verdict has been contested publicly by his family. He was twenty-six, and had released his final album, *Pink Moon*, more than two years previously.

His death was not entirely a surprise, but it shook the Martyns hard. Beverley felt she shared at least some understanding of the pain Drake had been in. 'I was taking antidepressants in 1972 or '73,' she says. 'I knew that he was ill and he needed help, but who could you go to? Sometimes he would talk, sometimes he wouldn't talk, sometimes he would have a cup of tea and hold it for three hours looking out at the sea. He would go out walking in the evening with me and the dog while someone babysat. He seemed to like the company. I think he felt safe. He would play me the odd song, and I would play him one. I tried to take care of him, and he knew I was suffering. He really knew. I think it upset him in the end, John's treatment of me. He knew what was going on.'

In contrast to the romantic myth that Drake simply dissolved passively into a kind of bleached nothingness, there is hard evidence which suggests he harboured a large amount of active anger towards the end of his life. 'I think Nick had gone beyond disillusion into rage,' says Paul Wheeler. Drake had stayed at 10 Cobourg Place not long before his death and seemed uncharacteristically confrontational. Returning from a visit to the pub, where he had observed his friend chatting up a barmaid, he called Martyn 'devious' and refused to hug Beverley when he left. 'It was as if John had said or done something that night that had really upset him,' she wrote.[20]

That visit was the last time Beverley saw Drake, although Martyn reportedly made a trip to Tamworth-in-Arden not long afterwards where, Martyn claimed, Drake disclosed the extent to which he felt he had failed with his musical career. 'I never realised Nick Drake was ambitious until he confided to me that he was, and it took me greatly by surprise,' Martyn told me. 'It crushed him that he was ignored, because he was used to excelling at everything: as a student, as an athlete. In his eyes, it was the first time he'd ever failed at anything. It astonished me that he actually valued commercial success, but then I'm not ambitious at all, believe it or not.'

This may have been the case. On the other hand, it may have been an instance where the perceived flaws of one man are projected onto someone close to them. Exactly who the ambitious one was in their friendship, and to what extent, is open to question. 'Nick was very honourable, and had the highest integrity,' says Wheeler. 'He really did believe in the ideals of the Sixties and he was very distressed at those ideals disintegrating... I felt that Nick felt that John had sold out [and] Nick really didn't want to sell out. That was my version of Nick.'

Island producer Phill Brown, Martyn's friend and neighbour during the second half of the Seventies, recalls Martyn telling him that he'd had 'this terrible argument with Nick Drake. Nick had accused him of selling out because he had gone electric and was using pedals and things. John did his usual, wiped the floor with him verbally, which was a tough thing to do to Nick – and they were the best of mates. Within a month he was dead, and John had never phoned up to say sorry. That really haunted John. I remember being with him not long afterwards, and he was just destroyed.'

It was Wheeler who called Martyn to tell him the news that Drake had died. 'I remember him just laughing, and I remember being totally disturbed at the time. The laugh scared me. John had a number of different characters which he would adopt in different circumstances. On first hearing about Nick's death, I think he adopted the character of a tough guy who had no time for those who rejected help, probably as a defence mechanism to guard his own sensitivity and fear of isolation.'

Speaking to the writer John Neil Munro, Martyn said: 'I laughed, for which my wife never forgave me. I don't think I've ever cried for Nicky. It seemed so obvious that it would come.'[21] According to Beverley, Martyn simply said, 'He did it,' and walked out of the room, not to be seen again for two days.[22]

There is no record of him attending the funeral on December 2, and by the middle of the month he was back on the road, playing a series of shows in Brussels.

Sunday's Child came out in January 1975, a woozy hit of filtered domesticity. It's a fine album, but there was a sense, which Martyn shared, that he was tilling over ground which was yielding a less bountiful harvest. The mellow vibes of 'Lay It All Down', 'You Can Discover' and 'One Day Without You' were uniformly gorgeous, but somehow predictably so. There was room for some surprises. The hard-edged abstract groove of 'Root Love' was his most extreme guitar statement to date, betraying a recent obsession with The Isley Brothers' fuzz-toned 45 'Summer Breeze'; the spacey background squalls in 'You Can Discover' are similarly indebted to that source. The elbows-out, chicken-scratch funk-blues of 'Clutches' is great fun. 'Call Me Crazy' aims for the stars but falls short.

Martyn spent the first half of the year touring the UK and Ireland with Danny Thompson and John Stevens, a wildly talented free-jazz drummer who had some years earlier formed the influential Spontaneous Music Ensemble. Stevens was a good friend of saxophonist Dudu Pukwana, which is probably where the connection to Martyn was first made. His intuitive playing, ranging from expressive ripples to arrhythmic explosions, complemented Martyn's increasingly stretched-out live shows.

The heights reached by their folk-jazz trio were frequently sublime, a testament to Martyn's belief that he always flew highest on stage rather than in the studio, buoyed by the energy and sense of risk of playing for a crowd. 'I can't work to my full capacity unless I have an audience there, it's a funny thing.'[23] A snapshot of the tour was released later in the year as *Live At Leeds*, although only 'Make No Mistake' and 'Bless The Weather' were actually taped at the Leeds show on February 13, which was held in the student canteen at the university. 'The Man In The Station' was taken from the afternoon rehearsal and later overdubbed with a new vocal at Basing Street. 'Solid Air', 'I'd Rather Be The Devil' and 'Outside In' were recorded in London, presumably at the Victoria Palace Theatre on February 2.

'If John Martyn had been the only person that I had ever done music with, it would have satisfied all of my musical ambition,' Danny Thompson told me. 'That would have done me.' You listen to *Live At Leeds* and understand why. 'Outside In', which covered the entire first side of the album, is revelatory, Martyn's very own 'The Creator Has A Master Plan'. It's a maelstrom whipped up by wave upon wave of music so rich, it seems impossible that there were only two men on stage (Stevens sat this one out).

For unexpurgated insight into the 1975 tour experience, the deluxe version of *Live At Leeds* released in 2010 offers another perspective. The album features the entire Leeds show in sequence, presented audio vérité style. Here, the sublime spell conjured by the music is repeatedly and consciously punctured by mumbling Cockney wisecracks, silly voices, rambling detours, bizarre internal monologues and copious swearing.

It was, on the one hand, an extreme evolution of the stage technique Martyn had cultivated from the early days – the anti-folk-club dazzle designed to keep the audience on its toes and to prevent the atmosphere settling into cosy reverence. With drugs and alcohol added to the standard adrenaline rush – on this occasion, 'the dressing room was awash with crème de menthe and brandy,' recalled Thompson – the effects were deeply tedious: scatological profanity masquerading as wit; Derek and Clive without the punchlines; the speed-babble of the indulged barroom bore.[24]

On another level, such deflections revealed Martyn's deep-seated refusal to lay himself open. 'He'd often play something incredibly beautiful and follow it with a belch to dismiss it, in case someone thought he was being frightfully artistic, a bit *poncey*,' says Thompson. 'Everyone loved him for that, because at that time there was an ocean of guitar-playing singer-songwriter blokes: James Taylor, Tom Paxton, all those guys. John comes along with those great songs and that innovative guitar technique – even now no one realises quite how incredible it was, how much he could do with it – and people had this [close] relationship with him because they knew he wasn't this patronising artistic type.

'He dismissed his feelings by being one of the blokes, pretending to throw people out of pub windows, and of course it's that side of him that gets taken up. I understand it because I did the same thing. He didn't want anyone to see that soft underbelly. He wanted to be portrayed as the hard man, and people thought he was a bit of a braggart, a bit arrogant, and of course he wasn't. He'd already told us what he is, by singing that beautiful song. He had already demonstrated the man inside. I can relate to that. We all put barriers up, we don't want people to know what's really going on.'

At Leeds, as they were throughout the latter stages of the tour, Martyn, Thompson and Stevens were joined on the encores by Paul Kossoff, who typically contributed lead guitar to three songs: 'So Much In Love With You', 'Clutches' and 'Mailman'. Kossoff was by now a mess. After Free disbanded in 1973, he had made a solo album, *Back Street Crawler*, before forming a band of the same name, which latterly included John 'Rabbit' Bundrick. His addictions, however, had steadily overshadowed his attempts to make music. 'Kossoff had a little mews, and all the people used to go to his house, which wasn't far from Island, and it became like a den,' says Bundrick. 'People fed off each other. Most of the people Koss hung around with were those kinds of people.'

Even Martyn seemed somewhat taken aback by his appetites. 'Kossoff engaged in an almost sybaritic desire to get every damn thing he could down his neck,' he said.[25] He duly cast himself in the unlikely role of saviour and determined to get Kossoff off heroin, a task complicated somewhat by the fact that he had started dabbling in the drug himself. With Nick Drake no longer around to mollycoddle, he and Beverley would invite the guitarist down to Hastings, feeding him up and weaning him onto bottles of brandy rather than smack. Kossoff loved to play, and Martyn's decision to take him on tour was a generous act, more so because he was aware that his contributions were not a particularly good or natural fit in terms of what he was doing musically.

He proclaimed Kossoff's 'martinet' father to be a villain and a bully, but Martyn hardly treated his friend with kid gloves.[26] He and Thompson would 'frisk' him to make sure he wasn't carrying heroin. Prior to the show at Leeds, *Melody Maker* journalist Allan Jones, in town to interview Martyn, observed a pitiful scene of self-abasement and simmering violence, near-Neanderthal in its wild-eyed lust for trouble. Before the show, Kossoff was shoved by a student as retribution for attempting to grope his girlfriend. Kossoff was then punched 'extremely hard' by Martyn for failing to deal with the student appropriately.[27] After the gig, Kossoff attacked Martyn with a bottle, whereupon Martyn took him into the dressing room and beat him up properly. The prescribed cure, clearly, was tough love. 'Paul told me that John pulled a knife on him once,' says Jeff Allen, who toured with Martyn in the Eighties. 'At the back of the Odeon.' In the end, Kossoff's contributions were not included on *Live At Leeds*.

Though Island had stumped up to record the tour on their mobile unit – and the tapes were mixed that summer at their Basing Street studios – they ultimately decided against releasing a live album. It is testament to Chris Blackwell's remarkable generosity that he allowed Martyn to take the tapes away and release the album independently, using the EMI pressing plant to print a limited edition run of 10,000 copies. Modelled on The Who's own *Live At Leeds*, and designed with budgetary limitations uppermost in mind, it was presented in a plain white sleeve with a plain white label, a primitive Post Office stamp proclaiming the title and artist.

Martyn announced it with a Cockney-themed advert in *Melody Maker* in September 1975: 'Look 'ere, I've made this album. Now keep schtum and don't tell de uvver mob. Just send free quid as soon as you like to my gaff and my latest live waxing can be yours.' The advert included his home address and a tear-off mail order coupon. In keeping with the barrow-boy spirit of the enterprise, he sold all 10,000 copies out of 10 Cobourg Place, for £2.50 plus 50p postage. Mostly it was done by mail, but more than a few punters turned up on the doorstep. He wasn't quite flogging fruit from a market stall, but the principle was the same.

'It was very profitable for me,' he recalled. 'I mean, every morning for months I woke and there was another couple of thousand quid lying on the floor. It was wonderful. It was also a nightmare. I never worked so hard in my life, opening all those letters, having to personally reply to every one of them, making sure all the right letters went into all the right envelopes.'[28]

His wife dealt with many of the orders. There was a delay in the album stock arriving, due to a faulty test pressing, and for much of September and all of November Martyn was on the road. The albums were numbered and often personally signed. It was rarely difficult for the recipient to tell which of the couple had done the honours: one might read, 'Sorry to be so long – John and Bev'; another, 'Sorry it's late – EMI fucked the first pressing up. Godblessyer – John Martyn.'

All 10,000 copies had sold out by early November, whereupon Brian Blevins at Island issued a press release announcing that the fun was over and reassuring those who had not yet received an album that it would be in their hands shortly. For all that it was an appealingly ramshackle endeavour, and for all its undoubted musical merit, *Live At Leeds* was a sincere and perhaps rather desperate attempt by Martyn to earn some money from his records. By this point, 'the music industry was driving me totally insane,' he said.[29] Essentially working hand to mouth, living off his gig earnings, he had begun to fully realise the implications and intricacies of the contracts he had signed years before.

The original deal between Island and Witchseason had involved an inadvisable degree of cross-collateralisation. In effect, sales by all Witchseason artists were set against the sum total of advances and expenses paid upfront by Island to allow the records to be made. This was extremely messy. It meant that if, for example, Fairport Convention sold ten times the number of records Nick Drake sold, the collective proceeds went towards servicing a single shared liability to the record label.

When Witchseason was bought by Island in 1970, this problem was eliminated, but the money spent on past, current and future recordings was still held against each artist. In Martyn's case, the £20-a-week salary he had been paid by Witchseason, and the record advances he had received from Island for all his albums since 1967, both as a solo artist and in tandem with Beverley, had been stacked against any royalties accruing on future album sales. The equation did not work out in his favour. When *Bless The Weather* and *Solid Air* started selling in reasonable amounts, he felt there was finally a chance for him to recoup and earn some royalties. Standing in the way, however, was all the money spent previously by Island and Witchseason, particularly the relatively lavish outlays on *Stormbringer!* and *The Road To Ruin*.

'I think he viewed that as my fault and he wasn't happy,' says Joe Boyd. 'He went to see Chris and was complaining about the fact that the success of *Bless The Weather* and *Solid Air* was being gobbled up by old debts. I spent a certain amount of time between 1973 and 1977 sitting down at meetings at Island Records with [people from] business affairs and accounts and artists. We did have some meetings with a very angry John Martyn, where an accountant would say, "Well, look, this is how much they [cost]..." I think I managed to help Island sort it so that half of the *Stormbringer!* costs and half for *The Road To Ruin* were set against John's solo career, and half against Beverley – which would never be recouped. That's my memory. I think it was quite generous, or fair anyway, in allowing him to be approached that way.'

Martyn did not necessarily agree. He was still railing against Boyd twenty-five years later. Late in life, he told me that, in industry terms, the musician is 'down there with the plankton. One vulture is much the same as another as far as I'm concerned; there's just fat vultures and thin vultures. Mine tend to be middleweight.'

By the end of 1975, he was struggling with other pressures. On tour, the setlist had become predictable. He and Thompson were expending so much energy on misbehaving, there was little time to change things around on stage.

He spent all of November on the road. 'I saw him when he was playing in Exeter [on November 3] with Danny,' says his old Hampstead friend Jo Watson, who had moved to Devon and hadn't seen Martyn for some time. 'He was snorting up lots of coke, and it was sort of like seeing somebody disappearing. That's what I felt. We had been so young and comparatively innocent.' It seemed a grim fulfilment of the haunting coda to 'Ways To Cry': '*Got no little boy left…*'

The impossibility of the lifestyle had its claws in him. There were moments when he recognised it and hated it. 'Make No Mistake' is soused in the self-loathing of the habitual drinker, lying '*dead drunk*' on the floor, who gets up only to ask for more. His weaknesses fuelled his anger, which in turned fuelled further excesses, which only increased his rage. His features took on a certain debauched air. It's possible to trace his physical decline through *Old Grey Whistle Test* appearances alone. As late as 1973, curly-haired and scruffy, he still retained a certain cherubic quality. By 1975, dressed like a middle-rank snooker player, he looked puffy, red-faced and sweaty.

Home offered little respite. Putting his address in a national music magazine had not been a wise idea. With her husband absent much of the time, Beverley was left at Cobourg Place with three small children and a parade of unwelcome visitors, many of them persistent and unsavoury. 'They would be coming from Belgium, all over, and I'd be answering the door and letting them in,' says Wesley Kutner.

It was one reason behind their resolution to move out of town, to the nearby village of Heathfield, the following year. Another was the fact that, when Martyn was at home, Hastings was not an environment where he could easily escape temptation. Numerous pubs were on his doorstep, and within them he was regarded as a local hero. 'He was very loved in Hastings,' says Wesley Kutner. 'He was like a god.'

'[He] would spend hours in the Hastings pubs telling stories to a bunch of piss artists, then bringing them all back home to party in our house,' said Beverley Martyn. 'It was horrible... it had become [a] non-stop party, with hangers-on banging on our door day and night.'[30]

The drug scene there was heavy. Wesley Kutner recalls seeing heroin being taken at home while they lived at Cobourg Place. 'They all got a bit messed up when they were in Hastings,' says Phill Brown. 'There was a massive heroin problem at that time. When we were doing *One World* with John [in 1977], we got hold of this opium, by chance – which is the same drug, if you like, but a lot more controllable – and it was then that the whole thing came up about heroin and Hastings. Back then, it was pretty seedy. There were a lot of musicians hanging out around the Old Town, there was a good music scene going on, and it was cheaper. It was a definite decision for him and Beverley to move out and try to live a cleaner lifestyle.'

Martyn kicked off 1976 with a hometown show alongside Danny Thompson at the Carlisle pub. His tolerance of a well-oiled Friday-night crowd, and one particularly vocal woman, quickly stretched to breaking point. 'Look, I've got a 2,000-watt PA here and I still can't hear myself for you talking, so shut up,' he told her. 'If my wallet was as big as your mouth, I'd be the richest cunt in Hastings.'

Time for a change.

8

In the back room of a tiny club in the catacombs of Edinburgh's Old Town, the air reels from the combined effects of reefer smoke, Guinness fumes and Chinese takeaway food. Lee 'Scratch' Perry, not quite eighty-two years old, holds my copy of *One World* upside down and back to front and signs his name on it. One more scratch.

He is quite the sight. His beard and hair are dyed chemical-waste red. His hat is festooned with badges, sphinxes and mirrors; his elaborately patterned jacket has a cartoon alien on the front, and a huge psychedelic sunflower on the back. The epaulettes display the colours of the Ethiopian flag. His fingers are ringed with massive rocks, his neck adorned with beads and jewellery. On top of a small blue suitcase lies a twiggy bush of pungent weed. Periodically, he snaps off a bud and stuffs it into the bowl of his pipe, lighting it and puffing away until it glows like a Belisha beacon.

Perry's aura is imperial imp, a mercurial and slightly menacing space-dub pirate. A pioneer at Kingston's Studio One in the early Sixties, he mentored Bob Marley before the Tuff Gong became a superstar, and made some of the most sonically innovative and enduring reggae records of the Seventies at Black Ark, the lo-tech, high-concept studio he built in his back garden which boasted 'four tracks on the machine, twenty from the extraterrestrial squad'.

From this base, he forged new frontiers in cacophonous dub production, playing midwife to some of the greatest reggae records ever made, among them groundbreaking albums by Max Romeo, The Upsetters, Junior Murvin, The Heptones and The Congos. Later, his maverick talents were sought by everyone from The Clash and the Beastie Boys to Adrian Sherwood, The Orb – and John Martyn.

I mention Martyn's name and Perry peers at me.

'How is John?'

'He's dead.'

He accepts this solemn news with admirable equanimity.

'He dead? Who kill 'im? The wife, that lickle girl?'

No, it was closer to the other way around, I tell him.

He sucks his pipe and takes a closer look at *One World*. 'He is a great artist, full of fresh ideas. I meet him with Island Records. "Big Muff" was the song, I write that for him. He was a good artist, a good musician, a good singer. A lovely Scots person. I write "Big Muff", and we also have big puff.'

I point out that Perry has no writing credit on the song. 'John wrote I write it, John didn't put John Martyn write it, [but] not all the people are honest like John.' This may be a dig at Chris Blackwell, who is now, seemingly, on Perry's long and slightly baffling shit list – something to do with Bob Marley and the Devil. Although he gained his nickname from his first recording, 'Chicken Scratch', cut in Kingston in 1961, Perry's other nom de plume, The Upsetter, is perhaps more fitting. 'My style is to criticise, to warn with rain and fire,' he says. 'Is a fire-style! I am the burner.' You can see why he and Martyn hit it off. The Upsetter meets The Disruptor.

It was Blackwell – the great facilitator-in-chief of Jamaican music – who first brought Martyn and Perry together. Recognising that Martyn was close to crisis point, Blackwell had recommended a break. Flush from the cash windfall of *Live At Leeds*, Martyn resolved to cut back on touring for the first time in a decade and work on getting his head straight. He spent the first few months of 1976 with his family in Jamaica, staying at Strawberry Hill, the historic 20-acre estate Blackwell had coveted since childhood and had finally bought in 1974, ten miles up a rough track from the capital Kingston in the rising foothills of the Blue Mountains. Now a hotel, it was to Strawberry Hill that Bob Marley was spirited following the attempt on his life later that year, in December 1976.

Blackwell sensed that Martyn and Perry's shared love of reverb might forge a bond. 'I'm a bit of a minimalist, and I wanted him to hear Lee "Scratch" Perry's records,' he says. 'They had this incredible atmosphere in them, but there wasn't a whole lot of stuff going on. It was a kind of floating effect. Lee Perry and John Martyn, who most people would say were equally completely nuts, became very good friends.' At the time, Perry was experimenting using two echoplex, generating vast waves of tape delay. 'Lee was into the echo thing like I was,' Martyn said. 'He loved to perform the dub. We had the same need for space in our music, but it still had to have a great big bitching anchor.'[1] They shared other interests, too, of course. Ganja, chaos, women, rum, knives.

Martyn spent an enjoyably frenzied time making music with Perry at Black Ark, but only after a period of decompression. He was burned out. On arriving in Jamaica in January, 'I actually didn't pick up a guitar for three months.'[2] He swam, rested, walked, relished the culture shock, observing the stratified hierarchy of day-to-day living, the sharp edges of Kingston. He took a keen interest in the island's febrile political life, which was simmering, soon to hit a rolling boil. The children hunted for caterpillars in the mountains, where the air was clear and thick with hummingbirds, and swam in the translucent sea. Uncomfortable with being waited on by the black staff who worked at Strawberry Hill, the Martyns asked the cook, Agnes, to make the family plain chicken and rice like everyone else, and some cornmeal porridge to build up Spenser, not yet quite a year old and small for his age.

In the sunshine, some of the tensions of life at home drained away. The children remember it as one of the happiest times of their childhood. 'It made up for all of the shit, being in Jamaica,' says Wesley Kutner. 'It was amazing. It opened my eyes that there was more to life than miserable grey England. It was the only holiday we had, the only time we had really been away as a family during those thirteen years. I thought it was always going to be like that. I thought,

All this shit has been worth it. I went back there in my mind when things got bad.'

Jamaica was perhaps not the most obvious place to clean up, and so it proved. Strawberry Hill was not a health farm. Martyn later recalled wild sprees in coastal towns and the bars of downtown Kingston, drinking white rum, playing cards and dice, and rubbing shoulders with a whole new level of gangster. It was hairy at times, but it was a different kind of crazy from the road, or the winding streets, rowdy pubs and dubious alliances of Hastings. It felt restorative.

After a spell of rest, he was compelled to investigate the music scene. 'I had some incredible fun with Mr Perry,' he said. 'We got loads done, recorded tons of stuff at Black Ark, but you'll probably never hear it until I'm dead and buried. I even played on a Max Romeo hit, but I can't remember for the life of me what it was called – [Lee would] cut three hit records in a single afternoon.'[3]

At the time, Perry was making *War Ina Babylon* at Black Ark with Max Romeo, a fellow Island artist and Upsetter. The classic album included Romeo's single 'Chase The Devil', which may be the track on which Martyn appears, though his presence is not obvious. He almost certainly played on 'Oh Me Oh My' by Bree Daniels, also produced by Perry, and recalled adding guitar to Burning Spear's *Man In The Hills*, recorded with Jack Ruby in downtown Kingston, though again he is uncredited. The recordings give away few clues, but on 'Black Soul' in particular it is feasible that Martyn is supplying some of the phased guitar.

He was paid in fistfuls of fake American dollars, pornographic videos and bottles of coffee liqueur. It wasn't always a smooth blend of cultures. A large, loud, invariably inebriated Scotsman in a suit pitching up uninvited to a session armed with a phase shift pedal and an echo box was not to everyone's taste. 'Up until quite recently, in certain Jamaican recording studios the very mention of John Martyn's name would scare staff and locals,' Blackwell later recalled.[4] No mean feat. His interaction with Perry, too, could be erratic. During the trip, Blackwell took the family to Nassau in the Bahamas. While there, he attempted to broker another session with Scratch. 'Very, very bad,' says Blackwell. 'I think I made a huge mistake. They were the worst influence on each other.'

There was plenty 'fire-style' and chaos in their exploratory fusion, but it reaped tangible rewards. He and Perry resolved to work together again, and Martyn left Jamaica with sketches for songs such as 'Dealer', 'Smiling Stranger', 'One World' and 'Black Man At Your Shoulder' – pieces that, lyrically and musically, had been inspired by the trip. He learned a lot and returned re-energised. He also added Jamaican patois to his repertoire of voices, recalls Danny Thompson. 'He'd come back like, "Jah, rasclat! Me feel nah pain."'

The family returned to an English spring shortly after receiving the news that Paul Kossoff had died on March 16, after overdosing on an aeroplane travelling from New York to Los Angeles. Martyn wrote 'Dead On Arrival' shortly afterwards, a song which he demoed and performed live but never officially released. It was a sour, surly requiem. Aggressively sung and performed in a crunching blues-rock style, it amounted to a pitiless post-mortem, judging that there was *nobody else in this world* to blame but Kossoff for his demise. Martyn was not good with loss. Listening to 'Dead On Arrival', I'm reminded of something he told me about Jimi Hendrix. 'I took it as an insult when he died. I don't like it when they do that.'

Shortly afterwards, they moved out of Hastings to Heathfield, a small market town in East Sussex, fifteen miles inland, built on higher ground with views over the surrounding countryside. They rented and later bought Kenana, a large detached house on Tilsmore Road. There was a Douglas fir in the large garden, a conservatory and lots of space for the children.

'It was a very conventional rural environment for very normal people,' says Vari McGeachy. 'I think we were definitely the black sheep. There was nothing cultural or interesting from Beverley's point of view. Wonderful for ours, because it was fantastic countryside. I loved it, but Bev was out of the loop. Big house, three kids, no money.' They lived at Kenana until the end of the Eighties, before it was knocked down to make way for what the brochure described as 'a fantastic development of executive homes'.

Though it was larger and more middle-class than their previous homes, 'there was still lots of rugs and incense and that slightly hippie type of layout,' recalls Ron Geesin, the experimental musician who lived within walking distance of Kenana in Broad Oak, a hamlet on the outskirts of Heathfield. Martyn would often visit, digging around in his compost heap to find worms to use as fishing bait. Island engineer Phill Brown and his family lived two villages away. Both spent time with Martyn after he moved from Hastings, Brown bringing his children over to socialise with Wesley, Mhairi and Spenser while he and Martyn talked, smoked and played or recorded music.

The move did not enact a magical cure on the marriage. 'It was always a little edgy, somehow,' says Brown. 'I met Beverley there a couple of times, and it was tricky. That's when I was aware that he would beat her up occasionally. She was very much like a skivvy, in a way. She was cooking, cleaning, running the house, doing everything so that John could have his life. Which was sad, because she gave up her career and never really got it back.'

Geesin was also well aware that 'they had fights and they had problems'. It was probably worse than anyone on the outside could have imagined. Wesley Kutner remembers Kenana as 'a battlefield. It wasn't a home any more; there were bazookas, landmines, claymores. They were fighting every day.' Martyn was the aggressor, but it was a combustible, deeply dysfunctional partnership. 'He wasn't all bad, and she wasn't all good,' says Wesley. 'It was a co-dependent relationship. She was an artist as well, and she had a crazy lifestyle, too. They were nocturnal people.'

In Heathfield, says Vari McGeachy, 'everything was amplified'. She and Wesley attended the local Church of England primary school, Cross of Hands, where they were more or less left to their own devices. Their parents were not the types to attend sports days or teacher consultation evenings. 'It just wasn't in their remit,' says Vari. 'Parenting was not a doing word at that time. I think teachers were aware we were coming from an unusual and dysfunctional environment, but I don't remember us getting any extra care or consideration because of that. I think we were a little bit stigmatised, to be honest.' Their friends would never come to the house to play. 'The other parents wouldn't have that,' says Wesley. 'We didn't look normal.'

When they woke in the morning for school, they were confronted with the chemical detritus of the night before. 'Everything was on the table: Charlie, hash, leftover alcohol,' says Wesley. 'It was all done in front of us and we would see all the incriminating evidence. My sister and I would have to wake up and make our own bloody breakfast; they would still be in bed. That was normal. If I had said anything at school, if I had grassed on my parents, John and Beverley would have gone to jail. Nowadays, the kids would be taken away from the parents and the parents would go to jail. I won't speak for my brother and sister, but I was subjected to abuse and neglect.'

Martyn had not released an album since January 1975. The hiatus was plugged with a compilation album, *So Far So Good*, released early in 1977, a decent summation of his career to date. 'I'd like the nasty bits to get nastier and the gentle bits to get more gentle,' he stated in Brian Blevins' sleevenotes, which promised that 'the electric guitar will become even greater in its dominance over his acoustic work'.[5]

Martyn played live infrequently in 1976, his year of recalibration. Whenever he did, the acoustic guitar was less prominent. At an open-air concert held in Regent's Park on July 4, he previewed many of the songs that would appear on *One World* using a Doctor Rhythm, a primitive form of drum machine. The shift was evident in the demos he started making at home and at Ron Geesin's house. On October 4, 8 and 26, November 3 and 4, 1976, and again on January 7, 1977, Martyn spent several hours at a time in Geesin's 'workshop' studio, an outbuilding at the end of the garden, where he recorded and experimented with electric guitar and a drum machine.

When Phill Brown came to Kenana, he and Martyn would work in a makeshift studio on the ground floor. 'He had a Revox and a basic four-track, I would take my machine and some good mikes over, and we would record stuff, copy it to a machine and add something else. It was very basic. It certainly wasn't a home studio as we would regard it now.' Brown frequently sensed that a song Martyn presented as new would have been 'going around in his head for a few months and then become something. He obviously honed things, but he seemed very spontaneous.'

Promoting *So Far So Good* with shows in 1977, the evolution continued. He performed a superb new song, 'One World', during an appearance on *The Old Grey Whistle Test* in March 1977. It was a truly extraordinary performance, dominated by Martyn's howling electric guitar and accompanied by a drum machine, Danny Thompson on bass and Gasper Lawal on congas.

From these beginnings, a new album took shape. Most of what became *One World* was recorded at Woolwich Green Farm at Sulhamstead, near Reading, a property owned by Chris Blackwell and available as a perk to artists signed to his Blue Mountain Music publishing company. The farm was almost entirely surrounded by water, the house and outbuildings overlooking Hosehill Lake. Close to the M4 motorway, it was accessible to London while also being a rural haven.

For the first time in their ten-year association, Blackwell was producing Martyn. It was relatively rare for him at this stage to play such a hands-on role, particularly with an artist so established and accomplished. The two men had always been close, though never in a deeply personal sense, and had spent a significant amount of time together in Jamaica. Working at Woolwich Green Farm was in some ways an extension of that trip, a recognition that the album was rooted in that experience. It was the act of a friend, but also the informed decision of a label boss who wanted to ensure his artist delivered.

'The reason for working at Chris Blackwell's house was that he knew where John was: he wasn't in a city where he could suddenly disappear and maybe not come back for two days,' says Phill Brown, who engineered the album. 'Chris was really trying to help him. Some of the madness had already impacted on his career, and Blackwell wanted to keep him focused. He really believed in John, he thought he was a great artist. A lot of people thought John was just too much trouble, but, if Chris believed in someone, he would stick with them.'

'Chris was always comforting John,' says John 'Rabbit' Bundrick. 'Patting his back, putting his arm around his shoulder. Maybe he just needed that confidence. "I'm still good, aren't I?" Most creative people have that.'

Martyn spent three weeks in residence at the farm through July and August 1977. The recording space was one of half a dozen former stables converted into guest apartments. In the final flat in the block, the small downstairs room was adapted as the main recording room for Martyn, where he settled in with guitars, pedals, amps and microphones. Outside was parked a mobile recording unit which became the control room, manned by Brown and sometimes Blackwell.

'You can really tell we were somewhere else when we made that record,' Martyn later said.[6] Woolwich Green Farm wrapped them in its arms. They arrived, parked up the cars, and stayed on site for a week or ten days. They would then take a break, Brown would drive Martyn back to Heathfield, and a few days later they would return to continue recording.

Invariably, they worked the night shift. Blackwell would use the mornings to tend to office work, make phone calls and from time to time throw a few pennies on the horses. The musicians and crew would sleep late and limber up by taking dinghies out onto the lake, playing darts or snooker.* Recording would never start before two or three in the afternoon; often it was as late as seven. They would then work through until five or six in the morning.

One can feel the nocturnal rhythms working through *One World*, an album tinted with the blue-black blush of twilight, the going down of things rather than the rising. Opium was part of the chemical equation, and that sweet, slow stickiness found its way into the music. 'We all broke off bits and stashed it in various locations,' says Brown. 'Once

---

* One outtake tape from *One World* simply features Martyn and Brown playing snooker.

165

we'd run out of our little treat for the week, we didn't bother getting any more.'

Brown recalls that Martyn was generally a joy to work with. There was only one flashpoint during the sessions, when he walked into the mobile recording truck and overheard Brown and Blackwell talking about him. The conversation wasn't derogatory, but he felt put upon and vulnerable and became instantly aggressive.

'I talked my way out of it,' says Brown. 'I said, "Come on, John, you've not had your breakfast, have you?" I found a little ball of opium we'd been keeping, and within half an hour all of that had been forgotten. We all loved the guy, but we were wary if he was in the wrong mood. If he was in a particular kind of mood, it was best not to say anything, or just agree with him, to defuse it. If he was in a state of mind where you could deal with him, he was such a great guy, who wrote these beautiful songs, but he could also just be a madman. Coke and alcohol together can be a really dangerous format, but I think alcohol really was his big demon. He had that dangerous element about him, a very aggressive, violent streak, and if you had the wrong kind of personality or said the wrong thing you could make that ten times worse. I have to say, I saw more of the lovely side of him than the madman.'

They pumped out the music through the PA system and across the lake, where dozens of microphones were set up as far as their leads would allow to capture the sound of the music as it travelled over water and across the countryside. Although it was summertime, this was England, and through the night a fine film of condensation would gather over the Neumann U87s. When the damp caused the microphones to stop working, Brown would dry them out on the Aga in the farmhouse.

This experimental recording method was deployed primarily on two songs. On the title track, the shimmering guitar solo midway through, with its echoes of Neil Young, was sent floating on the breeze and captured in the wild. It is a beautiful moment in one of Martyn's most stunningly beautiful songs, wherein he throws all the compassion he can muster at a 'cold and lonely' universe. Inspired by witnessing first-hand the racial and class divides in Jamaica, it is a weary benediction, casting Martyn as a tattered Everyman, hymning peace, acceptance and unity.

A self-declared socialist, he interacted with people daily in pubs, before and after gigs, and on the road, and habitually took each person as they came, affecting few airs and graces. There were times when he put his egalitarian beliefs into more direct action, inviting a homeless man into his house to wash and eat, or handing out fistfuls of money to street sleepers. He liked money as a means to enjoy himself but he never worshipped it and was rarely motivated by its acquisition. Indeed, he was typically careless with it. He hated banks – preferring cold hard cash in the pocket – and his takings from gigs went walkabout on more than one occasion. Listening to 'One World', his commitment to the collectivist cause seems beyond reasonable doubt. Hansford Rowe's busy electric bass brought the track into the realm of jazz fusion, similar to the terrain Joni Mitchell was currently exploring with Jaco Pastorius on *Hejira* and *Don Juan's Reckless Daughter*.

Martyn reprised the echoplex on 'Small Hours', a pre-dawn symphony scored in reverb. Here, he reined in the wild flights of 'Outside In' and refined his playing to a haunting swell which at times seems to hang suspended. Phill Brown estimates that 90 per cent of the track was captured on the outdoor microphones. Martyn recorded at three in the morning onto one 15-minute reel, Brown starting the tape while he was already playing – 'he was always playing' – hence the track's strange, garbled opening seconds. It is a genuinely ambient recording, in which the flight of passing geese flying low over the lake, the not-so-distant rattle of the passing mail train, the gentle lapping of the water, the rush of early morning air, all contribute to the pastoral aural tapestry.

A 'very quiet, very subdued' Steve Winwood had come from his home in Gloucestershire to play synths and keyboard. One of Martyn's great and relatively unsung studio collaborators, Winwood was never obtrusive, always finding his place in the song and determining the right thing to play. On 'Small Hours', he added typically empathetic trickles of organ.

For Blackwell, 'Small Hours' is 'like Gil Evans. It's in the top three of records I've ever produced. When I say I produced it, I mean I was there, so I get the credit, but the musicians produced that music. It just floats, and the sound of the geese on the lake and the train going by — it's so alive. I remember the whole experience as pure magic. The atmospherics were so great, and he was so excited about how it sounded, that he'd captured this fleeting magic. Winwood's playing is unbelievable. It's like leaves [falling] from a tree, the way he plays. It's one of those magical things.'

There are brief, loving lyrics, but it is the impossible beauty and compassion of the sound of 'Small Hours' that delivers on the communal ideal behind the album's title track. It brings humanity and nature into harmony — a glimpse, perhaps, of the soul-solace Martyn achieved while fishing, alone with his thoughts and momentarily at peace.

Into all this cultured mellowness came Lee 'Scratch' Perry, like a grenade tossed through an open window. He and Martyn worked together on 'Big Muff', less a conventional song, more a lean hustle, swaddled in reverb, fuelled by a mean minimalism and puerile innuendo. The largely nonsensical lyrics were inspired by Perry, who, while eating breakfast one morning with Martyn and Blackwell, began manoeuvring a tea set of china animal figures into a variety of sexual positions. 'He was going on about his big muff, and how it was going to get away with the powder puff and everything,' Martyn said. 'That guy's sense of humour is in the song. It's silly. Jamaican silly.'[7]

Though he isn't credited as a writer, producer or engineer, Perry's peculiar mad magic is smeared all over the track. 'It was very spontaneous, it came out of nowhere,' says Phill Brown. 'It was such a great day. Nothing was set up.'

Perry immediately took charge of the production, recording in mono and reducing the area of interest down to eight tracks. 'He wanted me to bring everything onto one channel, and then he would plug these things through phasers and reverbs and triggers and repeats, and then dance around hitting things!' says Brown. 'He was a real inspiration. We never got a mix that day that was used, but the vibe that he created, and his ideas, made you want to have fun and work. He thought the lyrics were hysterical; he was convinced it was all sexual. Then, at one or two in the morning, he disappeared.' He later came to visit the Martyns in Heathfield, where he obsessively watched the wrestling on television, ate nothing but ice cream, and ran around the local neighbourhood in his vest and blue silk shorts.

At a time when many white rock acts were adopting reggae tropes, Martyn wisely steered clear of anything too obvious.* The album revealed a wider taste for the exotic. There was an airy, Afrobeat lilt to the joyous 'Dancing', his light-hearted but unapologetic take on the carefree troubadour life. The bossa-nova-meets-Tropicália rhythms of 'Certain Surprise' evoked João Gilberto, Gilberto Gil, even José Feliciano, with a trombone solo from the great Rico Rodriguez, who would subsequently work extensively with The Specials. Harry Robinson's strings were another new texture: Hollywood high and swooning on 'Certain Surprise', dreamy and dramatic on the churning funk of 'Smiling Stranger', where they entered like an assassin, thickening the sinister atmosphere.

The influence of reggae was more subtle, perhaps more radical than mere imitation. 'Dealer', 'Big Muff' and 'Smiling Stranger' hotwired the malevolent, muscular minimalism of dub. These were grooves as much as songs, built on fat bass, echoing guitars and corkscrewing spirals of skyscraping reverb. Lyrically, they were soaked in drug imagery and reflected a slightly morbid fascination with the mechanics of street life. 'Black Man At Your Shoulder', written for the album but not included on it, mixed racial and cultural paranoia – *the language is strange* – with something more ominously figurative, the black man on the shoulder a variant of the black dog of depression, coming *closer with each passing day*.

One World was less personal in some ways, certainly less intimate, than Martyn's recent records. 'Couldn't Love You More' was the one direct connection to his former work, a simple acoustic performance

---

* 'Big Muff' bears more than a passing resemblance to Martyn's version of The Slickers' rocksteady 45 'Johnny Too Bad', which he recorded two years later. He had heard the original while in Jamaica.

featuring Danny Thompson's sawing bass undertow and dappled sprinkles of vibes. The lyric was one of his most tender, if ambiguous, declarations. 'On a simple level it's saying, "I gave you everything,"' says Ralph McTell. 'On another level, it says, "I didn't have any more that I could pull out to give you." He had a light touch, but there was a terrible, awe-inspiring darkness in him as well. He was one of those artists who could articulate what we suspect is this darkness we feel in ourselves. Sometimes we don't want to see it.'

One World synthesised the old and new, marrying Martyn's traditional heart and soul to a sinewy energy and fresh, luxuriant textures. Punk had broken through during the period in which the album was written and recorded, but it made little impact on him. He claimed to enjoy the Sex Pistols, and for at least one member of the band the feeling was mutual: John Lydon was a Martyn fan, spotted at several shows. But, for a man beholden to slow music, the abrasion of punk was never going to be his thing, even if he rather admired the attitude. When *One World* was released in November 1977, it reached number 54 in the British chart, the best position of any Martyn record to date.

Once the sessions were completed, in August he flew to Australia with Bert Jansch for a series of joint shows. The two men now shared a manager, Bruce May, who was Ralph McTell's brother. May had flown ahead and was waiting in Perth for them to arrive.

'There was some kind of hurricane and they ended up in Melbourne, four or five hours away,' he told the author Colin Harper. 'I got a call at 9 a.m. and it was John: "What do you want: the bad news or the good news?" he said. There was no good news. "I've got a busted lip, Bert's got a dislocated finger and the road manager's in prison." They'd had a fight on the plane. Bert had hit John Martyn. I said to Bert the next day, "Whatever possessed you?" He said, "Well, I knew before the tour was over John was going to hit me so I thought I'd get mine in first."'[8]

The tour manager had been arrested for stealing a life jacket, which in fact had been sneaked into his hand luggage by Martyn as a drunken prank. Jansch missed the first date due to his injured finger, but the pair were soon on good enough terms to play a few songs together at the conclusion of their show at Sydney Town Hall.

The strange blend of admiration and animosity lingered. Some years later, when Jansch was playing the Renfrew Ferry in Glasgow, Martyn and Hamish Imlach turned up drunk and began heckling. Jansch gamely resisted rising to the bait. At the interval, they met up and Martyn suggested they play something together at the end. When the moment came, Martyn walked onto the stage so drunk he could barely play a note. It was awkward and embarrassing, and seemed to sum up the tenor of their relationship. 'Bert was too quiet,' says Jacqui McShee. 'His personality was just incredibly insular, and John was too busy and noisy and loud for him.'

Danny Thompson had suffered a heart attack in the summer of 1977, shortly after appearing on two tracks on *One World*. The following year, he stopped drinking and in time converted to Islam, practising Sufism. Though he and Martyn played a handful of dates together in 1977 and reunited in the mid-Eighties and again in 2001, the high-water mark of their collaboration was over.

Instead, Martyn returned primarily to performing solo, sitting in his chair with an expanded effects box, alternating between acoustic and electric guitars, using primitive electronic rhythm on 'One World' and 'Small Hours'. He remained a mainstay on the university and college circuit, and, although he rarely upended expectations, on a good night he was still a captivating, charismatic and febrile spectacle in the flesh. In Hamburg, on March 17, 1978, the act of restringing and retuning his acoustic guitar became a performance in itself.

He made two appearances on British television in 1978, one of which, on January 10, was an *Old Grey Whistle Test* special taped at the Collegiate Theatre in London. Later in the year, his October 20 show at Reading University was recorded for broadcast on *Rock Goes to College*. He arrived on campus dressed for Wimbledon, in a cream V-necked sweater, cream trousers and white tennis shoes.

Between these appearances, he embarked on a desultory US tour supporting Eric Clapton in March and April 1978. The previous year, Clapton had covered 'May You Never' on the hugely successful *Slowhand*, released the same month as Martyn's *One World*. The break was thanks in no small part to Lulu's brother, Billy Lawrie, who worked as a plugger for Island. Lawrie had been instrumental in getting Clapton to record Bob Marley's 'I Shot The Sheriff' in 1976 and, according to Brian Blevins, he also helped 'May You Never' along. It was a tepid version, but nonetheless it 'probably made me more money than all my stuff put together,' Martyn said in 1980.[9]

In the wake of a healthy publishing cheque came the tour, another spin-off. Supporting Clapton wasn't quite as demoralising as opening for Yes had been in 1974, but it was dispiriting, nonetheless. Martyn played solo to largely uninterested crowds. At some shows, guard dogs and armed police patrolled the pit between stage and crowd. For a man who cared deeply about his music and the connections it made, this was an empty experience. He filled the holes with yet more drinking, drugging and one-night stands. 'Being a travelling musician, especially in America, I had more opportunity to go on the randan than one normally would,' he told me. 'Supporting Yes or Clapton, you only did half an hour and I wouldn't care how I went down. I'd get off the stage and hang out, and by the end of the night you're going to walk away with something.'

While on tour, Martyn and Clapton attempted to write a drinking song called 'The Brahms And Liszt Blues'. Back in England, they lived relatively close to each other, and for a while became something like friends. When Hamish Imlach came down from Motherwell to play at Dorking Folk Club, he stayed with Martyn in Heathfield and they dropped in at Clapton's stockbroker-belt country pile, Hurtwood, on the way to the gig. Clapton decided on a whim to come along, his wife Pattie Boyd acting as chauffeur in a Mercedes 500 limousine. He and Martyn ended the night on stage backing Imlach on his signature tune, 'Cod Liver Oil And The Orange Juice', and Imlach swore nobody recognised them. Afterwards, they returned to Hurtwood, where they stayed up all night, Clapton playing drums while they jammed.

At the end of the year, Martyn embarked on a long solo tour of British colleges and universities. He was spinning his wheels a little – settled into a comfort zone – and he knew it. 'Isn't it just the same tour of the college circuit it's always been?' wrote Ian Penman in his review for *NME*. 'Perhaps he plays the same songs as last time. Perhaps the same people turn up. He gives the dopes what they want, and they give him perhaps what he wants... John Martyn relaxes even further and moves away from the courage of earlier work.'[10] It was a little harsh but not a million miles wide of the mark.

His support act was Steve Tilston, who hadn't seen much of his old friend since the early Seventies. 'He'd changed,' says Tilston. 'The difference was quite palpable. He could still be charming and beguiling, but the edge became apparent, mainly in his dealings with sound men, for some reason. I found that a bit hard to reconcile against getting up and singing "One World". He could be absolutely charming and full of love, and then strutting around like a robber baron. By the end of it, I didn't want to be anywhere near him.'

The tour was an unorthodox one. Martyn had the romantic notion of travelling between gigs in a camper van with a gangster-turned-roadie whom he would introduce to people as 'my assassin'. Early on in this social experiment, his protector turned on him. 'In the dressing room in Southampton, this guy pulls his knife on John,' says Tilston. 'John's very balletically trying to kick the knife out of his hand. Silly stuff. The guy bailed. He said he couldn't take it any more.' Martyn replaced him with a younger man from Hastings who, according to Tilston, 'had a criminal case pending for bringing illegal immigrants in. These were the kind of circles he was moving in then. He was taking a hell of a lot of substances, drinking a lot.'

When he returned to Kenana, he would 'be really stir crazy,' says Wesley Kutner. 'There was nothing there. He would be up at the Star Inn, every day, lunch and dinner, in a taxi. They loved him there.' 'His coming home from the pub was like nobody else's coming home from the pub,' says Vari McGeachy. 'The whole street knew about John getting home from the pub.' If neighbours nearby complained about the noise, or the volume of Martyn's music, he became aggressive and abusive. By now, the two older children were aware that their father was an alcoholic. 'He would be back home, miserable, wake up and drink three-quarters of a bottle of vodka,' says Wesley. Whenever Martyn misplaced his drugs stash, he paid Wesley a pound to find it.

Early in 1979, the domestic war ended after one extremely violent confrontation too many. 'There was a series of events – just daily living – which led to a big explosion,' says Vari. 'Bev was so scared, she pegged it out the back door.'

'I'd had enough,' says Beverley. 'It was over, that was it. I could never go back.' Wesley was almost eleven and recalls that, as soon as his mother left, Martyn 'was immediately really sorry. Like, "Oh, what have I done. What shall we do?" He tried to get very clear-headed, very clean, very sober, very together. He knew trouble was coming.'

Beverley arranged for the children to be picked up and taken to stay with friends nearby for a number of days. When they finally returned to Kenana, Martyn was gone. 'Surgically removed,' says Kutner. Beverley took his 12-gauge and 6-gauge shotguns from the closet, wrapped them up in some old clothes, and asked a friend to dispose of them.

Martyn was served divorce papers on the grounds of gross negligence. He was also ordered by injunction to stay away from Kenana, an instruction which he broke at least twice. 'When he came to collect his belongings – he came and cleaned out all his pots, pans, rugs, ornaments, records – he put jam all over the doorknobs,' says Vari McGeachy. For Martyn, it all seemed to come as a terrible surprise. 'I mean, it had been going on for a while but... the end was just boom! That was that.'[11]

It was the end of a relationship which had passed through deep passion and love to toxicity and terror. 'First of all I trusted him with my life, and with my child,' says Beverley Martyn. 'It was a very quick bonding, and I thought, This is my soulmate – and I think he probably was my soulmate; it's just that he had enormous success and it went to his head, and he actually believed the things that people said about him. Some people still think that John can do no wrong. He could be

174

sweet, gentle, boyish and beautiful, but then you had the other side, which was manic and angry and totally helpless.'

'Beverley had a terrible rough deal of it all,' says Phill Brown, who lost contact with Martyn for several years after he left Heathfield. 'She lost her husband and she lost her career. He was madly in love with her, and it was very sad that he couldn't curb his anger.'

Martyn may have only had himself to blame, but it landed a terrible blow. 'I remember feeling that breaking up with Beverley was the most damaging thing for him and his life,' says Chris Blackwell. '[He was] derailed by the end of his marriage.' He unloaded an almost overwhelming torrent of emotion on his next album. It ended with a soul requiem called 'Our Love', on which he reflected on a relationship that made a *'man from a boy'* and a *'woman from a little girl'*.

9

In the early Eighties, night owls killing time on Goldhawk Road in West London witnessed a strange nocturnal ritual. A figure dressed in green-and-white-striped pyjamas, burgundy dressing gown, socks and slippers was keeping the night watch. In his hands he clutched a brand new Sony Walkman, the orange Styrofoam headphones gaffer-taped to his head to prevent them slipping off.

In such a fashion, padding through the sodium night, John Martyn would listen to the rough mixes of his latest album, *Glorious Fool*. A big man, more than a little lost.

By the close of the Seventies, many threads in Martyn's life had begun to fray. His much-loved grandmother Janet died on February 27, 1979, aged eighty-seven, while his father was experiencing poor health.

Following the collapse of a marriage he had tested daily but had not wanted to end, he became estranged from his children. Wesley Kutner would not see the man who raised him again for the best part of twenty years. Spenser and Vari, meanwhile, at the age of four and eight, were faded out of his life. There was one visit, and intermittent phone calls, before even they ceased.

'I thought my parents should definitely be separated, for everybody's welfare – including the neighbours – but I didn't realise that, when they did separate, I wasn't going to see him,' says Vari McGeachy. 'I saw him once or twice after he left. We went to London Zoo, Spenser came along, and I remember going back to his flat. That was the last time I saw him for many years. [His attitude] was, "Don't look back. Keep on moving." Just selfishness: "I've moved on." John was a coward on many levels. If things were too difficult, he would just ignore them.' It would be several years before contact resumed.

His drinking and drugging, already extreme, took on a pathological fervour, a kind of nihilistic intensity. He went on a furious binge which lasted several months. The varied strains of his sickness, guilt, grief and sorrow were sweated out into the last truly great batch of songs Martyn wrote, ending up on *Grace And Danger*, the album which acts as a hinge between his magnificent Seventies and less essential Eighties.

He left the family home in Heathfield in February 1979 and moved into the apartment Blackwell owned in Basing Street, above Island Studios in Notting Hill. A stream of highly personal songs poured out, some dating from his previous life. Beverley Martyn remembers that they had started writing the title track together, when it was originally called 'Grace In Danger'.

Martyn used the Island studio downstairs to demo material with bass player Chris Glen and drummer Timi Donald. On March 29 they recorded seven of the nine songs which would subsequently appear on the album – some more or less complete, some still evolving – as well as a handful of others, such as 'Small Hat', 'Running Up The Harbour' and 'After Tomorrow', which wouldn't make the final cut.

They were extraordinarily confessional pieces, even for a writer as unguarded as Martyn, constituting 'probably the most specific piece of autobiography I've written. Some people keep diaries, I make records. It's all very fundamental, really.'[1]

They were certainly autobiographical in terms of expressing Martyn's emotions, if not exactly factual in the strictest sense. The idea for 'Some People Are Crazy' had originated from a throwaway line Bruce May had said to him, observing that certain people '*draw conclusions like curtains*'. Eventually it would be placed at the start of the album, where it acknowledged upfront the divisive nature of Martyn's character and cleared a path for all that was to come: love me or loathe me, this is my truth.

The songs displayed a sincere desire to rewrite the narrative of what had gone wrong in his life. He imagined a parade of suitors taking his place in the family home, agonised over what his ex-wife was doing and with whom, pleaded for a hearing, settled scores, kicked around blame, anger, sadness and remorse. Jealousy triggered delusions. On 'Grace And Danger', he declared how good it made him feel that *'you've found somebody else'*. It was a victim scenario he reinforced in interviews.

'I mean, it only rankles when I see the kids and they call me by another man's name because they've got a new father. That hurts, but otherwise it's old history.'[2] The reality was rather different. He didn't see his children, and his ex-wife was virtually penniless, heavily medicated, and would shortly suffer a serious mental breakdown. Sadly, the pattern of choosing men who treated her badly continued even after her ex-husband was off the scene. Martyn, on the other hand, would shortly embark on a new relationship.

The songs worked through complicated emotions. On 'Lookin' On', he returned to the imagery with which he documented his break-up with Linda Dunning a decade previously in 'Would You Believe Me?' Once upon a time a woman had kept the wolves from the door. Now they were free to come prowling in, *'with their innocent grin'*, leaving him alone and empty, feeling nothing.

'Sweet Little Mystery' was the eerily calm late-night emergency call of a man who simply didn't know how to fill his time. Elsewhere he displayed gifts for bravado (*'I'll never be alone'*) and emotional self-preservation (Beverley didn't get all of him: *'I saved some for me'*). He aimed a particularly cutting swipe at what he clearly felt had been the hysterical domestic theatrics of his former drama student wife, portraying her as Ophelia in a shoddy repertory production of *Hamlet*, *'demented in a theatre absurd'*.

On the desperately sad 'Hurt In Your Heart' he bawled and begged, but the closest Martyn came to an apology for his behaviour over the years was on the pitiful 'Baby Please Come Home', where he acknowledged a degree of blame and swore blind he had no idea what *'made me hurt you so'*. For all the deep and sincere expressions of pain, there was little contrition on display. Instead, there was rather a lot of 'It's not me, it's you.'

These songs played a dangerous game, their compelling, crafted candour flirting with the maudlin self-pity of the spurned lover, sobbing into his Stolichnaya. The spectacle was ultimately engaging, if bruising. Here for public consumption were the distress signals of a man who had chanced his arm one too many times and seemed astonished to discover that it had finally been torn off.

In demo form the music was rawer, with more acoustic guitar. The finished record settled into its own particular mood, an upmarket blend of bereft R&B, skittish AOR synthetics and mournful jazz-fusion, dark and heavy as molasses. It was in many ways a logical progression from the slicker, softer parts of *One World*, shaped by a love of Weather Report, a curiosity for emerging technology and by a new friendship with Phil Collins, the drummer in Genesis and, since Peter Gabriel's departure in 1975, also their lead singer.

Collins had been a fan of *Solid Air* and didn't need to be asked twice when 'someone recommended me to John' as a potential drummer for the album.[3] The principal players on the album were linked via several existing connections. Producer Martin Levan was represented by Martyn's manager, Bruce May, and had recently made an album with Jim Rafferty, brother of Gerry. Levan had worked separately with Collins and bassist John Giblin, while Giblin had played on *Project*, the latest album by Collins' offshoot fusion band, Brand X. At the time, Martyn claimed to have had no idea who Collins was, which was absurd. Though he had not yet launched his solo career, Genesis were hardly an obscurity. Martyn would have been well aware of him, and his skill set. Linda Thompson believes he was acutely conscious of what Collins could potentially bring to both his music and his career. 'I remember going to the studio when Phil Collins was producing a record for him, and he was like, "This is going to be it."'

They met to discuss Collins' involvement. His capabilities were not in question; the crucial matter was one of temperament. Fortunately, he was an approachable man – down to earth, likeable and reliable, a multi-talented A-grade musician who wore his gifts extremely lightly. He also enjoyed a drink. He and Martyn bonded quickly over a shared love of glassy jazz-funk and their furious, masculine heartaches. At the time, Collins was going through his own painful break-up. His marriage to his first wife, Andrea, had recently ended and he was licking his wounds, beginning the process of writing the painfully sad songs that would end up on his debut album, *Face Value*.

Misery loves company, particularly company that buys a round. The two men became playmates. On occasion, Collins would visit Martyn at his flat in Brecknock Road in Tufnell Park in North London, where he had recently moved after leaving Basing Street. 'Him and Phil used to sit up late writing,' says Jeff Allen, who drummed in the 'Scottish Beatles', The Beatstalkers, in the Sixties; a respected session musician, he played with both Martyn and Collins during this period. 'You'd find them asleep on the couch in the morning sometimes, scraps of paper on the floor, with ideas for lyrics. John and Phil, I think they needed the angst of a break-up, or to ruin a relationship, in order to write great songs. That was sometimes the way I saw it. They would have a fight [with their exes], then go out together, have a drink, then [start] writing.'

In Martyn's local pub, directly downstairs from his flat, he, Collins and Allen turned out for the house darts team. One of their regular opponents was the local CID. 'They would be going back upstairs to the flat to "enhance their skills", then coming back down to play the police,' says Allen.

More frequently, Martyn would visit Collins at his house, Old Croft, in Shalford in Surrey, where he had installed an ad hoc studio in what was once the marital bedroom. He practically moved in for a time. Here, many of the songs for *Grace And Danger* were further developed, upscaling the demos into something plusher. 'I'd noticed that John was in something of a bad shape,' said Collins. 'I offered moral support by inviting him to stay here in the house where we recorded the basic tracks for *Grace* with bassist John Giblin.'[4]

In the studio, Martyn assembled a small band featuring Collins, Giblin and keyboard player Tommy Eyre of The Grease Band, who at nineteen had arranged and played Hammond organ on Joe Cocker's 'With A Little Help From My Friends'. He later played on Gerry Rafferty's 'Baker Street'. The ensemble recorded for ten days at Dick James Music Studios in Holborn in late May 1979. 'The arrangements were worked on a little bit in the studio, a lot was improvised,' says Levan. 'It was a very organic production. It was done live, playing together, with some overdubs added on.'

Levan was aware of the deeply personal context surrounding the album, but such high drama did not impinge on the session. 'He had let it out in the songs. It was clearly from the heart, and John was clearly going through a very emotional time, but I was twenty-eight, and you tend not to intellectualise it. We went to the studio and did the work. He was focused. It was a harmonious project – we had a good time in the studio. I kept my distance and I think that helped.'

The excesses were routine, businesslike, even: working rations of cocaine, mid-level drinking. They only lost one day of productivity to drug-related anxiety, when 'we had to abandon things after half an hour,' says Levan. 'No one could find their stash, they'd lost it. We had all the furniture out of the studio – nope, couldn't find it. That was it: they all went home. That was a bit of a disaster, but that was the only day. I did have to run a reasonably tight ship. It wasn't crazy hours. If there was a football match on, they would all clear off at eight o'clock. They were quite into football at the time, or at least Phil was.'

The mood between the musicians was upbeat, particularly the rapport between Martyn and his drummer. 'I fell in love with John and his music during these sessions,' said Collins. 'He and I seem to musically hit it off.'[5] The music they made gestured only faintly towards Martyn's previous work. Giblin's lyrical fretless bass was the dominant melodic texture, and synthesizers were more prominent than ever before. Both the echoplex and finger-picked acoustic guitar were largely notable by their absence.

'Hurt In Your Heart' floated on much the same reverberating drift as 'Small Hours', but the wash of ambient sound transcended its surface smoothness by virtue first of Martyn's wretchedly unhappy vocal, and later a guitar solo which fizzed like a fresh scar. *Grace And Danger* had many such moments, wherein passages which sailed close to easy listening were interrupted by the aural equivalent of a loose wire, a snagged tooth. It landed its punches covertly, in a series of ambushes.

'Save Some (For Me)' was the last song written for the record and bore the most obvious imprint of Phil Collins. The jittery pulse flitted erratically, a thin beam of infrared light being bounced around four white walls. As on the heavy funk-rock of the title track, Martyn swapped wounded soulfulness for a more barbative vocal and lyric. Another late arrival, 'Lookin' On', was cubist jazz, glitchy and restless. On stage, he would often stretch it to extraordinary lengths.

The weightiness of the themes was leavened by Martyn's decision to cut a cover of 'Johnny Too Bad', a rocksteady track originally recorded by The Slickers which featured on the soundtrack to the classic rude boy film, *The Harder They Come*, released in 1972 and starring Jimmy Cliff. Martyn had first heard the song in Jamaica, where he adopted it as 'my theme tune for a while'.[6] He embraced it as an extension of his personal mythology, adding another character to a list of alter egos which includes John the Baptist and John Wayne; like the bad man in the song, Martyn was also prone to walking down the street with a switchblade in his pocket. They worked out an arrangement in the studio and recorded it live, Martyn improvising additional lyrics. Singers from the British soul band Kokomo added uncredited backing vocals. Providing a window of light relief in an otherwise gloomy chamber, it later became the album's sole single.

Towards the end of the sessions, Martyn introduced Collins to Eric Clapton for the first time. Martyn had called Clapton looking to score drugs. Collins went along for the ride. They met in a pub in Guildford, Clapton having resisted a home visit. Collins sympathised. He had already recognised that 'John is the kind of chap who has a tendency to overstay his welcome'.[7] Shortly afterwards, Clapton came up to London to play on the final day of recording. 'It just didn't gel for some reason,' says Levan. 'Lots of different egos floating about. I tried editing some bits to try to get something, but I couldn't. I think having five destabilised the foursome.' They would make a more successful second attempt on the next record.

Martyn taped his vocals at Morgan Studios, where they also recorded synth overdubs and mixed the record in early June. He scatted around the central lyrical themes, seeking the truest tone and the turns of phrase most apt to give shape to his pain. 'He came in with a scrap of paper and sketched out ideas for lyrics,' says Levan. 'Whereas some people would improvise a guitar solo, he would improvise the lyrics. Not all of them, but quite often. It's the first time I had seen that. He would sketch out the ideas and then go in there and live it. Some of those lyrics were one-offs. It was very special.'

Beverley Martyn was given a joint songwriting credit for 'Our Love', a lush R&B groove not a million miles from Marvin Gaye at his most uxorious. According to Martyn, she had not been involved in the writing of the song, but he did it 'because it seemed a nice thing to do. It was a gesture.'[8]

For all that was left unsaid, and for all that it told one side of a very much more complex and disturbing story, *Grace And Danger* exerted a strange, sorrowful, almost narcotic pull. 'I would do that [album] different now; back then I was too busy being sad,' he said. 'It's all about Beverley.'[9] It wasn't, of course – it was all about him.

The bittersweet blend was an unsettling one, a series of near-suicidal torch songs dressed up in the plush clothes of languorous late-night mood music, with the occasional tinkle of cocktail-hour jazz. Heard in the correct context, it was emotionally searing and very powerful. If one wasn't so inclined, the second side in particular was hard work. In either case, the sadness it conveyed was overwhelming. Tracing the route from *London Conversation* to *Grace And Danger* was to travel from a land of hope and callow optimism to one flooded with bitterly hard-won cynicism. 'The gradual erosion of one's innocence is the thing,' he said. 'That's the one thing I detest, but it's a fact.'[10] The price of love, it seemed, was extortionate.

The album landed like a brick at Island Records. 'Chris Blackwell thought it was too miserable to release, which is very true,' said Martyn.[11] Martin Levan received messages from the label saying they thought it was too sad, too emotionally revealing. Blackwell concedes that 'it was the case', but he also felt that Martyn was writing himself into a 'jazz niche', which would be a hard sell in the prevailing musical climate. However gently and artfully the news was framed, in effect the record was rejected, damned to circle the release schedule, waiting more than a year for a landing slot.[12]

Astute enough to mark the way in which the wind was now blowing, and not yet ready to be pigeonholed as a kind of singing Zoot Sims, Martyn set about making some significant changes. Sandy Roberton, who ran the production, publishing and management company Worlds End, had been working with English singer-songwriter Iain Matthews. On Matthews' recent album, *Stealin' Home*, he had covered Martyn's 'The Man In The Station'. His previous record, *Hit And Run*, had featured 'One Day Without You'.

The song choices were largely down to Roberton, who had also produced Steeleye Span, Shelagh McDonald and Shirley Collins, and was 'besotted' with Martyn's music. Word of his affiliation filtered back to Martyn, who turned up out of the blue one day at Roberton's front door in West London and announced, 'Well, you must like my music because you've recorded some of my songs. Would you like to manage me?' 'Just like that,' says Roberton, who subsequently visited Martyn's current manager Bruce May to straighten things out. 'My gut feeling was that it was sort of a relief for him,' he says. 'He was fairly gracious about it, actually.'

Roberton's first visit to see his new client was instructive. Martyn stopped off at Oddbins for 'a crate of Mount Gay rum and some wine' and then proceeded to cook his new manager the hottest curry Roberton had ever tasted using Scotch bonnet peppers, before 'drinking himself to sleep'.

With *Grace And Danger* on ice indefinitely, Martyn continued to tour. He played a handful of fine solo shows in Italy in May prior to his appearance at the Glastonbury Festival on June 21, accompanied by Chris Glen on bass and Timi Donald on drums. The festival founder and organiser Michael Eavis later picked his set as one of his top five favourite Glastonbury performances. 'He was in a good mood for a change,' Eavis recalled. 'He was always drunk and slagging me off – we had quite a stormy relationship, really. But on that occasion, at that moment in time, he was perfect.'[13]

The following month Martyn played Festival Elixir on a piercingly hot day in Brittany. In the backstage trailer, he ended up in a fist-fight with John Renbourn. Jacqui McShee, who was singing with Renbourn's band, recalls that Martyn had asked, pleasantly enough, after his old friend Jo Watson, who had split up some years ago from John James and was now married to Renbourn. Detecting some ulterior motive or slight in the comment, and never Martyn's greatest fan to begin with, Renbourn growled and matters swiftly escalated.

'John Martyn went straight into his Glaswegian accent, and they grabbed each other's beards,' recalls McShee. 'John was very pissed, and he said to me, "You'd better get out of here, dear, you don't want to get hurt."' Moments later, Renbourn came tumbling out of the caravan, crashing over some beer barrels. On stage shortly afterwards, Martyn took an age tuning up, before leaning so far back on his chair he toppled over. Undeterred, he continued playing from a prostrate position.

However much Martyn was hurting, he was not mourning the end of his marriage in monastic seclusion. Solitude was not an option. 'He was totally helpless, useless, without a woman,' says Beverley Martyn. 'He never had any time without a woman. He couldn't be on his own at all.'

During the making of *Grace And Danger*, he had started seeing Gillian Allen, the younger sister of Jeff Allen. It quickly became a committed relationship. They shared the apartment in Basing Street, before moving together to the 'funky flat' in Brecknock Road.

'He was wonderful and terrible, and in a bit of a mess,' says Allen. 'He was upbeat, but profoundly sad about the break-up of his marriage. He was very emotional about his children, but really, I don't think he called them more than once a month when I was with him. Because he would get upset every time that he phoned them, I used to think he was very compassionate and caring, the perfect father. I was young and daft, and I didn't really realise that that's not how to be a parent.'

Allen was in her late twenties, Scottish, lively, and a match for Martyn. They partied, took holidays to Glendalough in County Wicklow and had 'a lot of lovely times with some lovely people. We had a lot of fun with Phil Collins. He was very supportive of John; they would spend days together. They bounced off each other really well.'

She went with Martyn to visit his mother in Surrey and gained the impression their relationship had cooled considerably over time. 'He didn't have much contact,' she says. 'When he took me to see her, I don't think he had seen her in years.' Vari McGeachy and Wesley Kutner recall meeting Betty no more than twice throughout their childhoods, and never formed a relationship with her, or her other children. Indeed, they had no meaningful contact with anyone on Martyn's side of the family. Tommy did not visit them at home, and they have no memory of ever seeing him in Glasgow or getting to know their extended clan of great-aunts and -uncles. When Martyn went back to Tantallon Road or spent time fishing at the estate in Carradale, where his uncle Robert worked as a forester, in general he did so alone or with friends rather than his family.

To everyone's relief, and only after Martyn had practically begged, *Grace And Danger* was finally released in October 1980, three years after *One World* and a year after it had been completed. It was another modest commercial success, again reaching number 54 in the UK charts.

When he took the album on the road in October and November, for the first time since the ill-fated show with Beverley at the Queen Elizabeth Hall ten years previously, he put together a full rock band, featuring Collins on drums and backing vocals, veteran session man Max Middleton on keyboards, Jeff Allen on percussion and Alan Thomson on fretless bass. Thomson was a gifted young Scottish guitarist who had spent the past years playing in The Arthur Trout Band with Martyn's cousin, David Roy. When he heard that Martyn needed a bass player for the tour, he swapped instruments, practised for two weeks flat, auditioned and got the job.

The band rehearsed diligently. On stage, Martyn typically wore a suit and cut down on his between-song patter. There was precious little joint-smoking or swigging from bottles. It brought to mind the Hunter S. Thompson maxim: 'When the going gets weird, the weird turn pro.'

Danny Thompson regarded the band format as part of a concerted business plan to rehabilitate Martyn. 'When he got a [new] manager, he called me and said, "They don't want me to work with you any more." They wanted him to get a band and make him the next Van Morrison or something. I understood that. The business side saw the potential. I used to say, "Why do you want to do that?" He'd say, "Well, I love Weather Report and those types of bands." I'd say, "But there already is a Weather Report; there's not another John Martyn." I always thought he was the geezer, sitting on stage with his Martin guitar. I was being very, very selfish [and] when he went on the road with the band, he really enjoyed it. He was still John Martyn, and all those great musicians he worked with had the same freedom. He told no one what to play. It was totally free, no rules.'

It's highly unlikely any outside agent could have persuaded Martyn to pursue a musical direction he did not believe in. The shift was a matter largely of instinct, curiosity and pragmatism. The material from *One World* and *Grace And Danger* was difficult to present satisfactorily on his own. He would continue to perform solo shows and acoustic segments his entire life, but they were rarely his preferred choice. He had become increasingly down-hearted with the limitations of the format. 'I can't tell you how frustrating it got,' he said, some years later. 'With the best will in the world, I couldn't play it like I meant it.'[14]

The echoplex was no longer fresh or cutting edge. As early as 1973, reviewers were writing of his 'self-indulgent little excursions' in reverb.[15] He came to over-rely on his signature sound, diluting its impact, while other musicians had followed in his wake, making it less distinctive still. 'It was innovative, it was great, but I think it was absolutely overused,' says Richard Thompson. 'That's the danger of toys. You fall in love with them and want to use it everywhere, and it's not always a good idea.' Having removed Martyn from many of the constraints of playing acoustically, it had ended up imposing several more. He used the technique to such a great extent that negotiating the waves of competing rhythms eventually skewed his ability to play guitar conventionally. It also raised the interesting question of which element in the partnership was leading and which following.

Martyn had started exhibiting a certain amount of bald disgust for his past. During the *Grace And Danger* tour, on November 2, 1980, he opened the band show at London's New Apollo Victoria Theatre with a solo 'May You Never', later admitting to playing it 'totally calculatingly... My one big number, ladies and gentlemen. I just did it totally cynically.'[16] When he received a gold disc for *So Far So Good*, a summation of his so-called folk years, he smashed it up, ostentatiously, in public.

Having never experienced the formative teenage rites of passage of playing in a band with his friends, in his thirties the notion seemed more exciting to him than it did to his peers, many of whom were busy going solo. The exchange of energy and ideas between a group of musicians was, he felt, now more likely to lead to something unexpected and exciting occurring on stage. He was also more protected in a band. He could do less. The musical stakes were no longer quite so high, but the possibilities were enticing.

'I know that the most fulfilling thing I could ever achieve would be to go on stage with a small unit of musicians and be so inspired that I could perform a whole set of spontaneously created music,' he told Nick Kent at the end of 1980. 'Just capture the moment at hand and perform completely impromptu, improvised music for a whole two-hour set... There have been glimpses, when I've got swept up in a mood that pushes me into going out on that limb. That's what keeps me going really. The very possibility – however slight – of finally arriving at that place where one can create pure music.'[17]

It was an honourable motive, if not the only one. In any case, what was the alternative? To continue in a diminishing circle, returning to the folk circuit with his pretty songs, was never going to be enough for Martyn, even if he occasionally harboured a fantasy that it might. Instead of resting on his laurels, he rose to meet the challenge of a new age. He had, at least, a head start, having pledged no affiliation to any specific musical cause. 'I wouldn't like to be sitting still,' he said, 'while everyone else is moving.'[18] Perhaps foreseeing that the Eighties would not be inclined to kindness towards hairy men clutching acoustic guitars, he sharpened his look and his elbows and came out fighting, shining himself up for the shiniest of decades: shiny sharp suits, shiny LinnDrum rhythms, shiny synths and a shiny electric guitar, with which he made strange, phased, shiny sheets of noise.

The only thing not shined up was his voice, which in the ensuing years began taking increasingly scenic routes around the melody, sometimes to the point of wilful eccentricity. 'Sandy Roberton and I used to get really frustrated,' says Jeff Allen. 'He started to get into this grunting and garbled singing style, which was a bit weird, because you couldn't really hear the vocal properly.'

For a while it worked. The early band shows were tight, inventive and punchy, while the albums he made in the early Eighties were the most commercially successful of his career. Martyn enjoyed a run of Top 40 chart placings in Britain, significantly better than anything he had achieved in the Seventies.

In exchange, the music lost a degree of swerve and swagger, and Martyn cashed in a fair chunk of his maverick status. The dedicated margin-hanger, the paid-up non-joiner, was now edging towards the centre. 'When he tried to become more commercial, I think he lost a little of that power,' says Richard Thompson. 'I always thought he should have clung to his great virtues as an individual. That was what made him stand out in a crowd.'

The *Grace And Danger* tour was a success, even if some nights it was possible to see the cogs whirring. 'He was trying,' says Mark Cooper, 'and I don't think I'd ever seen John try before.' Phil Collins found it a rejuvenating experience, but he would only do it once. Martyn was 'extremely, but lovably, unpredictable… it seems like he's hell-bent on self-destruction'.[19] Off the road, the two heart-sore friends played music, laughed hysterically, drank to excess and took turns calling their ex-wives to vent at them. 'It always end[ed] in shouting and the phone going down,' Collins recalled.[20]

At the other end of the line, Beverley remembered these late-night calls from Martyn as unwanted and sometimes disturbing intrusions, often culminating with him demanding to know whom she had left him for. The financial ramifications of their parting rumbled on for years. He paid the mortgage on Kenana, but nothing more. In the divorce settlement, 'I never received a penny from him,' wrote Beverley.[21]

'I think he was definitely seething about the fact of his past [records] with me and Beverley dragging him down, and that may have been part of the reason why he refused to send her any money,' says Joe Boyd, who visited Beverley in Heathfield after the marriage had ended. 'I got a call from Susie Watson Taylor, who had worked for Witchseason and stayed in close touch with Beverley, saying she was in terrible shape, that John hadn't given her any money for eight months or something… Susie and I drove down to visit Beverley and she was really almost raving. She was so disturbed. It was very disturbing to see her.' Boyd gave her money to buy groceries. Friends like Art Garfunkel, Roger Daltrey and Wilko Johnson also tried to help out where they could, but the combination of financial and psychological pressures caused the family intense hardship.

'We were left destitute,' says Wesley Kutner. 'I would have to go to the headmaster's office to ask for a food voucher. I'd wait to be last in the queue so I wasn't embarrassed. Mum didn't have any money for lunch. There was nothing.'

'Leaving us in poverty did a huge amount of damage on every level,' says Vari McGeachy. 'It put a huge amount of stress on Beverley, way too much stress, and we all suffered because of it. [We were left] in a big house that was falling down, freezing goddamn cold, everything was malfunctioning, mould was growing off the walls. It was tough. It was increasingly hard to make ends meet or give us any little treats.

That was probably the worst thing that John did – that, when he went, he didn't keep in touch and [he sent] no money. Again, that was about control. There seemed to always be money on hand when he wanted it and needed it, throughout his life, but if you asked whether he had any, or had enough, the answer would probably be no.'

Martyn spun a very different story while airing his dirty laundry in public. He told the writer Chris Salewicz that he was bound by the terms of a 'crippling financial settlement' and that, rather than the children seeing the benefit of his payments, 'it's all for Beverley,' whom, he added magnanimously, 'I still like'.[22]

Through the other end of the telescope, Sandy Roberton was under no such illusions. He was in at the deep end, dealing with the unremitting chaos of Martyn's financial and personal life. 'The phone would ring in my office and it would be the bank manager: "I need to talk to you about Mr McGeachy and the bank account." That was every day. John was writing out cheques and paying for food and drinks and they were bouncing. He was always in financial problems. Beverley was calling, she would be trying to get me to talk to him about stuff. It was just awful. I just sensed that she was permanently in financial straits. To this day I'm sure he didn't pay any alimony. John wasn't giving her any money. It was very strange.'

Managing Martyn had already become a white-knuckle ride, a daily attempt to pilot a safe route through extreme turbulence. In the early winter of 1980, the band played a short tour of Italy. In Milan, on November 23, Martyn refused to go on stage unless he was brought cocaine.

'Now, I'm not a drug dealer,' says Roberton. 'Somehow, I managed to find out from people around the hotel where I can find a dealer for him. I go to this building and it looks like one of those buildings in *Gomorrah*. I go up to the apartment and this guy comes to the door, wearing a wife-beater white vest. I go into the kitchen, I'm carrying the band's float, and I get some cocaine for him so that the show can go on. Going down the stairwell afterwards, I think, God, what have I just done? I could have been killed here. I got it to him and I said, "Look, I'm not managing you to deal with shit like this," and I had a bit of a barney at him. It was almost blackmail: "I'm not doing the show unless you get me this.'"

The following day, in the back seat of a car en route to an appearance on a local radio show, Martyn heaped a small hillock of cocaine onto the end of his flick knife, leaned forwards, and shoved it under the nose of the horrified young woman driving him.

Yet, no matter what drama was occurring in the wings, 'the music was always really important,' says Roberton. 'On a tour, if there was no sound-mixer, I would do it. He would never play each song the same every night, and it made you really listen and love it. I would just stand there listening to this amazing music, and it was almost enough to make you forget all the other stuff.'

alued his friendship. It was a classic father/daughter relationship, but it came later in life.' At home with daughter, Mhairi (now Vari), in Hastings, 1975. *(Brian Cooke/Redferns)*

ry big and wilful, we were.' Martyn on stage with his finest foil and fellow troublemaker, nny Thompson. *(Brian Cooke/Redferns)*

'I write "Big Muff", and we also have Big Puff'. Lee 'Scratch' Perry with a copy of *One World*, Edinburgh, 2019. *(Graeme Thomson)*

'The whole experience was pure magic.' Scenes from the recording of *One World* at Woolwich Green Farr summer 1977. *(Courtesy Phill Brown)*

or a while I had a reputation as a real bad boy. This man was going to punch you out, shoot you or fuck u.' Martyn not quite going straight in the early Eighties. *(Janette Beckman/Getty)*

'They were a bit self-destructive. They weren't a good couple to be together.' Martyn with his second wife Annie Furlong, and (above right) at their wedding in Edinburgh in 1983. (*Courtesy Volker Bredebusch*)

'They never had a falling out. It was just about the music and having a good time.' With his lifelong friend and mentor, Hamish Imlach, Glasgow, January 1981. (*Courtesy Fiona Imlach*)

... had a terrific eye for beauty, and a terrific love and respect for nature.' Making a new friend at ...erton. *(Courtesy Volker Bredebusch)*

...u would rock up and hear all this racket, and you knew where he was.' Martyn's base camp at Roberton. ...ckwise from top: his rehearsal outhouse; the church with one bell; and his cottage, pictured in more ...ent times. *(Graeme Thomson)*

'On a good night it was just electric. He was such a force.' On stage at the Shaw Theatre, London, March 1990. *(David Redfern/Redferns)*

`He had come to resemble the middle-ranking gangster of his youthful imaginings.' Martyn in the mid-Nineties. *(Andrew Lepley/Redferns)*

wards the end, it really felt like a proper band.' Post amputation, during rehearsals for the *Solid Air* tour,
ly 2007, with (L-R) Arran Ahmun, Martin Winning, Alan Thomson and Spencer Cozens.
urtesy John Hillarby)

's so far ahead of everything, it's almost
onceivable.' Receiving his lifetime achievement
:olade from Phil Collins at the BBC Radio 2
k Awards, February 2008. *(Richard Young/*
utterstock)

'He got a year for free at the end.' Teresa Walsh
and Vari McGeachy accept Martyn's OBE at
Buckingham Palace, March 27, 2009 – two months
after his death. *(Ian Nicholson/WPA Pool/Getty)*
Overleaf: *(Brian Cooke/Redferns)*

10

Martyn became a father again in January 1981. He and Gillian Allen had moved back to Scotland the previous year. They came first to 10 Tantallon Road. Now in his early sixties, Tommy was in poor health and exhibiting increasingly erratic behaviour.

When Martyn was touring with Steve Tilston in the winter of 1978, Tommy had turned up on November 30, St Andrew's Day, at the show at Glasgow Pavilion. Using a walking stick and wearing a deerstalker hat, he watched his son perform. 'He was quite theatrical,' says Tilston. 'He was in his cups a bit, and I remember while John was playing, he was bending my ear: "Why is he called John Martyn? Why has he called himself John Martyn? His name is Ian McGeachy. He's got a perfectly good Scottish name." Afterwards, John was really quite horrible to him and I was quite embarrassed. He was quite brutal with his dad.'

When Martyn and his band played another hometown show at Green's Playhouse a couple of years later, during a quiet number a voice rang out from the audience. 'It was his father,' says Jeff Allen. 'In the middle of the gig, this old boy stood up with a walking stick, waving it at the stage. "I'll see you later, son! I'm away to the pub!"' Sandy Roberton recalls that Tommy 'had a cane, and he walked along the front row seats and said, "See you later, my boy!" It was so eccentric.'

According to Gillian Allen, Tommy was often extremely difficult to be around in close quarters, as was Martyn, making relations frequently strained. Alcohol was a significant complicating factor. Tragically, Martyn's childhood fears had been realised: both father and son were now alcoholics. Tantallon Road had become a somewhat faded version of its former glory. 'It was absolutely falling to bits,' says Allen. 'Untreated floorboards, old lino. We got a few things in from the antique shop.'

After Allen discovered she was pregnant in May, she and Martyn moved a couple of miles away, to a cottage on Humbie Road, at the back end of Newton Mearns on the outer edges of Glasgow. It was while living here that Ruari was born by Caesarean section on January 14, 1981, in Rottenrow Maternity Hospital. 'John was there, hysterical, as I was being cut open,' says Allen. 'He had more people around him than me.' Martyn had insisted that the birth take place north of the border, in order that the child had a fighting chance of playing rugby for Scotland.

Living back in Glasgow seemed to bring out the nostalgist in him. Shortly after the birth, he turned up at the Star Folk Club on Waterloo Street on a cold Thursday night to see Hamish Imlach, still plying his wares, still top of the bill. Martyn arrived in double denim and stood at the back of the room watching the floor spots. The unfortunate act which performed an underwhelming and thoroughly ill-timed version of 'Over The Hill' muttered their apologies to him as they came off stage.

Martyn borrowed a guitar from Scottish folk singer Dave Dick – 'it would be an honour,' said Dick; Martyn winced and glared – to play with Imlach. Afterwards, he was invited by Dick to come along to the gig he and his partner, Jim Gilbert, were playing the following night in a vegetarian café in the West End. Not only did Martyn show up, he joined in, even backing the duo on some of their own songs. 'I never get to do this,' he told Dick. 'Give us some more of that slide.' Most of the clientele had no idea who he was and simply ignored them while they ate. 'He was friendly, kind and courteous to two unknown musicians,' says Dick. He was also sober.

Shortly afterwards, he and Allen moved to Moscow in Ayrshire, a tiny village five miles east of Kilmarnock. They saw a lot of Imlach and his family, who lived a short distance east along the motorway. Hamish's wife Wilma was the first person to babysit the new arrival.

His girlfriend and their son accompanied Martyn when he went to London to make his next album. For the first time in his career, he was recording for a label other than Island. Did he jump or was he pushed? A little of both. Island did not exactly drop Martyn, but they did not try terribly hard to keep him, either. The scuffles over *Grace And Danger* had been portentous. Their initial refusal to release the album had deeply upset Martyn, who had always understood that, no matter what else was up for debate, his creativity would be allowed to flow unfettered. The bottom line, however, was financial. 'They offered me a tiny amount of money for a new record,' said Martyn, who claimed he hung up on the 'minion' who phoned him with the grisly details. 'That was that, but I bear no ill will.'[1]

Performing with a full band and with a more sophisticated sound and lighting rig, the margins of profitability were far tighter than in the days when he had traversed the country's railways with a guitar, an amp and a few pedals. Often, he was struggling to break even.

'The deal that he had with Island was shockingly bad,' says Sandy Roberton, who reviewed the contract as part of a general audit of Martyn's career. 'The royalty rate was really low, overseas royalties were 50 per cent. I went to see Chris Blackwell to talk to him about it, but he was fairly non-committal.' Blackwell does not recall any conversations about Martyn leaving the label. Roberton ended up going to see Island's general manager, Tom Hayes, and exploiting a legal loophole. 'I found a way [out],' he says. 'I can't remember to this day, but there was something in his contract that they were meant to have done that they didn't do, and I was able to get him out.'

He signed with Warner–Elektra–Atlantic (WEA) for the next two albums. He had been writing steadily with a fresh sense of perspective. 'I want to play faster for a change,' he said. '[The new songs] are a breakaway from the general more ponderous rhythms I've been working on for most of *One World* and certainly *Grace And Danger*. A change is definitely desirable anyway and right now that more aggressive, speedier style is the sound I find most appealing.'[2]

Some of the new material had been bedded in live with the band. The dark, frantic jazz-funk of 'Amsterdam' and a new, electric version of 'Couldn't Love You More' were performed in concert at Stirling University on February 25, 1981, a show filmed and broadcast the following week on the BBC's *Rock Goes to College* slot. Jeff Allen, who had only recently started playing drums with Martyn in his touring band, saw first-hand how seriously he took the music.

'He made a mistake in one song, and at the end of the show he got really angry and rushed to the recording truck. He said, "We've got to do that again"… The producer said, "No, no, it's okay, John," [but] he made them do it. "No, you're not having any of this stuff unless we do it again." We had to go back on and do it again as an encore. He'd come in wrong with the intro or something, something that nobody would have really noticed but him. This one little thing irked him.'

The shows were generally sharp and almost disconcertingly well drilled but with a looseness that the musicians appreciated. 'You could play however you wanted to play, within the confines of his arrangement of the song,' says Allen. 'Even if you took it somewhere slightly different, it was interesting for him. There's not many people like that.'

As Steve Sutherland put it, only half-jokingly, in his *Melody Maker* review of a May 1981 concert at the Dominion Theatre, 'John Martyn has forsaken his traditionally tasteful low profile of protracted inter-tour siestas and legless hit-or-miss on-stage binges in a concerted effort to become, as he so lovably and laughably puts it, "a superstar in my spare time."'[3]

For the new album, he took his touring band into the studio – Alan Thomson on bass, Danny Cummings on percussion and Max Middleton on keyboards. They recorded at the Townhouse, where Nick Launay was in-house engineer. At twenty-one, Launay had just made *The Flowers Of Romance* with Public Image Limited and had been working on *The Dreaming* with Kate Bush, two pioneering and highly experimental albums. Martyn and his band offered a wholly different flavour – smooth, consummate musicianship.

Martyn wanted Phil Collins to produce as well as play drums, and he was happy to comply. Collins arrived at the Townhouse on the heels of a huge solo hit with 'In The Air Tonight', a stark electronic ballad with a gargantuan drum sound, recorded in the studio's famous 'stone room'. His number one debut album, *Face Value*, had followed in February. The blokey rock muso playing in a pub darts team with Martyn a year ago was now an internationally successful pop star.

Little wonder, perhaps, that the drums on *Glorious Fool* are prominent to the point of intrusion. Who could blame Martyn for hoping that a little of that commercial fairy dust might flutter in his direction? With Alan Thomson's floating fretless bass rarely settling in one spot for long, the arrangements bordered on big and busy. For some, the new rock dynamics and additional layering of instruments created a clinical distance between Martyn and the listener. For others, he was bravely embarking on a new creative venture, one in which distinctive songs and the old sense of intimacy would prove less important than the style, the sound, the overall sonic picture.

Collins and Martyn were a less natural fit as producer and artist than they had been on *Grace And Danger*, where they were simply two musicians and friends working together. They got on well, but Collins was organised to the point of anal retention, armed each day with a running order. Martyn, on the other hand, was long a creature of mercurial moods and whims who made it a point of honour never to play the same way twice.

'John at that time was slightly lost, very unorganised, and Phil stepped in with a lot of optimism,' says Launay. 'He had lists and a plan, whereas John's was completely a jazz approach. If we had to go back to fix something, even an hour later, he had already retuned his guitar to something else and couldn't remember what the previous tuning was. I think Phil sometimes was a little frustrated: "How can you not remember what you played?" It was absolute chaos, but it didn't matter because it all sounded good.'

Martyn was living on site, in apartments above the studio belonging to the Townhouse, often with Allen and Ruari, who was still only a few months old. While he was recording there, Jeff Beck had a party in the studio, attended by the great and the good of the British rock scene, including Jimmy Page. Martyn 'was very badly behaved,' says Allen. 'I took the baby and left, I was so embarrassed. He just made a fool of himself.' Her last memory of Martyn is him lying on stage singing old Scottish folk songs.

He drank steadily through the album sessions, to the point where he would be amiably soused at the end of each night. His instructions to the engineers were relayed in the dry, over-enunciated style of Chic Murray: "Excuse me, young man, would it be possible to have approximately 13 per cent more reverb on my vocal?"; "If it's not too much trouble, young man, could I have my guitar a notch louder?" 'I was always very amused by him,' says Launay. 'I thought he was great. Recording vocals with him, I was just transfixed by his voice. I remember thinking it was like treacle and honey, just beautiful.'

Often, he and Launay were the only ones left in the studio in the small hours. They would put the world to rights as the engineer tidied up. In his early thirties, Martyn already seemed older than his years and slightly world-weary. 'I remember him asking me about punk rock,' says Launay. 'He was touring a lot and playing the same venues as a lot of those bands. I don't think he listened to it, but he was interested. I used to wear brothel creepers and skinny jeans, and he said, "Tell me, are you a Teddy boy?" I said, "No, I'm more of a punk." He asked me to explain to him what that was about. I said it was about rebellion and not having rules and not doing what you're supposed to. He said, "Ah, I can understand that." I remember thinking he was a rebel at heart. He was a punk, he didn't conform to any rules.'

After these chats, Martyn would often wander away down Goldhawk Road in his night attire, listening to the day's work on a Sony Walkman. Launay would see him as he was travelling home on his motorbike in the first hours of morning. 'There he was, walking towards Shepherd's Bush in his dressing gown and slippers, with his headphones taped to his head. I thought, God, I hope he's all right. A lot of his songs had a melancholy and sadness to them, the lyrics were about very personal things. I definitely felt that, but I don't think I was old enough to understand that he might have been in pain.'

Glorious Fool was a creditable effort within the terms of its remit. The malevolently moody 'Amsterdam' was another angry death song, written for an unnamed spiritual brother who had committed suicide in the Dutch capital after falling in love with a prostitute. By the end of it, Martyn sounded emotionally wrung out. The title track cooked up a compelling mood over a shuffling rhythm, with a lyric which took aim at the lies of the current US president, Ronald Reagan. Sociopolitical themes were more overt than was customary. 'Don't You Go', a modern Celtic ballad created from little more than a keyboard and sound-pad drone, was a spectral anti-war lament. These were the highlights. Just as typical was the frantic vacuity of 'Didn't Do That'.

There was a sense of a new signing trying to impress, or at least not alienate, a new record company. WEA launched the album with a glossy colour booklet and a new biography, effectively introducing Martyn to a fresh audience. At thirty-three, he was now something of an elder statesman. In interviews, where he was already becoming as revered for his drunken exploits and wild ways as for his music – a red flag for any artist – he veered between proclamations of deep happiness and agonising over his divorce and its fallout. These conversations almost felt like extensions of his live performances – feverishly extemporised affairs filled with jokes, sudden detours, bad puns, fantasy, philosophising and great emotional splurges where no personal detail was deemed off-limits. He seemed satisfied with the music he was making inasmuch as it wasn't like anything he had made before.

Steve Sutherland's positive review in *Melody Maker* called the album a 'blatant bid for the long deserved big time, emphatically more mainstream than its predecessors, and reminiscent of Collins' soulful solo efforts', all of which was correct.[4] Graham Lock, in a scathing review for *NME*, heard only 'upmarket competence… the unruly maverick has become neat, tidy and polite. There is no drive, no depth to *Glorious Fool*; no grace or danger.'[5] This also had the clear ring of truth.

Martyn and the band took the album on the road on its release in October 1981. 'The tour did really well,' says Sandy Roberton. 'It was a step up for him and it was very well organised.' 'Well organised' was not a phrase many would have previously associated with Martyn. He was now in the world of morning calls, scheduled load-ins and thickly sheaved tour itineraries, playing major theatres in all the main British cities, including the Hammersmith Odeon in West London.

With Phil Collins now embarking on several years of pan-global ubiquity, Jeff Allen returned on drums. He and Martyn riffed on a recurring absurd joke which sustained them through the tour. *Two hippopotamuses are standing in the river. One turns to the other and says, Is it Thursday today?* It seemed to make as much sense as anything else.

'Everything with John was to the extreme: eating, drinking, smoking, women,' says Jeff Allen. 'Whatever was going on, he was at the absolute edge of his capabilities. Just keeping him alive. He would have dark rum and Coke for breakfast when he was drinking. He was a strange animal. There's a few Scottish people I know that turn into Dr Jekyll and Mr Hyde. John was a little bit like that. He'd do mad, off-the-wall stuff. I can remember sitting in a pub in Dublin. There was a couple of girls there and John started to eat the glass he was drinking out of. I mean, really eating the glass, with blood on his face and his lips. Cutting himself. He had these bizarre traits. He was a very complex character. I loved him dearly, although he wasn't very good to my sister, I'm afraid, in the end.'

By the end of the year, Martyn's relationship with Gillian Allen was in disarray. He had wanted them to marry but his decree absolute was not yet through. What had been a relatively happy and healthy relationship until that point changed following the birth of their son. 'I'd stopped doing everything he liked doing – smoking, drinking, everything – and I saw another side of him completely,' says Allen. 'He started on the vodka and orange for breakfast and all that. He'd come up with this thing: "Domesticity is the death of an artist." He quoted that to me, often.'

While he was away on tour, she was subjected to his extreme possessiveness. 'He was very jealous. He would ring me up in the middle of the night: "Who are you with? I expect you're out with your friends." "I think you're a lesbian." All kinds of things.' 'Call Me', a sweet soul song which appeared a decade later on *Cooltide*, is rooted in the deeply ingrained insecurity Martyn felt while apart from all his significant lovers. He and Allen fought frequently, and loudly, but the arguments never turned physical. 'I'd say, "If you ever touch me, I will stab you" – and he believed me. He never ever laid a finger on me, never even pushed me.'

They divided their time between London and the village of Moscow, with frequent trips to Ireland. Together, they found the cottage in Roberton which would become Martyn's home base for the next twenty years. A tiny dot in rural South Lanarkshire, Roberton lies just off a ribbon of country road, out of sight yet well connected to the M74 motorway. The village sits on the ridge of a steep ravine, with hills on either side, through which flows a tributary of the River Clyde. It is beautiful and peaceful, perfectly situated for hunting and fishing.

Martyn's cottage was twenty paces up a narrow lane running off the only road through the village, tucked behind a converted church. It was a characterful longhouse, painted white, with narrow windows. 'It was small, quite dinky, but John loved it,' says Foss Paterson, who played keyboards with Martyn during the last twenty years of his career. 'It was cosy, hippie-ish, with lots of nice bits and pieces.' Martyn had a near obsession with filling his homes with antiques, bric-a-brac and trinkets – he would rarely leave a junk shop or restoration yard empty-handed. They were not practical additions, intended instead to create a mood and perhaps start a conversation. His acquisitive impulses had an obsessive edge. He would buy items on a whim and then forget all about them. 'I remember on tour, leaving Holland, and I got in the bus and it was full of African spears and shields he'd acquired from somewhere,' says Gerry Conway, who played drums with Martyn in the Eighties. In the living room, above the fireplace with its iron wood-burning stove, he hung an ornate seventeenth-century French mirror, a portrait of Robbie Burns, two Buddhas and a china scroll displaying the Lord's Prayer.

The front door opened directly onto a staircase which led upstairs to three bedrooms. To the right of the stairs was the living room, to the left the kitchen, and in the centre a small room in which Martyn kept his instruments and equipment, a sound-mixer and a Fostex eight-track. Behind the house was an outbuilding, which he later converted into a cramped rehearsal space. 'You would rock up and hear all this racket, and you knew where he was,' says Phil Shackleton. During the many years he lived there, Martyn's impact on the local community could resemble that of a boulder tossed into a millpond.

The cottage wasn't habitable when he bought it. By the time it was ready to live in, Gillian Allen had had a change of heart. 'He went on a tour and didn't come back,' she says. 'I'd really had enough of him. I hired a car and just left.' She returned to London with their son. The relationship was off and on and off again for several months. 'He made me think I was going mad, because one minute I loved him and then I loathed him. He was exhausting. I had to cut off at some point, and I did. I fell out of love with him, thankfully.'

Matters reached a head in May 1982, when Martyn suffered a nasty accident at Roberton. He had been out fishing, and while trying to jump over a fence he had slipped and impaled himself on a post, which sliced through his chest and punctured his lung. It was a serious injury, 'like a grenade had gone off in his armpit,' says Roberton. He was admitted to hospital for several days, where he recovered in his own fashion. 'I went into the hospital to see him, and he had two 2-litre bottles of Bacardi and Coke, disguised in Coke bottles, beside his bed,' says Jim Imlach. 'He's got one of those builder's belts with loads of pockets, and it's stuffed full of black dope. I went in to visit him sober and left totally smashed.'

In London, Allen had heard about the accident from her brother, Jeff, who came around to tell her the news. 'I didn't love him, but I cared, so I phoned the hospital,' she says. 'They said, "Oh, you can't speak to him just now, his wife's in with him." I thought, *Beverley?* Then Jeff said, "Gillian, you are so naive. It's Annie." I had no idea. It had been going on for a year.'

The woman in the hospital was Annie Furlong, who in 1983 would become Martyn's second wife. They had first met in the summer of 1980 at Lisdoonvarna, an annual Irish music festival held in the tiny spa town in County Clare. According to Martyn, their relationship had started in May 1981, when Ruari was five months old. They had been seeing each other for a year before Martyn punctured his lung and Allen belatedly found out, although it was already common knowledge among his friends.

'He called me and said, "Okay, Jim, my name's going to be mud. I've met this beautiful woman..."' says Jim Imlach. Furlong had been staying with him at Roberton, a situation that caused a cooling in relations between Martyn and a disapproving Wilma Imlach. 'My mother had known Beverley, and liked Gilly,' says Imlach. 'She said, "That's it, I'm finished with it."'

Furlong was originally from Wexford but was based in Dublin. She had done some modelling and worked in the entertainment industry, initially as a PA for the Irish film-maker and producer Tiernan MacBride. In the late Seventies, she was appointed manager at Windmill Lane on Dublin Quays, the recording studio used by U2 throughout the Eighties. As manager, Furlong was the interface between the artist and the technical staff, handling the bookings, scheduling and social functions, making sure the wheels turned smoothly and that everyone felt comfortable.

'She was the first studio manager at Windmill Lane, and a good one,' says the producer Brian Masterton, who, as director of the studio at that time was Furlong's boss. 'She brought a bit of glamour and pizzazz to it. She really knew how to celebrate the end of an album! She was vivacious, outgoing, very beautiful, and a lovely person. Quiet in her own way.' Vari McGeachy, who got to know Annie in the mid-Eighties, saw her as 'complicated. Very beautiful. Intelligent. Kind of fragile. A little bit brittle as well...'

Once she started seeing Martyn, their relationship developed quickly. 'There was a going-away party at Windmill Lane, and [John] was the reason she was leaving,' says Masterton. 'There was a bit of trepidation, among her girlfriends particularly, who warned her that it was dangerous to commit that much. But she was in love.' Furlong left the city, gave up her career and moved into the cottage at Roberton, and the talk turned to marriage.

During this period, perhaps inevitably, Martyn struggled to focus on making his second album for WEA. Sandy Roberton was producing this time at RAK Studios on a considerably tighter budget, following the relatively modest returns of *Glorious Fool*. Martyn was now swimming in the world of hit singles and hit albums. 'They wanted a much more commercial or semi-commercial record,' says Roberton.

Pre-production had begun in Martyn's music room in Roberton, but the momentum was halted when he was hospitalised. 'It was sounding really great up there, and if that had continued it might have been a little bit more of an adventurous record, but John was just not that well,' says Roberton. 'It was one of those situations [where] the tour was getting booked, and the album was going to come out on this date. It was in this big machine.'

Such was the poor state of his health, some of the backing tracks were recorded without him. 'Without Alan Thomson and me and the engineers, that record would have never been made,' says Roberton. 'We sort of made that record without John, really.' The band at RAK comprised Thomson, Jeff Allen and Danny Cummings, with Jim Prime and Geraint Watkins adding keyboards. When he did come to the studio, Martyn scribbled notes on a cardboard record sleeve, filling it with alternative lyric ideas and discarded song titles: 'Driftwood'; 'Suck It And See'; 'Try It On Your Teeth'.

His least committed record to date, *Well Kept Secret*, was released in August 1982 and, as is the manner of such things, gave Martyn his only Top 20 album. 'Gun Money' and 'Love Up' raised a little heat at one extreme, while the slurpy sax and twinkling tastefulness of his cover of Johnny Ace's 1954 single 'Never Let Me Go' cast a sleepy fireside spell at the other. 'Hiss On The Tape' was a dead ringer for Robert Palmer. The rest was the sound of Martyn sounding cool and relatively contemporary, but it lacked the imprimatur of his unique musical personality. There was plenty of craft, but no longer much room for the sublime. The view in *Melody Maker* was that it represented 'a troubled stab at relevance... a mixture of heady experiment and gratuitous change for change's sake', which seemed about right.[6]

Whereas previously one simply took it as a matter of faith that Martyn had been moved to make music out of some urgent necessity, now it felt more like he was trapped in the industry cycle and learning a whole new set of skills on the job. Embracing the techno sheen of the times was a bold move for someone as deeply rooted in the human-divined power of music as Martyn, but the results were not anywhere near as radical as that shift might suggest. The irony was that going outside his comfort zone ultimately brought Martyn into a world of greater orthodoxy. *Well Kept Secret* was not terribly far removed from the work of every other sharp-suited male with a seductively grainy voice singing slickly processed R&B and soul, among them Palmer, Collins, Paul Young, Michael McDonald, Joe Cocker and a similarly rebranded Steve Winwood. The difference was that almost all of them were recording stronger material.

The tour that followed was the biggest of Martyn's career: five weeks traversing the UK, playing twenty-nine shows at venues ranging from capacities of 1,200 to 3,500. Beforehand, he spent two weeks staying in the Chelsea Cloisters hotel, conducting interviews and rehearsing with the band every day at John Henry's studios. This was followed by two days on a sound stage at Shepperton fine-tuning the set with the lights and sound board.

At the final show at Hammersmith Odeon on October 22, Phil Collins flew in from Sweden, where he had been promoting a solo album by Frida from ABBA, which he had produced earlier in the year. He played drums on a few songs, sang 'Sweet Little Mystery' with Martyn and made sure everything was shipshape. 'Phil was sorting the sound out, running around in the sound check,' says Jeff Allen. 'It was already a good gig, but it went through the roof when he came on and sang.'

Philentropy, a live album released independently late in 1983, gives a strong flavour of the dynamic of Martyn's shows during this time: synths and keyboards to the fore, Martyn's electric guitar loud and harsh on a fussy rearrangement of 'Johnny Too Bad'. With its spare reverbed guitar notes and hectic melodic bass, 'Lookin' On' was reminiscent of The Police. There was plenty of virtuosity and attack, but in terms of intimacy his voice was left to do much of the heavy lifting. His phrasing, always idiosyncratic, had now reached the point where words and melodies were mere benchmarks for wider exploration. The style divided opinion, both then and now. Those who had once loved him most fervently often felt the keenest sense of betrayal.

'In this dislikeable group, with its flat-handed drummer, superfluous percussionist and preposterously insensitive keyboardist, Martyn simply plugs in his heavy metal guitar,' wrote Richard Cook in his *NME* review of the Hammersmith Odeon show. 'It's tiresome, it's lazy, it's wasteful.'[7] Cook went on in similar fashion for some time. Martyn forever enjoyed a degree of critical goodwill, but he was seen increasingly as an artist who had chosen a path that seemed counter-intuitive to his gifts and slightly baffling.

The tour stretched into 1983, with solo shows in Australia and New Zealand. Sandy Roberton and his partner at Worlds End, Paul Brown, drew lots to see who would accompany Martyn to the Antipodes. The loser had to go with him. Brown picked the short straw and packed his bags. Having run his keeper ragged throughout the tour, Martyn drank for the entire flight home. 'When I went to pick them up at Heathrow, I'll never forget Paul's face,' says Roberton. 'He said, "I just can't deal with that guy any more." Paul never had anything to do with him after that.'

The final act was also nigh for Roberton. It arrived on the American leg of the tour in May 1983. The entourage was due to leave New York in the morning for that night's show in Chicago, but Martyn refused to get up. Roberton got hold of the pass key for his hotel room, went in and started pulling off the bed sheets.

'He leaped at me and started punching the hell out of me. I retaliated and started punching him. He broke or cracked a rib on me, and I closed one of his eyes. I said, "That's it, that's it. We're going to drive to Chicago, we're going to do the gig without you, John. Bye." Somehow, he paid for a driver and he and Annie got to the gig and he did that show with one eye half closed. I thought, I can't be involved in this. I went back to London and he came back and nothing really changed. I got these phone calls from his bank manager and then there would be a message from Beverley. I thought, I can't deal with all this, so I resigned. He never forgave me for that. He was really, really annoyed. I left him. Not allowed.'

There were other farewells. After the *Well Kept Secret* promotional cycle came to its conclusion, Martyn parted ways with WEA. His time there had been defined by two commercially successful records and the most organised and orthodox tours of his career, with fine musicians in prestigious venues. It had reaped tangible rewards, yet in the end it felt like a theoretical experiment in accessibility, playing with the idea of commercialism rather than really committing to it. Somehow, at the end of it all, Martyn was left in a more precarious position than before.

At the end of 1983, he released *Philentropy* independently – a throwback to *Live At Leeds* almost a decade earlier and done for similar reasons – to turn a quick profit. The album effectively drew a line under Martyn's big-band era, which in the end couldn't pay its way. He contemplated returning to solo performance and didn't relish the thought, although he was sometimes left with no option, as when he performed alone at Glastonbury in June 1984. Fans were always delighted to see him in what many felt was his purest natural state, but he regarded it as a retrograde step.

The entire period was, he said later, 'a sticky bit'.[8] During this time, Martyn had no contact with any of his four children. Wesley, Vari and Spenser were still living in Heathfield with Beverley, who was raising them in impoverished circumstances. His youngest son Ruari had been living in London with his mother since she and Martyn split up. In the autumn of 1982, after several months without contact, Martyn asked for a meeting with them. They went for lunch in Soho, during which he told Gillian Allen he was going to marry Annie Furlong (at the same time saying explicitly that he knew it would be a mistake). Marriage seemed to be the only means by which he felt secure in a relationship. He and Annie wed the following year, in Edinburgh.

At the end of the lunch with Allen, as they said their goodbyes, Martyn started to weep. His son was barely eighteen months old, and he would never see him again. 'That man, with such compassion, with such a beautiful heart and the beautiful words he used to write, never got in touch with Ruari,' says Allen. 'Not a birthday card, not a Christmas card, not a penny.'

When Gillian Allen married six years later, her husband adopted Ruari, who took his surname. In the mid-Nineties, when he was entering his teens and exploring music, the boy grew curious about his natural father. His mother told him she had no objection to him contacting Martyn if he felt he would like to. Allen still had a phone number for the cottage at Roberton and called to talk it through with him. Although it was the first time they had spoken in more than a decade, Martyn acted as though they had last met the previous week. He asked her to tell him a joke. 'I'm not phoning to tell jokes,' said Allen. 'It's Ruari – I think maybe he might like to meet you.' There was a short silence, then a response: 'Tell him I'm dead.'

PART TWO

Rolling Home

I

We are in the beer garden, John Martyn and me. Two decades have passed. Ample time to reflect and repent.

'I'm not nearly as wild as I should have been, really,' he says. 'Could have had *more* fun. I did frolic for a while, but, as for being a wild man, that's been overplayed. I don't rob banks, I don't steal. The average yob on a Saturday night outdoes me a thousand times. I've been a bit of a Jack the Lad, but what do you expect?'

In the movie that will never be made of Martyn's life, there would have been a redemptive arc, a sharp right angle on the road between then and now, a turning towards the light. If there had been no such pronounced change, of course, there was, at least, a gentle curving movement here and there as the path narrowed. It would be hard for an intelligent man who had lost his leg and his looks, who grew apart from many friends and most of his family, not to reflect. The albums released directly before and after his death, *On The Cobbles* and *Heaven And Earth*, are patchy at best, but it is possible to hear on them a man grappling with the meaning of his three-score years.

Today, sucking down his vodka-infused cider, he tells me of his dislike of organised religion. 'I practise Buddhism. You meditate as and when you feel right, which for me is two or three times a week. I do it outside; I prefer to meditate by running water. I find Buddhism very comforting. It's basically the difference between good and evil, which is always a good thing to observe. If religion has a function, it should be to teach the difference between good and evil, and if it does, then life will become more bearable.'

There was selective spiritual comfort, perhaps, but no repentance. No 'my-drug-hell' renouncement of wayward ways, no public confessions or tearful apologies. For better and for worse, Martyn lived his life as he chose and expected neither pity nor forgiveness, nor offered any excuses. Though plenty of people paid the price, he was not spared. His predicament in later life bore testament to that.

'A lot of people got wounded in John's vicinity, but he damaged himself more than anybody else – there is no question of that,' says Vari McGeachy. 'I don't mean to diminish Beverley's experience of John, but he really hurt himself. He really did.'

By the mid-Eighties the best of Martyn was behind him, and the worst of his trouble lay ahead. 'Beverley left and it all fell apart for John,' says Phill Brown. 'I remember he said to me in the Nineties, "You know, I've never written a great song since Beverley left." Which is partly true, I think, but also terribly sad. Up until that point he was just making brilliant records.'

To place the blame for his artistic decline on the wife-muse who Martyn drove away seems an overly dramatic line in wounded male artistry. It seeks to pin some specific external cause on the perfectly natural shape of a creative falling off, which was at times steep but by no means absolute, and which did not follow a neatly descending trajectory. Martyn encountered peaks and troughs throughout the last twenty years of his life. Some of the best music he made in that period came nearer the end than the beginning.

It is true that *Grace And Danger* marked the end of his run of truly essential records, but it is also the case that he wrote some fine songs after the end of his marriage. Although the musical emphasis changed and his delivery became more erratic, his power as a performer ensured he was capable of brilliance right up until the months before his death.

The wider truth of his diminishment, however, is undeniable. Whether it was attributable to some sort of soul-sickness, waning energy, the toll of alcoholism and drug abuse, misguided creative choices – one, some or all of these – the loss of an essential spark is plain enough to hear. He later felt that he gave too much away on *Grace And Danger*. Thereafter, he took his own advice and seemed to always hold something back for himself.

The closing line of Glyn Brown's gentle review of Martyn's 1986 album, *Piece By Piece*, was both revealing and prophetic. 'I think Martyn can be indulged a while yet,' wrote Brown.[1] He still benefited from an enormous amount of critical goodwill stored up from his Seventies records, as well as sentimental fealty to his maverick persona, but no one save the most diehard supporter was getting terribly excited about his records any more – very possibly including the man who made them. Little changed in that regard up to his death. We were glad he was around, gratefully embracing the occasional offerings which reminded us of his unique power and tolerating the rest. It was really no more or less complicated than that.

The glossy, oddly empty aesthetic of *Glorious Fool* and *Well Kept Secret* continued with diminishing returns on *Sapphire*, in 1984, and *Piece By Piece*, in 1986. He had re-joined Island Records, after his split from Sandy Roberton had been followed by a parting from WEA. Chris Blackwell, ever willing to help his friend, took him back into the family and sent him on a sun cure to Nassau.

Having effectively disbanded the group of musicians he had worked with during the past five years, Martyn made the record with the Compass Point Allstars, a group of session players led by the guitarist Barry Reynolds, who was also producing. The pair fell out badly – there was, says one friend, a 'massive ruck' – and Martyn fell into predictable bother.

'I had already resigned,' says Sandy Roberton. 'The mad thing was he called me from Nassau one day and started talking to me like nothing [had changed]. He was asking, "Have you got health insurance for me?" I said, "John, I don't work with you any more. I didn't take out any health insurance for you to go and make a record in the Bahamas." It was just bizarre. That was probably the last time I spoke to him.'

Robert Palmer was drafted in to finish the Nassau sessions, and Martyn completed the album at CaVa, a small studio in Glasgow. The fractured jazz balladry of 'Rope-Soul'd' stood out from the coke-rock sheen, itchy, intimate and restless. The elegiac 'Fisherman's Dream' harnessed the smooth soulfulness of Van Morrison's early Eighties output. There was a twinkling, almost lazily pretty version of 'Over The Rainbow'. Little else cut through. So it went. *Sapphire, Piece By Piece, The Apprentice, Cooltide.* Middling records, tasteful and clean, with the occasional song sufficiently strong to rise above the fray.

The Apprentice was a painfully drawn-out affair, pieced together over the course of three years. It was released only after first being rejected by Island, Chris Blackwell having finally lost patience. 'It became very difficult,' he says. 'He was just very difficult; some of his actions were totally indefensible. He became really like a split personality. That voice he had, like an angel, but there was devilment in him. He took things to extremes.' Blackwell would not be there to post bail next time around. In August 1989 Island was sold to PolyGram for £180 million. There was never anything as formal as a falling-out, but they saw very little of one another in the remaining twenty years of Martyn's life.

The Apprentice was eventually released in 1990 on the independent Permanent Records. With it, Martyn left behind any semblance of a mainstream music career. The Island Years, part two, were a final hurrah to big budgets, lavish studios and the degree of creative freedom such things could bring. He returned to the margins, where he was perhaps best suited.

The albums which followed were a mixed bag. There were bold and sometimes ill-advised revisions of his classic compositions on *Couldn't Love You More* and *No Little Boy*, two near-identical albums shoddily and confusingly released within twelve months of each other in an unedifying game of industry tit for tat. There were semi-official live releases, a solid covers album, compilations which ranged from the lovingly curated to the cheap and gratuitous, collaborations with new kids on the block and fond old faces. A generous critic would commend Martyn's willingness to continue poking around with technology while refusing to rest on his laurels, but a clear-eyed view of the material he released between *Glorious Fool* and his death in 2009 is that it could fill a decent compilation album. It would contain songs such as 'Fisherman's Dream', 'Wildflower', 'Under My Wing',

'Angeline', 'One For The Road', 'So Sweet', 'Suzanne', 'Hole In The Rain', 'The Sky Is Crying', 'Call Me' and 'Sunshine's Better'.

There is a sense that Martyn grew tired of record making as the budgets got smaller and the labels became more 'selective'. He recorded frequently but without any great focus. He seemed to tire of writing, too, in time. He claimed that he needed to be completely out of it – 'blootered' – in order to compose. He grew into his calling as a jazz and blues elder statesman, exploring the catalogue on stage each night with a coterie of sympathetic musicians.

His regular foils were Alan Thomson, Foster Paterson, Spencer Cozens, Arran Ahmun and John Giblin. Dozens more musicians came and went, among them Dave Ball, Andy Sheppard, Danny Cummings, Gerry Conway and Martin Winning. In the years following the end of the band era, Scottish keyboard player Foss Paterson became Martyn's closest partner. His first meeting involved 'this big naked man glaring down the stairs: "You're early. I'll just get dressed."' Paterson was broken in during a three-day initiation ceremony in Roberton, where he quickly realised the folly of trying to keep up with Martyn's industrial-strength recreational habits.

'He had no band, no Alan [Thomson]; it seemed a bit of a lean period,' says Paterson. 'I didn't really know what he was after. He'd have the drum machine, and he kind of wanted me to play everything. He didn't want to go back to the old acoustic thing, he was totally anti that. He wanted to do something new with his electric guitar, which was always in his own tunings. He actually struggled to play a conventionally tuned guitar. He didn't want Rhodes or piano, he wanted colours. He wanted it to be big.'

They fuddled around at Roberton before going on the road as a duo early in 1985. There was no attempt to recreate the smooth textures of *Sapphire*, the album Martyn had recently made in Compass Point. This was something else. 'I was astonished when I saw him in action, outside the music room,' says Paterson. 'I thought, "Jesus Christ, this is amazing!" His line of Bacardi and Cokes on top of the amps, and the spliff hanging from his guitar strings. It was just electric. He was such a force.'

From here on, Martyn worked to a jazz sensibility. He was focal point and bandleader, around which he could form a duo, trio, quartet or, occasionally but infrequently in the latter years, a full band. Paterson left active service in 1990, though they remained friends and played together often in the following years. 'He demanded loyalty, and he got loyalty – you just had to hang in. They were some of the best gigs and some of the worst nightmares, and it would largely depend on him. I worked solidly with him and then I jumped ship. It was time to get out of the washing machine. It really *was* a washing machine. Full spin. It burned you out.' Even after he had moved on, Paterson would get panicked phone calls from Martyn over some rogue piece of new equipment. 'He was hopeless with technology.'

Classically trained at Berklee College in Boston and Goldsmiths in London, Spencer Cozens took Paterson's place on keyboards, as well as co-writing with Martyn and producing. He started early in 1990 and was still there at the final concert in November 2008, with time off for good behaviour in between. Cozens arrived at Martyn's doorstep in Roberton one dark February night, alongside Alan Thomson and Welsh drummer Arran Ahmun, following a nine-hour drive from London. Martyn made them queue up outside, a recruiting sergeant inspecting his new troops. After fingering their collars, checking their shoes, running his eyes over their garb, they passed muster and were allowed in.

The cottage at Roberton was base camp. It was where he wrote, rehearsed, drilled musicians, inducted them into the fold. Inside, the fire would be lit, a bottle opened, a meal prepared. Many of his band members still recall the finer culinary details today. Monkfish steamed in vine leaves and coconut sauce. Joints of beef from the local butcher. Slices from the ham hanging behind the kitchen door. Curried goat. Spanish tapas. Moules marinières. Jerk chicken. Herby dumplings. He was not averse to eating roadkill. Martyn didn't do fast music and he didn't do fast food. 'He abhorred McDonald's,' says Cozens. 'There were times on tour when there was nothing else, and he just wouldn't eat. No pizza and chips for

Johnny. He opened up our palate to an awareness of good things. It made everything so much more three-dimensional, that quality of life.'

Musically, he warmed to Cozens only when the keyboard player ceased trying to emulate the parts of his predecessor and started trusting his own instincts. 'That's what it was with John,' says Cozens. 'Don't go in and play pretence; he would spot it a mile off. You had to be truly what you were, or else he wasn't interested.'

There were times when the music he made with the band was inspired. Other times, it could be clanging, harsh, offhand and ugly. The difference often hung on the levels of stimulation at hand. The sight of Martyn in the theatre bar or a pub across the road before a show was rarely good news; if he was too drunk, the gig was a bust. When it was 'tooting time' and cocaine entered the scene, 'he'd become a bit distant and aggressive, and the music would go out of the window,' says Cozens. 'Certain characters would come to gigs and you knew why. As soon as you saw them, I thought, Oh well, that's tonight's gig gone! It was so predictable. The chemical thing was no good. People would just appear around John, some pretty strange characters. They weren't part of our team, they weren't helping, and it could be a pain. They were there for their own reasons.'

It was hand to mouth, gig to gig. Managers came and went, some more reputable than others. 'He was always firing them,' says bassist Dave Ball. 'He was his own worst enemy in that respect.' There was a point where representatives of a prestigious management company flew to Scotland to meet Martyn with a view to representing him. 'John decided to go to the pub and get drunk at twelve o'clock,' says Ball. 'By the time they got there at four, he was non compos mentis. He was frightened of what they would do to him. He sabotaged it. I know that, because he told me he was going to do it. That was John being John. He was his own man.'

'He didn't help himself,' says Linda Thompson. 'There is that slightly self-destructive Glaswegian thing – Billy Connolly had it, too, but he drew back from it. My friend Gerry Rafferty had it in spades. He was successful, but he shot himself in the foot constantly, and he was nasty to people, like John was. John tested a lot of people's patience.'

He was by now a man whose habits were set. From the outside, his life may have seemed romantically piratical and wildly spontaneous. In reality, it settled into the reliable rhythms of dysfunctional relationships, functioning alcoholism, relentless touring, recreational drugging, punctuated by wild, frightening binges which brought out the worst in him. 'A bender on the road was a nightmare,' says Foss Paterson. His band mates recall tours in Germany and Spain where they stopped at every bar they passed. Nights off were always dangerous.

One well-known drummer wasn't offered the job following an impressive audition because he drank orange juice when the band went to the pub, behaviour divined as an advance warning of some insurmountable personality defect. The musicians who bonded with Martyn stuck around longer than they might have in often trying circumstances because the music never stopped changing and offered something that they could not get anywhere else.

They loved him, cared for him, saw him at his most extreme. At one point or another, he took a swing at most of them, sometimes connecting. There were scuffles in the Saracen Head in Glasgow and hotels in New York, at Roberton and in the Chelsea Arts Club. At these times, says Cozens, 'you looked at him and he wasn't there. It wasn't John. It was just awful and scary.' He always apologised profusely the next day. The other Martyn, meanwhile, was warm, funny and excellent company, reading Julian Barnes' *A History of the World in 10½ Chapters* and engaging in wide-ranging philosophical conversations between shows.

He was not oblivious to his behaviour. His pleas for forgiveness in the aftermath of a flashpoint could be lucidly self-aware, just as his more extreme transgressions were not always spontaneous acts. There were times when it was obvious that he enjoyed unnerving people, or when his desire to cause an emotional disturbance was clearly premeditated. Mark Cooper booked Martyn on the first series of

Later... with Jools Holland in 1992, where he played upcycled versions of 'The Man In The Station', 'May You Never' and 'Sweet Little Mystery'.

'He came barrelling in, and it was a big drama,' says Cooper. 'He made everything around him feel insecure, and it was quite compulsive on his part to do that. You didn't know what was coming next, and I think he liked that. It was fantastic, but quite nerve-racking.'

The walls of Martyn's Eighties and Nineties are papered with tales of his disgrace, humiliation, generosity, violence, humour, kindness. Some stories are told with a kind of grim admiration, others with deep sadness. Some with anger, many with love. A fond exasperation is common. In isolation, many of them are wildly funny, like the night at Roberton where Martyn stood up from the dinner table, stripped off naked and ran into the snow wearing only his boots. Fifty minutes later he returned, lobster red, icicles forming on his extremities, and asked his companions, 'What are you looking at?' before sitting down to finish his meal. Or the time he burst into a Lake District pub, long after closing time, dressed in his pyjamas, and ordered a quadruple brandy, washed down with a lump of hash 'the size of a golf ball' which, recalls Dave Pegg, who was in attendance, he swallowed whole. Or the night he left his £1,500 fee in a stranger's coat and demolished his hotel room when he realised his mistake. Or the Spanish tour during which he bought a plastic trumpet and played it non-stop in the van. Or the time the specialist in prosthetics told him the technology for false legs was 'coming on leaps and bounds'.

His fellow adventurer was Kenny MacDonald, whose roving brief covered roadie, chauffeur, drug dealer, courier, social secretary, minder, drinking buddy, nursemaid and sparring partner. An Edinburgh man – remembered by Foss Paterson as 'a lovely, gentle giant' – MacDonald accompanied Martyn on many furious sprees. They were regulars at the Elphinstone Arms in Biggar, the nearest town to Roberton, where they drank, played pool and misbehaved. When they got bored, they sometimes fought one another for sport.

'I went down to John's one day,' Paterson recalls. 'He said to meet in Biggar, at the Fleming Arms, not the Elphinstone. I thought that was odd – he never drank in the Fleming Arms. He walked in covered in scratches and bruises. He claimed Annie had crashed the car but, just prior to that, the guys in the bar had been telling me about the massive fight John and Kenny had had in the pool room in the Elphinstone last night, rolling about the pool table, a full-blown scrap. John had knocked one of Kenny's teeth out and, apparently, he had bent down, picked it up and crunched into it.' The fight spilled out onto the street and ended when MacDonald was taken away in an ambulance. When Paterson went back to the cottage, MacDonald was lying on the couch beneath a blanket as Martyn tended to him gently.

The police were involved, home and abroad, on many occasions. 'There are a couple of things I won't tell,' says Paterson. Martyn became the scourge of Biggar, until eventually he was more or less forced to drink elsewhere, in Crawfordjohn, Lanark and Abingdon. His neighbour in Roberton, Gavin Stott, who eventually bought the church across the lane from Martyn's house, recalls his revels around the tiny village with a kind of rueful amazement: the New Year's Eves where 'you had to shut the door on him. He was in and out, in and out, looking for white spirit'; the battered BMW parked up the lane; the litre bottles of Bacardi arriving long after midnight in the back of taxis; his calling the proprietor of the local bed and breakfast 'Mrs Miggins'.

Yet there was a shadow hanging over it all. Bad drug deals, money that went missing, ill-advised dalliances. For a while in the mid-Nineties, Martyn spent a lot of time in Chicago. There was also a period living on a narrowboat in Chester. Some friends believe he was deliberately making himself hard to find.

Martyn invited Phil Shackleton around to Roberton for lunch one day. 'He said he was going to pop into Lanark to get some food. When we got to the cottage, there was no one in. We sat there for a couple of hours – nothing. Eventually they came back, and Kenny said, "Sorry we're late, we had a bit of an incident." John came in and, man, he was smashed to fuck. I thought he had gone through the windscreen of the car. He was in a real state. He could hardly talk, he was black and blue and blowing blood bubbles from his nose. According to Kenny, they had pulled up in the car park of the supermarket and, as they got out, another car pulled up beside them, two guys got out, dragged John out and gave him a good pounding with an iron bar. It looked like he had upset somebody somewhere.'

They are good stories. When they are extracted from a single night, or a weekend, or a tour, however, and strung together into a life, the cumulative effect is sobering.

II

One positive Martyn salvaged from his first marriage was a close and loving relationship with his daughter. After several years without contact, Vari took the bus from Heathfield to see him when he played at Brighton Dome at the end of November 1984.

'I needed that relationship,' she says. 'I do realise if I'd left him to his own devices, he might have never stuck his head above the parapet, [but] once we were back in touch, it took about thirty seconds to catch up and get back to where we were, which was father and daughter. It was very easy.'

The past was dealt with quickly and consigned to history. 'When I first spent an evening with John in his home, I kind of vomited my [complaints and bad feelings]. Once I'd blurted it all out, there was this almost clown-like expression, like, "What can I say? How can I make it better? How can we go back and do it all again?" I thought, It's happened, it's in the past; there's no point in being angry and sad for ever. Very pragmatic. How that came about, I've no idea.

'I think Beverley would see it as [me letting] him get away with it scot-free, and she probably resented me for that for quite some time, but I never saw it as forgiveness. It was more practical and rational than that: "You're my father, I would be happier with you in my life in some way, and if in order to do that it takes me to be a little bit bold and brave, then fine." It was never "I forgive you, Daddy, don't worry." It was never that. He did some awful terrible behaviour, inexcusable... [and] he definitely felt guilty about it. Like a lot of drunks, he would get terribly sentimental. Sometimes he would misconstrue something I would say and get a little teary [but] I wasn't accusing him of anything. I came to terms with his behaviour quite early on, and I was way past the point of being angry or upset about it.'

As a sequel of sorts to 'My Baby Girl', Martyn wrote 'Look At The Girl', a track on *The Apprentice* which communicated his pride in the young woman his daughter had become: cool, smart and beautiful, *'hasn't she turned out fine'*. When the criminal convictions of one of his many shady helpers prevented him accompanying Martyn to the States, Vari took his place, and stayed on for a small UK tour as well. 'I went under the guise of tour manager, but really just to take care of John,' she says. 'It wasn't for me, it was all about getting this big man on stage every night, but I'm glad I did it.'

She describes her connection with Martyn as 'one of the best relationships of my life, in terms of how you relate and communicate and share. I valued his friendship. I think it was a classic father/daughter relationship, but it came later in life, so it may have looked a bit peculiar [and,] to the women in [his] life, possibly a bit OTT.'

The woman in his life when Vari first reunited with her father was Annie Furlong. Martyn's second marriage had taken a predictable course, becoming as dysfunctional, abusive and damaging as the first. There were no children involved this time. Otherwise, it was a variation on a theme. Alcohol was an accelerant, as Furlong at first attempted to keep up with Martyn's appetites and then succumbed to them. At the start of the marriage, there was one alcoholic in the house; by the end, tragically, there were two. Drink exacerbated a tendency to push and provoke each other. 'I think they were driving each other mad,' says Vari. 'It was the nature of a toxic relationship. It was a little bit like the Punch and Judy show with Annie and John sometimes; it could be constant bickering and haranguing and slagging off of each other.'

They spent little time apart. Furlong came with him on tour: he was too insecure to leave her at home alone. When friends stayed at Roberton or in adjoining hotel rooms, they 'heard goings-on in the bedroom at night that resulted in black eyes and swollen lips,' says Phil Shackleton. 'I was aware he often didn't treat his women well. It wasn't a secret, but nobody ever mentioned it.' Jim Imlach remembers them as 'a bit self-destructive. They weren't a good couple to be together.'

Yet there were times of happiness and contentment at Roberton, when Annie would forage in the woods for chanterelle mushrooms and Martyn would cook. Vari would come to visit and they 'would do a lot of Scottish jaunts. Annie drove us right to the top a few times, up the Drumbeg road' in the far North West of Scotland, near Unapool.

Martyn recorded 'Annie Says' on *Cooltide*, a sweet, scatted ode to his wife, who says '*I'm just a loony*'. It gentrified the no-go zones of their relationship, turned their dysfunction into something palatable. The same year as *Cooltide* was released, in 1991 Furlong ran away from the marriage, leaving behind almost all her possessions when she did so. She left Roberton a 'broken and anxious woman' and would never fully recover.[1] Her family viewed her as collateral damage in Martyn's raging fight with the world and himself, and never forgave him.

Martyn ran, too, embarking on a month-long summer binge in 1991 around his old haunts in Hastings, where he seemed permanently ensconced in the Lord Nelson pub in the Old Town. He left the bar to play a spectacularly boozy impromptu concert on the shingle beach, raising funds for the RNLI. Greeting families in his best Glaswegian with 'All right, you English bastards?', he dedicated 'Big Muff' to his mother-in-law. In terms of pure, unfiltered self-expression, it may have been one of his most truly honest performances.

During this period, Martyn got to know his son, Spenser, who wasn't quite four when his first marriage ended and with whom he'd had little contact since. Aged sixteen, he caught the bus up to Roberton from Brighton, where he and his mother were now living. Later, he went on the road with Martyn. 'He was too young, but he insisted on going,' says Beverley Martyn. 'He adored his father. They were very close.'

They developed a musical bond. On tour, Spenser learned the ropes of sound engineering, and Martyn arranged work experience with

Fish, the former singer with Marillion. In exchange, Spenser opened his father's ears to contemporary dance-based music and urged him to record. He turned up in the dressing room one night with a box of goggles from an army surplus store. 'Of course John would automatically gravitate towards such a thing,' says drummer Gerry Conway. 'He said, "Right, when we go on, I want you to put the goggles above your heads, and when I say, 'Gentlemen, adjust your goggles!' that's when we'll play." Sure enough, he gave us the order, and we put our goggles over our eyes. The only trouble with mine was they misted up immediately, and so I couldn't see anything.'

He took his son fishing to the dam at Patterton in Glasgow, accompanied by his old friend Davie MacFarlane. 'I was a wee bit disappointed with him there, because John spent most of his time fishing and I spent most of my time helping Spenser,' says MacFarlane. 'I felt John should have been the one doing that.'

They had fun, but 'with John's lifestyle there were just certain things that couldn't happen,' says Spencer Cozens. 'He didn't talk about it much, I think he found it quite painful. He loved children, and he would have loved to be a good dad, but he wasn't there to be a dad, and that was a bit of a tragedy.'

It was an often heavy scene around Martyn on tour – tough, macho and excessive – and 'Spenser got into bad habits,' says Beverley. He has struggled with addiction for much of his adult life. While his sister Vari is naturally wary about speaking on his behalf, she says, 'blame is a funny word. I don't think John can be blamed for Spenser. I think all of us are a product of our experience and our genes.'

Martyn and his stepson Wesley Kutner met again in the Nineties, backstage at a concert, after almost two decades without contact. 'I told him that I forgave him, and he broke down crying,' says Kutner. 'He [knew] exactly what he [had] done. He was a bad boy.' Their relationship thereafter was distant, with sporadic contact. After Martyn lost a leg, Kutner invited him to come to stay with him in Spain, where he now lives, but it proved logistically impossible.

Many of Martyn's oldest friends had fallen away or saw him infrequently. 'He didn't want anyone coming in who was too close from way back,' says John James. 'He got a bit more distant. Some people remain the same. He didn't, I think.' His schoolmates from the Southside of Glasgow still touched base occasionally. Their names were added to the guest list at every hometown show, but increasingly they found close contact difficult. 'He would phone the house and I couldn't understand a word he was saying,' says Donnie Barclay. 'I got quite worried about him.' They lost touch in the Nineties. 'We approached him a few times later in life, and he was either so high or so pissed he wasn't making sense,' says Brian Stanage. 'You'd think, What's the point? We drifted away from that.'

He saw his cousins Kirk and Fiona McGeachy whenever he played Canada, where they lived, but many others in his extended family, who loved him dearly, were kept at arm's length. 'It was too painful for those who loved him to watch his inner demons take hold,' said his younger cousin, Janet.[2] The last time Martyn saw Alison McGeachy, in Newcastle, he 'didn't seem himself,' she says. 'I think he did recognise me, but he only said, "Do you live here now?"'

His mother, Betty, died of lung cancer in a hospice in Esher on April 26, 1993, aged sixty-eight. Martyn was touring with his band in Europe at the time. In Brussels, on April 27, he came on stage an hour late, miserably drunk. The show was 'horrible', according to one eyewitness.[3] The next day he was in Paris for a show at the Passage du Nord-Ouest club. Spencer Cozens remembers: 'He said, quite proudly, in the lobby, "Right now, my mum is being burnt to a crisp." I was a little shocked. I thought, Crikey, I'm not going there. He didn't use to speak much about it all; it was too dark and deep to go into.' An audience member that night remembered it as 'an awful concert. John was in a terribly bad mood.'[4]

At the beginning of 1996, Hamish Imlach died. The pair had remained close through their various upheavals: Imlach had split up from Wilma in the mid-Eighties and moved to the eleventh floor of a council tower block at Netherwood Tower in Motherwell. The two men saw each other regularly, at home and on the road. On one occasion, they recorded a clutch of old blues tunes at the cottage with a view to making an album.

A few months before his death, Imlach had suffered an injury to his foot while swimming in Dubrovnik. It hadn't healed, and his immune system gradually began failing. He died in his living room in the early hours of New Year's Day. Martyn was devastated. 'I drove up on New Year's Day and I called into John's place and stayed with him for three or four hours,' says Phil Shackleton. 'He was just out of it. I said, "Are you coming up [to Motherwell]?" and he said, "I can't face it, I can't face it." He said, "I'll be late for my own funeral." He wasn't functioning at all. He just went quiet for the next few weeks. I called a few times and he was away with the fairies.'

Imlach was sent on his travels with a six-piece jazz band leading the funeral line, New Orleans-style. Hundreds turned out at the wake at the civic centre in Motherwell for ceilidh and curry. Martyn was beside himself. 'He was just so upset,' says Ewan McVicar. 'He seemed to be out of control with grief, really.'

Annie Furlong also died in 1996. After leaving Martyn, she had returned to Dublin and remarried, to a doctor. They moved to Kenya for his work and, while there, Furlong died of cerebral malaria. She struggled with alcohol abuse until the end of her life and is remembered by friends and family as a complex woman, with her own troubles and insecurities, who never recovered from the decade she spent with Martyn. 'Years later her brother contacted me, and my heavens he was so angry about John,' says Brian Masterton. 'When you see that happening to such a lovely, gentle person, you see her life pretty much ruined, it's hard.' Though she and Martyn had parted in 1991 in desperate circumstances, her death 'knocked him sideways', says a friend.

Martyn's own health was poor, his body assailed by a variety of internal and external attacks. A prostate cancer scare towards the end of the Eighties had been cause for considerable concern. His lifestyle, too, put him in occasional peril. Martyn's claims that he was shot while in America should be taken with a pinch of salt – most close friends don't credit it, chalking it up as another tall tale – but Wesley Kutner insists that 'something did go down somewhere, but I can't say. He was in a pretty bad fight in America. He got stabbed with his own knife.'

Alcohol, as ever, was his primary aggressor. In 1996 he suffered a perforated pancreas. 'He called me up to say that he had been to the doctor and he had pancreatitis,' says Jeff Allen. 'The doctor said, you drink, you die. He called me up from Inverness Airport for a chat, first thing in the morning, drunk. This was a day after he told me about the specialist. He was on a collision course with the Grim Reaper.'

'For me, John was always unwell,' says Vari McGeachy. 'The drinking had got him, and it affected him greatly. His drug use was fairly recreational. He was probably piggish with it, but he was piggish with everything he liked. It was the booze that got its claws in him. His health wasn't good for years and years.'

There were periodic attempts to curb his drinking, or even stop altogether. He might water down his wine for a few days or even a week, drink coffee instead of spirits for breakfast, and then be back in business. 'His idea of detox was just chaotic,' says Vari. '"I'll just drink cans of lager and take loads of Diazepam." It might have just been sheer stubbornness and laziness. It was a big task to take on, and he wouldn't find the commitment. Any kind of diversion, like a new tour, would be the perfect reason not to start. He was very day-to-day. Not terribly pragmatic.'

Physically, Martyn had come to resemble the gangster of his youthful imagining. Heavily bearded, with his receding hair slicked back, wearing suits, sunglasses and Crombie coats, he could have passed for a middle-ranking crime boss come to collect his protection money.

III

If his lifestyle was by now governed by his addiction, the one thing that never settled into comfortable repetition was the music. Martyn never again hit the heights he reached between 1969 and 1980, but neither was he content to defer to its magnificence. 'Emotionally, he was certainly lost,' says Spencer Cozens. 'As an artist, he wasn't lost.'

There were shows throughout the Nineties and Noughties which are fondly remembered by those who were there – nights which reaped memorable, unrepeatable versions of a classic song, sustained bursts of inspiration, moments of magic when everything clicked. On a good night, Martyn could still change your life, and the good nights made up for the bad ones – of which there were plenty: shambolic shows and drunken misfires where he short-changed the paying public while performing under the false flag of rebellion.

One was an Ethiopian famine benefit concert at the Usher Hall in Edinburgh in December 1984, on a bill which included Jack Bruce, Charlie Watts, Rory Gallagher, Bert Jansch and Rick Wakeman. Martyn was spotted in the pub beforehand with blood on his face, rarely a good omen. Later, after playing a short solo set, he ambushed the all-star finale, taunting Gallagher from the side of the stage before unplugging the Irishman's guitar and playing deliberately inappropriate solos. Roadies tried to physically restrain him, to no avail. Unusually for a Scottish concert, where Martyn was generally free to misbehave at will, some of the crowd turned on him.

Another was the notorious Mean Fiddler show in September 1987 where he started three hours late, vomited into a bucket after the first song and then departed, not to return. He later pleaded sunstroke. There were people who went to see Johnny Thunders in the Eighties half-hoping the former New York Doll might OD in front of their eyes. A little of that dubious appeal latterly attached itself to Martyn. 'I always thought that towards the end a few of the people that came to see John were going to see how fucked up he was,' says Ralph McTell. 'I don't like that aspect much. That's not entertainment for me.'

It was often messy, but there was stubborn pride in his determination to present a moving target. Only rarely did he succumb to the pressure – and there was a lot of it – to return to the style of music with which he was most closely associated.

His collaboration with Danny Thompson was reprised sporadically. They played several shows together in 1986 and 1987, proving that Thompson remained capable of coaxing Martyn into stellar work, particularly vocally. Together, they made some of the richest music of his later career for the BBC Scotland show *Transatlantic Sessions*, which invited British, Irish and North American musicians to come together and find common ground. In 1995, performing with Kathy Mattea and Jerry Douglas, he and Thompson conjured a spellbinding version of 'May You Never' which breathed new life into an old chestnut. Their duo take of 'Solid Air' from the 1998 sessions was sublime: slow and sensual, the more expansive jazzer of Martyn's later years given free rein.

In May and June 2001 Martyn and Thompson came together again for the Sunshine Boys tour, a knowing nod to the 1975 movie starring George Burns and Walter Matthau, about the less-than-convivial reunion of two cranky old comedians. The reference was perhaps a little too on the nose. There was some friction behind the scenes over management and money, the pair travelled separately, and ticket sales weren't what they might have been. An unshakable affection remained, however, and on a good night the musical empathy was evident in abundance.

At most gigs through the years, whatever the format, Martyn would pull out 'May You Never', 'Spencer The Rover' or 'The Easy Blues' and play them straight, but as a rule he resisted the lure of slipping back into his troubadour shoes. 'He had moved on from the acoustic guitar,' says Cozens. 'Would you want to go and do something you did when you were nineteen? Anyone who is going to last are people who do the true thing. His stuff with the acoustic guitar was fantastic, but he felt it was rote. It was from a gone time, it was finished, and he wasn't going to do something as a performing dog. He might do it sitting around at the house or at the hotel, and it was beautiful, but it wasn't where his cutting edge was at that time.'

As late as 2006, critics were still puzzling over what many regarded as wilful musical contrariness. 'Keyboardist Spencer Cozens marshals the kind of slick, jazz café outfit you'd expect to have cosseted the likes of Sade twenty years ago rather than the more rough-hewn yet vulnerable Martyn,' wrote Mat Snow in his *Guardian* review of the May 10 show at Shepherd's Bush Empire. 'Mysteriously, that is the way he wants it.'[1]

He never stopped listening. The sounds on the tour bus would shift with his obsessions: Chet Baker, hip-hop, Annie Lennox, Willie Nelson. When he loved something, he loved it intensely, and would play it over and over again. Much of the recording he undertook in the early Nineties took place in Chicago with producer Jim Tullio and engineer Stefon 'Bionik' Taylor, who during the same period was recording with the likes of R. Kelly and Aaliyah. Some of that urban influence rubbed off. Chicago opened his ears to programmed beats and the energy of crisp hip-hop rhythms. His son Spenser, who was involved with producing dance music, stretched his tastes further. Martyn not only dropped an enthusiasm for drum 'n' bass, acid house and jungle into interviews, he added some of these ingredients to his music, with mixed results.

The generational churn helped orientate him following a period in the wilderness. He was picked up first by Go! Discs, making *And.* for the label in 1996, an album which reunited Martyn with Phil Collins on big drums and thin backing vocals. In tandem, it deployed programmed beats to create its plush twinkling grooves, flirting with fashionable trip-hop rhythms and chill-out ambience. Smooth, mellow, mid-paced, cossetted with curlicues of fluttery soprano sax, *And.* was rather too polite in places, but it nevertheless showed that Martyn remained an artist to be reckoned with. It contained some fine songs in 'Suzanne' and 'Sunshine's Better' and raised the energy levels with the funky pitch and roll of 'Step It Up'. On 'Carmine', a toxic love affair reduces him once again to '*some little boy*' who never knew anything.

The lilting 'The Downward Pull Of Human Nature' cut particularly close to the bone, a very personal litany of misadventures – hurting the ones you love, sirens roaring in the night, eyeing up your best friend's wife, excessive pride, drinking until you fall over – which included a glimpse into the void, the '*six foot destiny*' beckoning him into its arms. In the song, Martyn attributes his transgressions to some internal yet universal human impulse pushing buttons far beyond his control. As a writer and as a man, he was beholden to his emotions without analysing or perhaps even understanding them very well. He acted upon his feelings, sometimes rashly, and moved on. 'He would live with his heart on his sleeve, you could tell if he was up or down,' says Phill Brown. 'He was honest all the time, he said what he thought.'

An idealist, an optimist and a romantic, he seemed unable to deal levelly with life's routine rations of disillusionment. 'I think I'm possibly prone to unhappiness more than some people,' he said. 'I just see a lot of things other people don't see or don't want to see, and I can't close my eyes, you know, so I get hurt and sad and a whole lot of other things.'[2]

After *And.*, Martyn found his most sympathetic home since his first stint at Island Records. Independiente was a new company formed by Andy Macdonald, who had sold Go! Discs to PolyGram and taken Martyn with him. Among his new label mates were Paul Weller, Travis, Gomez and Martina Topley-Bird.

Independiente understood the ways in which he fitted into the contemporary musical landscape. *Solid Air* had become a set text for many rap, hip-hop and post-rock artists interested in experimenting with space, atmosphere and decelerated psychotropic rhythm – among them Massive Attack, Faithless, Portishead, Tricky and The Verve. Martyn was marketed, somewhat spuriously, to a post-rave, post acid-jazz generation as a spiritual godfather of trip-hop, the come-down cooler king for assorted stoners and pillheads. It was this theory which underpinned Talvin Singh's clubby remix of 'Sunshine's Better', as well as Martyn's cover of Portishead's 'Glory Box' and his appearance as guest vocalist on 'Deliver Me' by Sister Bliss from Faithless. 'He could fit into most musical scenes because that integrity was there,' says Cozens. 'Jazz, funk, hip-hop, reggae. It works, because it was John delivering John.'

The mashing of cultures didn't always convince. Portishead were reportedly less than impressed with his lethargic take on their signature song. In May 1998 Martyn supported The Verve at the band's request at their hometown show at Haigh Hall in Wigan, where he was on the receiving end of a brutally inhospitable reception from the crowd.

His deal with Independiente involved the label acquiring the deconsecrated Scots Congregational kirk across the lane from Martyn's cottage in Roberton and leasing it back to him. Plans to convert the building into a fully functioning studio never came to fruition. Nor did a delusional rum-fuelled pipe dream to turn six local cottages into 'an orphanage-cum-retreat for underprivileged city kids who've never seen the countryside'.[3] Instead, Martyn started living in the church in a manner not too far removed from vagrancy. 'He basically slept on the balcony,' recalls Gavin Stott, who now owns the property.

The quid pro quo in this arrangement was for Martyn to record an album of cover material for his new label, which provided a list of thirty-five songs for consideration. It was an uncharacteristically pragmatic undertaking and the results were strong, if not necessarily inspired. Released in March 1998, *The Church With One Bell* was coherent in a way that many of his later records are not. In CaVa studios, Martyn led a four-piece band of Cozens, John Giblin and

Arran Ahmun. 'We had great fun,' says Cozens. 'They [gave us] a load of tunes, we sat and routined them up in Roberton for a few days. It soon became clear which ones worked, and then we went into the studio for about ten days. It was very clear, very clean-cut.'

The ten tracks he recorded ranged from those by artists who were relatively contemporary – Dead Can Dance, Ben Harper, Portishead – to enduring loves like Bobby Charles, Elmore James, Lightnin' Hopkins and the Reverend Gary Davis. He gargled through Randy Newman's 'God's Song' and sank his soul into Nina Simone's sacred 'Strange Fruit'. The generally soporific mood lifted with a spirited swing through Hopkins' 'Feel So Bad', although a fixation on songs concerning death and decay was perhaps inevitable given the series of losses Martyn had endured in recent years. His closing version of Davis's sepulchral blues staple 'Death Don't Have No Mercy' seemed particularly wracked: *'look in the bed, your mother will be gone'*.

The upturn in his fortunes in the later Nineties was attributable in large part to his girlfriend, Daisy Flowers, who also became his business manager. They had met in 1993 and were a couple for five years, living together in Roberton. Flowers is widely credited among Martyn's friends with making sense of his chaotic finances and getting his career back on track. A petite can-do Londoner, who knew the industry and understood how it could work for a critically respected artist in his late forties, she was focused, good-humoured, organised and determined on Martyn's behalf.

Her attempts to address Martyn's alcoholism proved more challenging. When things became too rough at home, she would move into a local bed and breakfast until the storm passed. Sometimes it took longer to blow through than others. 'He did have a quite vicious streak,' Flowers told John Neil Munro. 'He could be quite violent, but it didn't affect me because I used to do kickboxing before I met him. He never landed a punch on me.'[4]

Phil Shackleton was the support act on Martyn's tour throughout November 1997. Kenny MacDonald was no longer on the scene, and Martyn was driving down to the night's show in Whitehaven with his personal assistant, George McCallum. Shackleton was following in his own car. When he arrived, 'George told us that John was in jail. Most tours, there would be a point where he would be in the cooler for the night. [At the hotel,] the sound engineer had gone haywire, he had barricaded himself in the bedroom and ripped the radiator off the wall. Daisy had a massive bruise on her head from nutting John, and the landlady was going crazy. He arrived at the gig with these wrap-around shades on, he looked like a panda. He and Daisy didn't speak for the rest of the tour.'

The relationship ended shortly afterwards, with catastrophic consequences. The title and cover image of *The Church With One Bell* turned into a requiem for a building that would shortly slip through his fingers. In short order, the kirk was returned to its owner and the cottage was eventually sold to pay off debts to the tax man. When he left Roberton, Martyn abandoned numerous tapes, later discovered in the rehearsal shed and at the back of the church. They were, believes Gavin Stott, simply thrown away in his absence.

After parting from Flowers, his finances again descended into disarray. 'I think there was an element of, when things were too stable, John didn't like it, because it meant he had responsibilities,' says Cozens. 'I think there might have been a reaction there.' His taste for cocaine and crack, a taste he shared with some of the people who were now in theory responsible for looking after his business interests, ensured a constant leakage of money. Tens of thousands of pounds were squandered, whether through carelessness or exploitation. Martyn was ripe for being ripped off, but his appetites were compulsive in many things.

'As soon as Daisy was gone, it reverted back to the same old chaos,' says Vari McGeachy. 'He was never going to fill in a tax return by himself. It just wasn't on his mind. As long as he had some money in his pocket and a guitar and he could bang a tune out, he was all right. It was a strange kind of tightrope walk and it gave him the lifestyle he needed.'

The situation gradually worsened, to the point where his fifty-third birthday arrived with a series of unpleasant surprises. 'On 9/11 it was all "Happy birthday to you", then, bloody hell! Bang go the

Twin Towers. Then there's another bang at the door: "Mr McGeachy, we have a summons for you." Some sort of bankruptcy thing. Fantastic. What a day! It wasn't funny at the time. I just went out and got drunk.'

His album *Glasgow Walker*, released in 2000, spanned these life changes. It was started in the shed at Roberton and at the Washoose, a small studio in nearby Crawfordjohn, and completed in Ireland after Martyn had moved to Thomastown in Kilkenny to live with his new girlfriend, Teresa Walsh – his partner, and latterly his carer, until his death in 2009. A former nurse, 'Teresa was strong, and really, really good for him,' says Foss Paterson. 'You had to be strong to live with John. She was his pillar. There was genuine love there. She just took him as he was.'

The album started strongly with 'So Sweet', 'Wildflower' and 'The Field Of Play' but faded as it went on. Much of the material was written by Martyn on the Korg Trinity keyboard, rather than the guitar. The odd ill-advised digital detour aside, it was an engaging blend of sounds, styles and songs, containing some of his best work for almost two decades. It ended with a sumptuously sad version of the American standard 'You Don't Know What Love Is', recorded with the Guy Barker International Quintet for Anthony Minghella's acclaimed film *The Talented Mr Ripley*. If Martyn's later career never quite translated into one last great record, *Glasgow Walker* perhaps came closest.

During this period, he offered a platform to several emerging solo artists. Kathryn Williams sang on *Glasgow Walker*, and he gave support slots to John Smith and James Yorkston. On the Sunshine Boys tour, English singer-songwriter Rosalie Deighton was the opening act. 'I know people had problems with him, but John was nothing but kind and sweet to me,' she says. 'He'd always give me a thumbs up before I went on.' When Deighton left the tour early, having been invited to support Roxy Music, Martyn gave her his blessing and a bottle of champagne wrapped in brown paper with the message, "Thank you for your lovely musk." 'It took me a few hours to realise he had meant to write "music",' says Deighton. Kathryn Williams took her place.

He toured *Glasgow Walker* in 2000 with a dislocated shoulder, to add to his other woes. The decade had taken a considerable physical toll. In the summer of 1998, Martyn and Richard Thompson had been booked on the same bill at the Fleadh Festival in Chicago. Martyn appeared with one side of his face swollen and bruised. He told an interviewer at the time, 'I got hit on the side of my head with a baseball bat in New York a few days ago. Mugged just a few yards from my hotel.'[5] Thompson was sceptical.

'It was great to see him, but I was slightly disturbed at the same time. He gave me this total bullshit story about having been attacked by someone on the streets of New York and [how he] had beaten the shit out of him. It was a typical John story, but the bullshit he gave me was toned up a few notches. I didn't challenge him on it. I was really disturbed to see the state of him. I had heard stories from Danny, about how he had become a serious alcoholic, and I was really saddened to see him. He did not seem in a good way. He still performed really great, but as a human being he seemed in a disturbing state.'

He was now carrying a lot of excess weight, and his right foot was badly infected. '[While] mixing the album, his foot was really bad,' says Cozens. 'It had basically died. It was poking out of the end of a cast and it looked awful. He drew faces on all of his toes.'

Martyn cancelled shows throughout 2002: first due to the infected foot, then the after-effects of a road accident in August, where he suffered a broken nose and whiplash when the car in which he was travelling collided with a cow. The shattered glass damaged his hands. Matters reached a head when a cyst the size of a cricket ball burst at the back of his right leg, leaking poison into his bloodstream.

Such was his condition, he was left with no further options. In April 2003 his right leg was amputated just below the knee. 'I could see it coming,' he told me. 'I had myself resigned to it well before it happened.'

'It could have been avoided, no question,' says Vari McGeachy. '[In the end,] he had absolutely no choice. He had pushed the circumstances to the limits.'

He was operated on in Waterford Hospital, where he recuperated in traditional fashion as a stream of visitors came to see him. 'Teresa was bringing him in cans of Guinness and curries, because the food wasn't very good,' says Spencer Cozens. 'You thought, Jesus, John! They would bring his dog in, Gizmo, wrapped in a blanket or smuggled in a jacket. It all went on.'

IV

We are back in the beer garden, John Martyn and me.

I ask him about the leg that is no longer there. 'Fuck me, it's still painful,' he said. 'You can still feel your toes and everything – it's very odd. It still catches you by surprise in the middle of the night. "Ha-ha! Still here!"' Phantom pains. The suffering inflicted by absence.

'What can I tell you? I was very angry for a while, very pissed off that it happened to me, but the initial shock wore off and I'm cool. It could have happened when I was fifteen and changed my life entirely. Even if I popped my clogs tomorrow, I've had a wonderful time. I can't argue at all about the way that life's dealt me.' Truth or bravado? I'm still not sure.

Martyn was in hospital for two months and recuperated for six. During his recovery he was on morphine and wheeled in and out of hospital for a number of secondary procedures. 'I've this natural aversion to small, square rooms,' he said. 'Cells, for instance.'[1]

'If there was going to be a time for John to straighten out, that would have been it,' says Vari McGeachy. 'He could have taken the opportunity to say, "Okay, I'm having a major operation, I'll be in hospital, I can detox, then go straight to a rehabilitation centre and deal with the drinking." It could have saved his life, potentially, or given him some more years... [but] this is in another world! You could never explain to a surgeon what kind of a creature you were dealing

239

with. The idea that you could just remove a major limb from this creature and send him home and he would fare okay – it's not their fault, you wouldn't know. John was quite personable, quite pleasant and rational if you were a doctor dealing with him. After the amputation, it was pretty much downhill, [with] the weight gain and the mobility.'

On November 7, 2003, after a year off stage, he made a comeback at Connolly's in Leap, County Cork, backed by Spencer Cozens and John Giblin, with a 'Welcome Home' banner strung on the wall behind him. He made no fuss, the sound was messy, but it was a quietly heroic appearance, nonetheless, and one which proved a point, not least to himself. The gig was filmed as part of a BBC Four documentary directed by Serena Cross, *Johnny Too Bad*, which followed Martyn at close quarters during the period before and after his operation. Captured at home, he played the clown for the cameras, messing around with his prosthetic, dissembling in a Jamaican patois, at one point lurching around with a mitre on his head. It was an eccentric and essentially lovable portrait, fringed with only an occasional sense of his deeper complexity and darkness.

He was back in the swing of touring by April 2004, when a new album, *On The Cobbles*, was released. The number of studios used, the unusually high number of musicians and its interruption by serious illness betrayed a rather tortuous genesis. Martyn told me the year after it was released that he didn't like it much, that 'it was literally cobbled together'. An entirely tin-eared revision of 'Go Down Easy' in particular left one wondering about Martyn's aesthetic judgement. Nonetheless, its very existence felt validating, with morale-boosting appearances from Paul Weller, Mavis Staples and Verve guitarist Nick McCabe. His faithful trio of exemplary bass players – Danny Thompson, Alan Thomson and John Giblin – appeared together on one track, 'My Creator'. The last song on the final LP released in his lifetime was a version of Lead Belly's 'Goodnight Irene'.

Touring in a wheelchair was complicated. Foss Paterson recalls 'moments where it was awkward for him. He couldn't walk away.' Another friend remembers a post-gig scene in the Yorkshire town of

Beverley, where Martyn was surrounded by twenty or more hangers-on and left with a bar bill which totalled more than his fee for the gig. When I met him in 2005, he was blunt in his distaste for the reverence he often received from well-meaning fans. His illness had only made it more intrusive.

'I used to be more forthcoming, but I retreated. My health is not good. I do a two-hour set, and by the end all I want to do is get out the back door. Otherwise, you get your ear bent and told how wonderful you are and what a privilege it was for them to be there. I find it very embarrassing indeed. I mean, I wouldn't do it if I didn't think I was good at it. I've already got the odd nutter sending letters and turning up at gigs to make cow faces at you, being strange and generally overdoing your importance in their lives. Because of the romance in the songs, they think, "Ah, *he* knows!"'

There were unexpected positives. Being wheelchair-bound made Martyn less likely to go off the rails before a show and enabled a certain amount of sobriety to enter the proceedings during one. It brought a new quality of focus to the music. Though his voice was adversely affected by his extreme weight gain and the effects of being compressed in a chair, the change in emphasis during what Cozens calls 'the post-leg years' was marked. 'I thought the music revived quite a lot. There were times [before] when we would go out and it would just be a noise. I think we got more of the fantastic stuff later on. There were times when he would just sit back in his chair and listen. His ears were always on the case. Towards the end, it really felt like a proper band.'

V

When he was finally forced to stop running, the melancholy that Martyn had spent much of his life expressing in his songs and dodging in his life seemed to catch up with him. His physical predicament meant he spent a lot of time on his own, which was not his natural state. 'He couldn't bear being alone,' says Vari. 'I think [towards the end] he would have been lonely for some good company.'

His compulsion to tour was partly about the camaraderie of being around people he liked. Off the road, a little off the beaten track in Thomastown, he became more isolated. He would telephone friends in the early hours of the morning to discuss the day's snooker coverage or the trash TV he got a kick out of watching, such as *The Deadliest Catch* and *Ice Truckers*. He followed *The X Factor* avidly, he told me. 'Love it, love it, love it! Tears roll down my face. The standard of music at the moment is so atrocious, it's almost fantastic. I really like bad music on a certain level.'

His behaviour has echoes of Peter Cook's later days of ennui and alcoholic solitude, when the comedian would call LBC Radio for company in the small hours, chatting to presenter Clive Bull in the guise of his alter ego, a lonely Norwegian fishing fanatic called Sven. It was both funny and tragic. Martyn called Danny Thompson at three in the morning to tell him he loved him. He checked in on other friends and old adversaries. 'He would call me occasionally,' says Beverley

Martyn. 'When he was really ill, he said, "Nobody will remember me when I'm gone." That's what he said to me.'

He became more reflective. He still loved to cook, but more than ever he was an executive chef, overseeing the proceedings with an often infuriating eye for detail. He spent time with Gizmo, he told me, watching birds in the garden, taking life at a 'slower, sweeter pace. I'm becoming more and more withdrawn from the world. I have a lot more peace and composure. I like being on the road still, but I prefer doing sweet fuck all, listening to the trees. I don't drive fast cars, I don't have a swimming pool, but I don't miss them. I've got a lovely girlfriend and a pub around the corner. I don't need much, really.'

'He was quite Zen,' says Vari McGeachy. 'As wild and chaotic and destructive as he could be, he could also be as creative and gentle and as sweet, sympathetic and honest. Most people walk the line between the two. He was very extreme.'

As ever, these twilight feelings and cosmic contemplations found their way into the music, imbuing several songs on his final two records, *On The Cobbles* and the posthumously released *Heaven And Earth*. 'My Creator' was a valedictory reckoning on an un-compromising life, a vow to keep on fighting until one could '*fight no more*' and to '*never bend the knee*'. 'Heaven And Earth' was a prolonged meditation on the peace to come, when '*all of my sorrows*' will drift away '*over heaven*'.

'Willing To Work' and 'Colour' felt like alternately wry and bitter reflections on his experiences in the music industry, which had left him, in the words of his daughter, doing the rounds 'like an old carthorse'. Here was the logical conclusion of the childhood dream of living the imagined life of Robert Johnson, the troubled troubadour roving from town to town, measuring out their pain for the purpose of entertainment and taking their due in hard cash. 'I remember somebody shouting out to him at a gig not that long [before he died], "Lighten up, John, take it easy,"' says Ralph McTell. 'And he said, quite aggressively, "It's not my fucking job to take it easy!"'

'Under My Wing' threw a protective embrace around a vulnerable loved one, conceivably Martyn himself, who kept their most intimate feelings under lock and key. 'I put on accents; I put on a front, because I'm a very private person,' he told an interviewer in 2002, in a rare moment of unvarnished candour. 'That's what I'm about. I hardly let anyone get close.'[1]

On the BBC Scotland programme *Scotland's Music*, broadcast in 2007, Martyn sang 'Hurt In Your Heart' with tears in his eyes. The song was written originally as a plea to Beverley, and watching him relive it felt like witnessing an old wound rupturing in real time. Foss Paterson played keyboards at the taping and recalls it came at the very end of a difficult day, during which Martyn had drunk furiously, forgotten lyrics and disrupted proceedings with testy recalcitrance, before he finally nailed the performance. He sang it in a high, cracked bluesy keen, an ageing animal in primal pain.

He hadn't entirely mellowed. His performance in August 2006 at Fairport Convention's annual festival at Cropredy in Oxfordshire, celebrating the band's fortieth anniversary, was made of darker stuff. 'I probably hadn't seen John for a good fifteen years,' says Dave Mattacks. 'I remember him coming down in a van, and seeing the state he was in. I thought, You silly bugger!'

'He was a complete arsehole at Cropredy,' says Dave Pegg. 'His guitar was total distortion, and he just blamed everybody around him, the crew and everybody... but it was actually that the battery had gone in his guitar. Eventually he sorted it out, but it didn't endear him to people. It was never fun for me to be with John, because you never knew which way he was going to go. He could be absolutely charming or a complete arsehole. We all loved and admired him so much, but it was always disturbing to be in his company.'

Since 2005 Martyn had been talking up his next album, provisionally titled *Willing To Work*, but, despite recording several songs at home and with Jim Tullio, he couldn't quite get it together. Instead, he followed the fashion for artists performing entire albums from their back catalogue. Setting aside any historical distaste he may have felt for his most acclaimed record, he toured *Solid Air* early in 2007 – spinning off an original commission for the Celtic Connections festival in Glasgow – and did the same with *Grace And Danger* at the end of 2008. 'He felt that was a good compromise,' says Spencer Cozens. '[Playing] half of those albums, and half new stuff. He could play bigger venues and everyone was happy.'

Where previously he was booked into small clubs, pubs, hotels, provincial theatres and arts centres, the popular selling point of the album tours enabled Martyn to fill venues such as the Royal Concert Hall in Glasgow, the Sage in Gateshead and the Roundhouse in London, where the DVD of the *Solid Air* tour, directed by Gavin Taylor, was filmed. He and the band played the entire album, out of sequence, sandwiched between half a dozen other songs. The music remained a living thing, subject to endless variation rather than faithful reproduction.

The *Solid Air* tour was part of a wider curve towards a cussed kind of respectability. The Establishment recognition Martyn received in the final year of his life now resembles an augury, a divination that something unique was coming to its conclusion. He had cancelled a series of shows towards the end of 2007 due to a brush with pneumonia and played little for much of 2008. However, there was, more importantly, the matter of an auspicious birthday in September 2008, marking his sixtieth year. He had also reached the point where it felt safe to offer up a summation of an artist's career in the belief that what is yet to come is unlikely to significantly alter the narrative.

In February 2008 Martyn was honoured with a lifetime achievement award at the BBC Radio 2 Folk Awards. The citation heralded his 'heartfelt performances' and 'idiosyncratic genius'.[2] At the ceremony at the Brewery in London, he made a funny, breathless speech which contained a good-natured dig at Danny Thompson, and performed terrific versions of 'May You Never' and 'Over The Hill' – for once doing what he was told – the latter with John Paul Jones of Led Zeppelin on mandolin. Phil Collins presented the award and kissed him affectionately on the crown. Eric Clapton sent a message acknowledging Martyn's profound influence on 'everyone who ever heard him... he's so far ahead of everything, it's almost inconceivable'.

Later in the year, to mark his birthday, Island released a four-disc compilation titled *Ain't No Saint*. Spanning essential performances, deep cuts and rarities, it was a commendable attempt to bridge the full span of a multi-faceted career.

The following month, he sailed to New York to test a new prosthetic, assembled following consultation with a team of specialists at Columbia University Medical Center and with the help of Danny Thompson, who flew out to attend the fitting. 'It was fantastic. It was the first time he'd stood up in years,' says Thompson. 'I've got pictures. We had a fantastic time together.'

The pair played together, despite Martyn feeling that he was not well enough, at Joe's Pub, his first New York gig for a decade. Reviewing for *The New York Times*, Jon Pareles described Martyn as 'One of the most idiosyncratic British innovators... He joked, gruffly, that he is now a "living leg end," and at times he seemed to be in pain. But when he played, his music was intact. He picked taut, spiraling triplets in "The Easy Blues," stretched and teased the vocal phrases of "May You Never" and "Solid Air" toward abstraction, and played hide-and-seek with the beat amid the Echoplexed layers of "Big Muff."'[3]

While in New York, Martyn caught up with his old friend Bridget St John, now living there with her husband. He surprised her after her show at the Stone club. 'We hung out after the gig and then hung out the next day. It was sort of a lovely ending. I didn't know it was the end, although he was clearly so uncomfortable.'

Martyn's health was by now precarious. He was in a state of almost constant pain. On his return to Britain in November, he caught up with another old friend, Paul Wheeler, in Brighton, during the UK and Ireland tour revisiting *Grace And Danger*. 'I was living just a few doors down from Beverley,' says Wheeler. 'It was pointed out to me that if I wanted to see John alive, it might be a good idea to catch him. I went to see him and we had a kind of parting meeting. Maybe he kind of knew he was near the end, I don't know. It was touching, a retrospective farewell.'

Nevertheless, when his old renegade socialist friend accepted an OBE in the New Year Honours list in 2009, Wheeler was rather horrified at his willingness to toe the line. Martyn's motives proved mercurial to the end. Viewed from a certain angle, accepting an offer to join the bejewelled Establishment was less a measure of conformity and closer to one final act of rebellion.

VI

'He got a year for free at the end,' says Spencer Cozens, who played the final show, at Vicar Street in Dublin, on November 25, 2008. Martyn died just over two months later, on January 29, 2009, of pneumonia and acute renal failure, at St Luke's Hospital in Kilkenny.

Many of those who were in contact with him towards the end believe he made a concerted attempt to clean up at the beginning of 2009. He wanted to lose weight for the OBE investiture ceremony, and he was also determined to give himself the best chance of making the new prosthesis a success. If so, the shock of withdrawal may have been too much for his system. More likely, his body had simply taken as much punishment as it could withstand.

His death didn't make the major television bulletins. A sign, perhaps, that, despite the baubles, Martyn remained an unclubbable and essentially underground proposition to the end. Among musicians, critics and fans, however, the news hung heavy. The writer and radio broadcaster Danny Baker heard of his death just before coming on air at BBC Radio London for his afternoon show. He decided to dedicate the entire two hours not just to Martyn's music, but to the memories and meanings it evoked.

'I was floored,' Baker told me the following day. 'There was something so terrifically personal in that melancholy. There was a truth in that spirit and that soul – it's a one-on-one thing. We all held in there for the last twenty years, waiting for the acoustic guitar to come back, but it's cold to look at it like that. He wasn't a performing chimpanzee. He had that Mozart thing; this clown, this fool, who could do "Small Hours" on the turn of a dime. Maybe it frightened him. He fostered the myth; otherwise, you're left with people worshipping at his feet.'

I was on death-knock duty that day. As well as Baker, I spoke to Ralph McTell, Chris Blackwell, Bert Jansch, Phil Collins – and a distraught Danny Thompson, who at first was too choked to speak, but soon found some comfort in talking about the bad old, good old days. Almost exactly ten years later, I spoke to Thompson again. I wondered whether Martyn's most simpatico musical companion felt that on some level his friend had ended up squandering his enviable gifts.

'No,' he said. 'I understand other people feeling that, but you have to be true to yourself and live your own life. He never thought, "Oh, I can't do that, because what would my audience or fan base think?" It's all part of your make-up. You are what you are, you can't pretend to be anything else. However frustrating that is for you – and I've been there, I've been in that situation where alcohol and alcohol abuse has completely taken over – there is only one person who can do anything about that, and that is yourself.

'One thing I can say about my curly-haired boy is that he never pretended to be anything that he wasn't. Just listen to the songs. People call it folk, or contemporary folk, or whatever, and I understand the reasons people put boxes on it, but for me it was music from the heart. People hear all these different stories and say, "What was John really like?", and I say, "If you really want to know what he was like, listen to his songs!" That tells you everything about the man.'

His funeral was held in St Mary's Church, Kells, on February 1, with family, band mates and close friends in attendance. There was music and readings, and the ensemble sang 'May You Never' as he was carried from the church. He was cremated the following day at Newlands Cross in Dublin. No flowers. The snow was so bad that night, all the flights out of Ireland were cancelled.

Perhaps inevitably, given the manner in which Martyn led his life, in the aftermath of his death there was some disquiet over the distribution of his estate, a dispute eventually resolved in the courts. He left £82,000 and was probably amazed it was that much. Initially, Teresa Walsh was bequeathed 75 per cent and Vari 25 per cent. This was later adjusted, with Spenser receiving 25 per cent and Teresa 50 per cent. Wesley Kutner would have liked Martyn's buck knife but received nothing. He bought his own, instead. Notwithstanding the difficulty in their relationship, Wesley felt 'total and utter grief when he died. I was very sad that he died and [about] the way he died. You can still want to be loved by someone that you admire, who shows their love for you in a strange way.'

In 2014 Beverley Martyn released her first record for decades. *The Phoenix And The Turtle* was well received and sparked a brief renewal of interest in her music and her story. She played shows around the UK and in Germany, and finally gained a degree of closure on a career that had been curtailed forty years before. I met her during this time and we spoke at length about her ex-husband. There was a residue of affection, along with bitterness, hurt, an ambiguous ache. She had suffered through the years from depression, hypoglycaemia, kidney disease and financial hardship, as well as the pain of dealing with an addicted son. She exuded an air of sadness, damage, even, but told her story with clarity and good humour.

She recalled the moment she heard the news that Martyn had died. 'My first reaction was shock, and then sadness because of his children,' she says. 'I was going to have to pick up the pieces of the kids, who knew that one day it was going to happen but never quite believed that it would, because he was this mythic superhuman who could drink more than anyone and all that. So I was sad. The next couple of weeks I was dreaming of him constantly, like he was trying to get through...'

After his death, the trajectory towards respectability continued. In May 2011 his final recordings were released as *Heaven And Earth*. Produced by Jim Tullio and completed by Gary Pollitt, the nine tracks contained moments of interest and beauty, but bore witness to the struggle Martyn had endured in those hard, final years to get his creative fires burning. Three months later, *Johnny Boy Would Love This* appeared, a tribute album comprising cover versions of thirty of Martyn's songs. The cast list was stellar, a testament to how far his music had travelled through genres and generations. David Gilmour, Robert Smith, Phil Collins, Beck, David Gray, Snow Patrol, Beth Orton, Paolo Nutini, Joe Bonamassa and Bombay Bicycle Club were among the participants. Only three of the thirty tracks had originally been recorded after the end of the Seventies.

Martyn's catalogue was too erratic, his persona too unwieldy, his life too long, for him to be granted posthumous cult superstardom of a type similar to his friend Nick Drake. Instead, his music continues to mean a tremendous amount to a relatively small number of people. It is celebrated at the John Martyn Gathering in Yorkshire, an annual grassroots event for musicians, friends and fans to convene in the convivial atmosphere of a local pub. He has a Facebook fan group numbering thousands of followers. Two excellent websites are dedicated to tracing the details of his career.

To mark the tenth anniversary of Martyn's death, a tribute concert was held at the Royal Concert Hall in Glasgow on January 27, 2019, as part of Celtic Connections. 'I've always thought of him as much more of an expansive mind, musically, than a straight-ahead acoustic singer-songwriter,' says Donald Shaw, the festival's artistic director. 'There is so much going on in terms of experimentation, electronica and jazz, as well as folk music. He was an innovator and extremely influential for a lot of the new guard of singer-songwriters in the last twenty years – for his sense of freedom, and for creating his own vocal style.'

The house band was made up of old friends: Foss Paterson on keyboards, Alan Thomson on electric bass and Arran Ahmun on drums. At the centre was Danny Thompson, proud as punch, if creaking around the edges somewhat at the age of seventy-nine. Wearing a kilt and an expression which flitted between joy and pain, Thompson regaled the audience with the old war stories as he hosted a sentimental journey down memory lane.

251

On a superlative 'Go Down Easy', he and John Smith sparred with guitar and string bass, rolling back the years to Martyn's heyday. The Blue Rose Code divined the often painful soul-searching at the heart of the music on expressive renditions of 'Fine Lines' and 'Make No Mistake'. Martyn's friend Eddi Reader added some uptown sparkle on 'Dancing' and 'Certain Surprise'. There were moving contributions from younger artists such as Katie Spencer, Lucy Rose and Rory Butler, who performed 'A Day At The Sea'.

The headline turn, Paul Weller, appeared under-rehearsed, singing 'Don't Want To Know', 'Going Down The River' and 'Sweet Little Mystery' with his eyes locked on the lyric sheet. He was all business, but then that was not unusual, as Martyn had observed when he and Weller had worked together early in the millennium on 'Under My Wing'. 'He's a Mod, he's got the Mod ethos. He's very full-on, he likes to get a thing done, which is great.'[1] Weller didn't join the cheerfully chaotic communal finale of 'May You Never'.

Throughout the evening, old photographs of Martyn in the company of friends, family, lovers and children filled the video screens behind the performers. They depicted him as a child, a young man, as an artist in his pomp and an elder statesman in stubborn decline. Footage of him performing 'Over The Rainbow' played while the audience filed out, and it was impossible not to be moved. It was a night, appropriately, when the warmth and magic of his music was celebrated, yet the mood of cosy consensus seemed somehow to sell short his furious contradictions, his profound pain, his unsettling intimacy, his capacity for inflicting great damage, and to gloss over the darker colours in his paint box.

It was left to the American bluesman Eric Bibb to strike the one appropriate dissenting note. Explaining why he would not play the song initially suggested for him, 'The Easy Blues' – the word 'slave' was non-negotiable, he said – Bibb instead performed a stunning solo acoustic blues on St Louis Jimmy Oden's 'Going Down Slow'. It is the lament of a thrill-chasing low-roller whose wheels have finally stopped turning, who is facing an impending reckoning alone, with a sure knowledge of the life he has lived and the cost it has exacted.

The words cut through the air in Ian McGeachy's hometown, breaking skin somewhere between tribute and rebuke. John Martyn, I think, would have approved.

I done had my fun
If I don't get well no more
I done had my fun
If I don't get well no more
My health is failin' me
I'm goin' down slow

Would you write my mother
Tell her the shape I'm in
Would you write my mother
Tell her the shape I'm in
Tell her to pray for me
Forgive me for my sins

I don't need no doctor
He can't do me no good
I don't need no doctor
He can't do me no good
It's all my fault
I did not do the things I should

I done had my fun
If I don't get well no more
I done had my fun
If I don't get well no more
My health is failin' me
I'm goin' down slow

Notes & Sources

All quotations in *Small Hours* are taken from interviews conducted by the author unless credited otherwise in the text or marked with a reference number corresponding to the sources listed below.

The vast majority of interviews were conducted by the author exclusively for this book between January 2018 and December 2019. The exceptions are as follows: Beverley Martyn was interviewed on September 25, 2013 for *The Herald*, and on April 1, 2014 for *The Guardian*; Danny Thompson was interviewed on January 30, 2009 for *The Word* and on November 13, 2018 for *Uncut*; Bert Jansch was interviewed on January 29, 2009 for *The Word*; Danny Baker was interviewed on January 30, 2009 for *The Word*.

Footnotes are marked with an asterisk and listed at the bottom of the same page.

Prologue: The Road to Ruin

1. Steve Sutherland, *Melody Maker*, October 23, 1982

PART ONE: THE WINDING BOY

Chapter 1

1. Mat Snow, *John Martyn in Person*
2. Janet Heads, Whatever Happened to the Fisherman's Dream? McGeachys of Dalintober and John Martyn, *Kintyre Magazine*, issue 77, spring 2015

3. Mat Snow, *John Martyn in Person*
4. Ibid.
5. Beverley Martyn, *Sweet Honesty*
6. Mat Snow, *John Martyn in Person*
7. Nick Coleman, *Mojo*, October 1994
8. Mat Snow, *John Martyn in Person*
9. Andy Childs, *Zig Zag*, issue 41, 1974
10. Ibid.
11. Trevor Dann, A Conversation with John Martyn, included with the *Piece By Piece* promotional box-set, 1986
12. Andy Childs, *Zig Zag*, issue 41, 1974
13. Mat Snow, *John Martyn in Person*
14. Ibid.
15. John Neil Munro, *Some People Are Crazy*
16. Janet Heads, Whatever Happened to the Fisherman's Dream? McGeachys of Dalintober and John Martyn, *Kintyre Magazine*, issue 77, spring 2015
17. Hamish Imlach & Ewan McVicar, *Cod Liver Oil and the Orange Juice*
18. John Neil Munro, *Some People Are Crazy*
19. Beverley Martyn, *Sweet Honesty*
20. Trevor Dann, A Conversation with John Martyn, included with the *Piece By Piece* promotional box-set, 1986

Chapter 2

1. Trevor Dann, A Conversation with John Martyn, included with the *Piece By Piece* promotional box-set, 1986
2. Andy Childs, *Zig Zag*, issue 41, 1974
3. Mat Snow, *John Martyn in Person*
4. John Neil Munro, interview with John Martyn, May 10, 2004, published on Big Muff website: https://www.johnmartyn.info/node/1436
5. Chris Nickson, *Solid Air: The Life of John Martyn*

Chapter 3

1. John Renbourn in Mick Houghton, *I've Always Kept a Unicorn: The Biography of Sandy Denny*
2. Robin Frederick: https://robinfrederick.com/nick-drake-place-to-be
3. Rob Young, *Electric Eden: Unearthing Britain's Visionary Music*
4. Hamish Imlach & Ewan McVicar, *Cod Liver Oil and the Orange Juice*
5. Andy Childs, *Zig Zag*, issue 41, 1974

6. Mick Houghton, *I've Always Kept a Unicorn: The Biography of Sandy Denny*
7. Philip Ward, *Sandy Denny: Reflections on Her Music*
8. Ibid.
9. Andy Childs, *Zig Zag*, issue 41, 1974
10. Andrew Male, *Mojo*, March 2, 2009
11. Rob Fitzpatrick, *The Word*, October 2008
12. Jerry Gilbert, *Sounds*, August 18, 1973
13. Rob Young, *Electric Eden: Unearthing Britain's Visionary Music*
14. Trevor Dann, A Conversation with John Martyn, included with the *Piece By Piece* promotional box-set, 1986
15. Ibid.

Chapter 4

1. Rob Fitzpatrick, *The Word*, October 2008
2. Beverley Martyn, *Sweet Honesty*
3. Andy Childs, *Zig Zag*, issue 41, 1974
4. Beverley Martyn, *Sweet Honesty*
5. John Neil Munro, *Some People Are Crazy*

Chapter 5

1. Andy Childs, *Zig Zag*, issue 41, 1974
2. Beverley Martyn, *Sweet Honesty*
3. Rob Fitzpatrick, *The Word*, October 2008
4. Barney Hoskyns, *Small Town Talk*
5. Happy Traum, interview with author
6. Barney Hoskyns, *Small Town Talk*
7. Mat Snow, *John Martyn in Person*
8. Pamela Marvin, *Lee: A Romance*
9. Beverley Martyn, *Sweet Honesty*
10. Ibid.
11. Mark Powell, liner notes, *Stormbringer!* remaster reissue
12. *Melody Maker*, March 7, 1970
13. *Beat Instrumental*, issue 85, 1970
14. Rob Young, *Uncut*, October 2008
15. Jerry Gilbert, *Sounds*, August 18, 1973
16. *Melody Maker*, December 26, 1970
17. Andy Childs, *Zig Zag*, issue 41, 1974
18. *Melody Maker*, December 26, 1970
19. Ibid.

Chapter 6

1. Mat Snow, *John Martyn in Person*
2. Joe Boyd, *White Bicycles*
3. Mat Snow, *John Martyn in Person*
4. Beverley Martyn, *Sweet Honesty*
5. Mat Snow, *John Martyn in Person*
6. Beverley Martyn, *Sweet Honesty*
7. Ryan H. Walsh, *Astral Weeks*
8. Rob Fitzpatrick, *The Word*, October 2008
9. Trevor Dann, A Conversation with John Martyn, included with the *Piece By Piece* promotional box-set, 1986
10. Rob Young, *Electric Eden: Unearthing Britain's Visionary Music*
11. Andy Childs, *Zig Zag*, issue 41, 1974
12. Andrew Mearns, *Melody Maker*, February 20, 1970
13. Stephen Holden, *Rolling Stone*, December 9, 1971
14. Mat Snow, *John Martyn in Person*
15. Ian Anderson, *All-night Fever*: https://www.ianaanderson.com/les-cousins
16. https://www.johnmartyn.com/1970s/solid-air-1973
17. Trevor Dann, A Conversation with John Martyn, included with the *Piece By Piece* promotional box-set, 1986
18. Rob Young, John Martyn: Feeling Gravity's Pull, *The Wire*, June 1998
19. *Sounds*, April 4, 1973
20. Trevor Dann, A Conversation with John Martyn, included with the *Piece By Piece* promotional box-set, 1986
21. Ian MacDonald, *NME*, July 21, 1973
22. Geoff Brown, *Melody Maker*, October 13, 1973
23. Interview with author, September 2005

Chapter 7

1. John Neil Munro, interview with John Martyn, May 10, 2004, published on Big Muff website: https://www.johnmartyn.info/node/1436
2. Nick Kent, The Exorcism, *NME*, November 29, 1980
3. Geoff Brown, *Melody Maker*, October 13, 1973
4. Ian MacDonald, *NME*, July 21, 1973
5. Geoff Brown, *Melody Maker*, October 13, 1973
6. Jerry Gilbert, *Sounds*, August 18, 1973
7. Ian MacDonald, *NME*, July 21, 1973
8. Geoff Brown, *Melody Maker*, October 13, 1973

9. Ian MacDonald, *NME*, July 21, 1973
10. Trevor Dann, A Conversation with John Martyn, included with the *Piece By Piece* promotional box-set, 1986
11. Ian MacDonald, *NME*, September 29, 1973
12. Ian MacDonald, *NME*, July 21, 1973
13. Rob Young, *Uncut*, October 2008
14. Mat Snow, *John Martyn in Person*
15. Andrew Male, *Mojo*, March 2, 2009
16. Rob Fitzpatrick, *The Word*, October 2008
17. Ibid.
18. Ibid.
19. Trevor Dann, A Conversation with John Martyn, included with the *Piece By Piece* promotional box-set, 1986
20. Beverley Martyn, *Sweet Honesty*
21. John Neil Munro, *Some People Are Crazy*
22. Beverley Martyn, *Sweet Honesty*
23. Trevor Dann, A Conversation with John Martyn, included with the *Piece By Piece* promotional box-set, 1986
24. John Hillarby, liner notes, *Live At Leeds* deluxe edition, 2010
25. Mat Snow, *John Martyn in Person*
26. Ibid.
27. Allan Jones, *Can't Stand Up for Falling Down*
28. John Hillarby, liner notes, *Live At Leeds* deluxe edition, 2010
29. Rob Fitzpatrick, *The Word*, October 2008
30. Beverley Martyn, *Sweet Honesty*

Chapter 8

1. Rob Fitzpatrick, *The Word*, October 2008
2. Ibid.
3. Ibid.
4. Brian Boyd, *The Irish Times*, April 29, 2008
5. Brian Blevins, liner notes, *So Far So Good*
6. John Neil Munro, *Some People Are Crazy*
7. Rob Young, *Uncut*, October 2008
8. Colin Harper, *Dazzling Stranger*
9. Nick Kent, The Exorcism, *NME*, November 29, 1980
10. Ian Penman, *NME*, November 18, 1978
11. Nick Kent, The Exorcism, *NME*, November 29, 1980

Chapter 9

1. Nick Kent, The Exorcism, *NME*, November 29, 1980
2. Ibid.
3. Phil Collins, *Not Dead Yet*
4. Nick Kent, *NME*, March 21, 1981
5. Phil Collins, *Not Dead Yet*
6. Daryl Easlea, liner notes, *Grace And Danger* deluxe edition, 2007
7. Phil Collins, *Not Dead Yet*
8. Daryl Easlea, liner notes, *Grace And Danger* deluxe edition, 2007
9. John Neil Munro, interview with John Martyn, May 10, 2004, published on Big Muff website: https://www.johnmartyn.info/node/1436
10. Steve Sutherland, *Melody Maker*, October 23, 1982
11. John Neil Munro, interview with John Martyn, May 10, 2004, published on Big Muff website: https://www.johnmartyn.info/node/1436
12. Chris Salewicz, *NME*, October 10, 1981
13. *The Guardian*, June 21, 2009
14. Trevor Dann, A Conversation with John Martyn, included with the *Piece By Piece* promotional box-set, 1986
15. *Sounds*, April 4, 1973
16. Nick Kent, The Exorcism, *NME*, November 29, 1980
17. Ibid.
18. Steve Sutherland, *Melody Maker*, October 23, 1982
19. Phil Collins, *Not Dead Yet*
20. Ibid.
21. Beverley Martyn, *Sweet Honesty*
22. Chris Salewicz, *NME*, October 10, 1981

Chapter 10

1. Rob Fitzpatrick, *The Word*, October 2008
2. Nick Kent, The Exorcism, *NME*, November 29, 1980
3 Steve Sutherland, *Melody Maker*, May 30, 1981
4 Steve Sutherland, *Melody Maker*, September 19, 1981
5. Graham Lock, *NME*, October 10, 1981
6. Steve Sutherland, *Melody Maker*, October 23, 1982
7. Richard Cook, *NME*, October 30, 1982
8. Trevor Dann, A Conversation with John Martyn, included with the *Piece By Piece* promotional box-set, 1986

PART TWO: ROLLING HOME

I

1. Glyn Brown, *Sounds*, March 8, 1986

II

1. John Neil Munro, *Some People Are Crazy*
2. Janet Heads, Whatever Happened to the Fisherman's Dream? McGeachys of Dalintober and John Martyn, *Kintyre Magazine*, issue 77, spring 2015
3. Patrick Teugels, *Big Muff*, March 18, 2002: https://www.johnmartyn.info/content/john-martyn-90s-giglist#1993
4. https://www.johnmartyn.info/content/john-martyn-90s-giglist#1993

III

1. Mat Snow, *The Guardian*, May 12, 2006
2. Sineve Soe, *The Sunday Independent*, August 4, 1996
3. Rob Young, John Martyn: Feeling Gravity's Pull, *The Wire*, June 1998
4. John Neil Munro, *Some People Are Crazy*
5. Mitch Myers, *Magnet*, September 28, 1998

IV

1. Paddy Kehoe, *RTE* website, January 29, 2009

V

1. Adam Lee Potter, *Scotland on Sunday*, September 9, 2002
2. www.bbc.co.uk/radio2/events/folkawards2008/
3. Jon Pareles, *The New York Times*, October 10, 2008

VI

1. Paddy Kehoe, *RTE* website, January 29, 2009

Select Bibliography & Further Sources

Of all the material available on John Martyn, special mention goes to the official website – www.johnmartyn.com – a labour of love maintained by John Hillarby which constitutes an enormously rich archive. Big Muff: The John Martyn Pages – a fan site run by Hans van den Berk at www.johnmartyn.info – is another treasure trove of audio, visual and written content for anyone interested in this subject. My sincere thanks to both platforms.

I drew extensively from decades of magazine and newspaper coverage of John Martyn, much of which is referenced specifically in the *Notes & Sources* section. Of particular note is the feature writing of Andy Childs, Ian MacDonald, Nick Kent and Steve Sutherland. Many of these, and other excellent pieces on John Martyn, can now be found in one place at the online music library, Rock's Back Pages: www.rocksbackpages.com. The archives of the National Library of Scotland in Edinburgh, as well as www.britishnewspaperarchive.co.uk and www.ancestry.co.uk, were valuable.

The documentary *Johnny Too Bad*, directed by Serena Cross and first shown on BBC Four in 2004, is a vivid character study and a useful career overview.

The following books proved most helpful:

Barry, Lee, *Grace & Danger* (Lulu, 2006)

Boyd, Joe, *White Bicycles: Making Music in the 1960s* (Serpent's Tail, 2006)

Brown, Phill, *Are We Still Rolling? Studios, Drugs and Rock 'n' Roll – One Man's Journey Recording Classic Albums* (Tape Op, 2010)

Clapton, Eric, *Eric Clapton: The Autobiography* (Century, 2007)

Collins, Phil, *Not Dead Yet: The Autobiography* (Century, 2016)

Connor, Richard, *Solid Air: An In-Depth Look at the Classic Album by John Martyn* (Richard Connor, 2014)

Dann, Trevor, *Darker Than the Deepest Sea: The Search for Nick Drake* (Piatkus, 2007)

Harper, Colin, *Dazzling Stranger: Bert Jansch and the British Folk and Blues Revival* (Bloomsbury, 2006)

Heron, Mike & Grieg, Andrew, *You Know What You Could Be: Tuning into the 1960s* (Riverrun, 2017)

Heylin, Clinton, *Bob Dylan: Behind the Shades* (Viking, 1991)

Hoskyns, Barney, *Across the Great Divide: The Band and America*, new ed. (Pimlico, 2003)

Hoskyns, Barney, *Small Town Talk: Bob Dylan, The Band, Van Morrison, Janis Joplin, Jimi Hendrix & Friends in the Wild Years of Woodstock* (Faber & Faber, 2016)

Houghton, Mick, *I've Always Kept a Unicorn: The Biography of Sandy Denny* (Faber & Faber, 2015)

Humphries, Patrick, *Nick Drake: The Biography* (Bloomsbury, 1998)

Imlach, Hamish & McVicar, Ewan, *Cod Liver Oil and the Orange Juice: Reminiscences of a Fat Folk Singer* (Gallus Publishing, 2015)

Jones, Allan, *Can't Stand Up for Falling Down: Rock 'n' Roll War Stories* (Bloomsbury, 2017)

McVicar, Ewan, *One Singer, One Song: Old and New Stories and Songs of Glasgow Folk* (Glasgow City Libraries, 1990)

Martyn, Beverley, *Sweet Honesty: The Beverley Martyn Story* (Grosvenor House, 2011)

Martyn, John, *Open Window Songbook* (International Music Publications, 1982)

Marvin, Pamela, *Lee: A Romance* (Faber & Faber, 1997)

Molleson, Kate, *Dear Green Sounds: Glasgow's Music Through Time and Buildings* (Waverley Books, 2015)

Munro, John Neil, *Some People Are Crazy: The John Martyn Story* (Polygon, 2007)

Nickson, Chris, *Solid Air: The Life of John Martyn* (Creative Content, 2011)

Salewicz, Chris & Newman, Suzette, *The Story of Island Records: Keep on Running* (Universe, 2010)

Snow, Mat, *John Martyn in Person* (Mat Snow, 2010)

Walsh, Ryan H., *Astral Weeks: A Secret History of 1968* (Penguin Press, 2018)

Ward, Philip, *Sandy Denny: Reflections on Her Music* (Matador, 2011)

Young, Rob, *Electric Eden: Unearthing Britain's Visionary Music* (Faber & Faber, 2010)

Acknowledgements

I would like to thank everyone who spoke to me about John Martyn between 2009 and 2019. Their memories, insights and honesty were invaluable in the writing of this book.

They include: Gillian Allen, Jeff Allen, Jon Anderson, Danny Baker, Dave Ball, Donnie Barclay, Chris Blackwell, Brian Blevins, Joe Boyd, George Boyter, Sandra Bradley (née MacEwan), Harvey Brooks, Phill Brown, John 'Rabbit' Bundrick, Martin Carthy, André Ceelen, Tim Clark, Billy Connolly, Gerry Conway, Mark Cooper, Spencer Cozens, Tommy Crocket, Rosalie Deighton, Dave Dick, Richard Digby Smith, Linda Dunning, Archie Fisher, Alison Floyd (née McGeachy), Tristan Fry, Ron Geesin, Andrew Greig, Stefan Grossman, Claire Hamill, Mike Heron, Jim Imlach, John James, Van Johnson, Mike Kowalski, Wesley Kutner, Nick Launay, Martin Levan, Tod Lloyd, Davie MacFarlane, Gordon MacIver, Norrie MacQueen, Donald McGeachy, Fiona McGeachy, Pat McGeachy, Vari McGeachy, Sean McGhee, Rod McLeod, Jacqui McShee, Ralph McTell, Ewan McVicar, Beverley Martyn, Brian Masterton, Dave Mattacks, Brian Miller, Christy Moore, Andy Newmark, Rab Noakes, Tony Palmer, Foss Paterson, Dave Pegg, Lee Perry, David Philip, Tony Reeves, Sandy Roberton, Phil Shackleton, Donald Shaw, Andy Sheppard, Bridget St John, Brian Stanage, Gavin Stott, Danny Thompson, Linda Thompson, Richard Thompson, Steve Tilston, Happy Traum, Jim Tullio, Keith Warmington, Jo Watson, Paul Wheeler, Robin

Williamson, Ali Wilson, John Wood and Ruthie Zorgenlos. Thanks also to those who preferred to speak off the record.

Many others took time to assist in various ways, from setting up interviews and passing on contact information to sharing music, organising concert tickets and forwarding material of interest. Their goodwill is much appreciated. Thank you to John Hillarby, Richard Williams, Stevie Horton, Philip Ward, Jim Tullio, Barney Hoskyns, Liam Doherty, Barbara Dickson, Ronnie Simpson, Sarah Jane Morris, Ann Grant at Shawlands Academy, Siobhan Miller, Donald Shaw, Joe Black, Norrie MacQueen, Ted Cummings and Suzette Newman.

To everyone who provided personal effects, photographs and memorabilia – in particular, John Hillarby, Brian Stanage, Sandy Roberton, Phill Brown, Jim Imlach, Fiona Imlach and Linda Dunning – I am indebted to your generosity.

I am grateful to David Reed and Brian O'Gorman at the British Music Hall Society for their kind assistance; to everyone at Morningside Library, Edinburgh; to Josephine Sillars and Lola Smith-Welsh for transcription services; and to Alison Rae for her attentive copy-editing and for making many improving suggestions. Any mistakes which remain are my own.

The subtitle to this book is an homage to James Gavin's superb biography of Chet Baker, *Deep in a Dream: The Long Night of Chet Baker* (Knopf, 2002). Thanks to James. Thank you to Imogen Gordon Clark and David Barraclough at Omnibus for their patience, assistance and enthusiasm; to my agent, Matthew Hamilton, at the Hamilton Agency, for his advice and support; and to Aitken Alexander Associates. I'm immensely grateful for the generous input of the family of John Martyn.

Finally, love and thanks to my own family, particularly to my wife Jen and our three children. May you never lay your head down without a hand to hold.